HARRY POTTER

PLACES

BOOK ONE

LONDON AND LONDON SIDE-ALONG APPARATIONS

A Novel Holiday Travel Guidebook

By CD Miller

Harry Potter Places BOOK ONE
London and London Side-Along Apparations
A Novel Holiday Travel Guidebook

by CD Miller

Published by:
A Novel Holiday Travel Guidebooks
16614 226th Street
Ashland, NE 68003
http://www.anovelholiday.com

The publisher and author(s) of *Harry Potter Places* Book One have taken great care to ensure that all information provided is correct and accurate at the time of manuscript submission. However, errors and omissions—whether typographical, clerical or otherwise—do sometimes occur, and may occur anywhere within the body of this publication.

Changes in real-life site information will inevitably occur. As aptly stated by the Internationally-renown travel guidebook author, **Rick Steves**: "Guidebooks begin to yellow even before they're printed." This rule holds true for eBooks, as well.

Users of any *Harry Potter Places* travel guidebook are advised to access the Internet links provided within each Site entry in order to obtain the most up-to-date information during the planning of your UK Potter holiday. For instance, the ticket and entry fees cited are those that were in effect during our last pass at researching each site.

Currency equivalents are offered only to provide an *approximate idea* of what British Pounds (£) equals in US Dollars ($). Currency exchange rates change daily. Check current foreign exchange rates by using a free Internet currency converter such as the one offered by **Oanda**:
http://www.oanda.com/currency/converter/

The publisher and author(s) of *Harry Potter Places* travel guidebooks hereby disclaim any liability to any party for loss, injury, or damage incurred as a direct or indirect consequence of errors, omissions, or post-manuscript-submission information changes, whether such errors, omissions, or changes result from negligence, accident, or any other cause.

Copyright © 2012 by Charly D Miller
A Novel Holiday Travel Guidebooks Publishing Company
Printed in the United States of America
ISBN 978-1-938285-16.-5

Publisher's Cataloging-in-Publication Data
Miller, Charly D, 1956 -
Harry Potter Places Book One (Color)—London and London Side-Along Apparations by Charly D Miller.
     p. cm.
     includes index
     ISBN 978-1-938285-16-5 (softbound) $45.99
     1. Travel Guides—United Kingdom—.
I. Title.
DA650.H75 M460 2012

DISCLAIMERS

J.K. Rowling's *Harry Potter* books are so popular, that an amazing number of **unauthorized** *Harry Potter* guidebooks have been published over the years.
http://harrypotter.wikia.com/wiki/List_of_Harry_Potter_unofficial_guidebooks

In order to avoid the threat of litigation related to copyright or trademark infringement, all unauthorized *Harry Potter* guidebooks publish at least one **Disclaimer**. Below are the **several** important *Harry Potter Places* Disclaimers.

An Unauthorized *Harry Potter* Travel Guidebook

Harry Potter Places Book One—London and London Side-Along Apparations, is an unauthorized *Harry Potter* travel guidebook.

Harry Potter Places Book One [hereinafter referred to as **HPP Book One**] is not authorized, approved, endorsed, nor licensed by J.K. Rowling [hereinafter referred to as **JKR**], Warner Brothers Entertainment, Inc. [hereinafter referred to as **WB Inc**], the Scholastic Corporation, Raincoast Books, Bloomsbury Publishing Plc., nor by any other persons, entities, corporations or companies claiming a proprietary interest in the *Harry Potter* books, movies, or related merchandise.

HPP Book One is not officially associated with the seven *Harry Potter* novels written and copyrighted by JKR. Nor is *HPP* Book One in any way officially associated with the eight *Harry Potter* movies produced and trademarked by WB Inc.

The Purpose of Book One

HPP Book One is written solely for the purpose of providing an historical review of, and directions for finding, the **real-life** London and nearby-London locations that:
- Were mentioned within one or more of the *Harry Potter* novels.
- Are sites where Harry Potter filming took place.
- Significantly influenced the design of studio sets built for filming one or more of the *Harry Potter* movies.

HP-Associated Names, Places, Titles or Terminology

HPP Book One does not claim, nor does it intend to imply, ownership of, or proprietary rights to, any of the fictional character or place names mentioned within JKR's *Harry Potter* novels, nor any of the titles or terminology used or created by JKR within her books or within the movies made thereof.

More information about Potter and Potterlike terminology found within *HPP* Book One is provided in the **Prior Incantato** section.

Publication of *Harry Potter* Movie Screenshots

Screenshots are split-second still photos captured from a movie. Several of the twenty-eight (28) *HPP* Book One Potter Site entries include one or more small movie screenshots. The sole purpose of including them is to enhance the experience of *Harry Potter* fans [**Potterites**] who visit a real-life film site, or a real-life place that strongly influenced movie studio set design. By having one or more screenshots to observe while visiting, Potterites are better able to recognize the specific areas where filming occurred, and are armed with a guide important to assuming positions similar to that of the actors in the scene(s) filmed at the site when snapping their personal photographs.

To be an effective site identification and photography guide, however, *Harry Potter* movie screenshots had to be substantially *altered* in a variety of ways so that the site location's **background** could more easily be recognized.

All eight *Harry Potter* films were produced and trademarked by WB Inc. *HPP* Book One does not claim, nor does it intend to imply, ownership of, or proprietary rights to, any portions of the *Harry Potter* movies. The caption of every screenshot and screenshot segment that appears within *HPP* should read "™©WB Inc." Because this info is given here, we instead have captioned *HPP* screenshots with identification of the movie from which it was captured.

Use of Google Maps UK Images to Create Potter Maps

In order to assist visiting Potterites to find multiple filming locations within one Site (such as the Knight Bus Pickup Playground, or the Ministry of Magic Area), a few **Potter Maps** were created for *Harry Potter Places* Book One.

When using Google Maps UK images to create Potter Maps, *HPP* Book One authors strictly adhered to the *Google Maps and Google Earth Content Rules & Guidelines*, and appropriately attributed Google with credit for the full-sized Potter Map included within a Supplementum PDF posted on the Internet, as well as for any thumbnail-sized Potter Map images published within the travel guidebook.

HPP Book One does not claim, nor does it intend to imply, ownership of, or proprietary rights to, any of the Google Maps UK images used within the guidebook or the Supplementum PDFs posted on HarryPotterPlaces.com.

Author vs Authors of *Harry Potter Places*

The **A Novel Holiday** travel guidebook publishing company concept was solely conceived by Ms. Charly D Miller in 2007, as was the concept of the first series of A Novel Holiday (**ANH**) travel guidebooks, **Harry Potter Places**. However, during the researching and writing of *HPP* travel guidebooks (as well as during design of the ANH and *HPP* websites), Ms. Miller was so generously assisted by other individuals, that she feels unworthy of claiming sole credit for authoring the text's or websites' content. Thus, **plural terms**—such as, "authors" … "we" … "our"—are used throughout the *HPP* travel guidebooks, as well as throughout the ANH and *HPP* websites, when referring to the writers or creators of same.

However, for all legal purposes, every A Novel Holiday *Harry Potter Places* travel guidebook was solely written and published by CD Miller. She, alone, is responsible for all the content ultimately published within any eBook or print versions of the *HPP* travel guidebooks, as well as all the content posted on ANH and *HPP* websites.

Ms. Charly D Miller hereby avows and affirms that any and all other individuals who participated in or contributed to the researching, writing, or publication of *Harry Potter Places* travel guidebooks and associated websites, are **indemnified and held harmless** from and against: any and all demands, claims, and damages to persons or property, losses and liabilities, including attorney's fees arising out of or caused by any form of litigation brought against the A Novel Holiday *Harry Potter Places* travel guidebooks or websites.

CREDITS AND ACKNOWLEDGMENTS

Thank you, Tara and Wolfgang!

The two most generous and dedicated Contributing *Harry Potter Places* Researchers are Ms. Tara Bellers of the US, and Mr. Wolfgang Mletzko of Germany.

Tara Bellers traveled from the US to the UK on three different occasions between 2009 and 2011. During each of those trips, she voluntarily spent personal time investigating answers to Potter Place questions that couldn't be found on the Internet. In addition to snapping location pix for us, Tara discovered and reported info important to enhancing other Potterites' enjoyment of a similar visit.

When not traveling, Tara continued to significantly contribute to this project. While at home, she independently performed hundreds of hours of Internet research, leading to the discovery of several important Potter Places we might have missed. Thanks to Tara, Potterites will have no trouble finding even the most obscure UK Potter Places.

Wolfgang Mletzko began visiting UK Potter Places long before A Novel Holiday travel guidebooks (let alone *Harry Potter Places*) were even a concept. Since 2002, Wolfgang has performed several well-researched UK Potter treks, and always has freely-posted his marvelous photos and Potter travel tips on his website—which is how we found him!
http://www.bdyg.homepage.t-online.de/index.html

If you can't read German, go to **Google's Translation** website and paste-in Wolfgang's website address.
http://translate.google.com/

Thank You, to the Many Other Contributing Researchers

Below is a list of people who generously contributed important info and/or pix to the *Harry Potter Places* **Book One** (*HPP* Book 1) project.

Conny Rhode of Germany earns a *Very Special Mention* for providing loads of London Zoo and Grimmauld Place pix and info.

Duncan Smith: Thank you for being so very helpful with Saint Paul's Cathedral information.

Marc Lechtenfeld of Germany: Thank you for your Surbiton train station pix and info.
http://www.harrypotter-xperts.de

Murali Menon and **Sarah Moore** each deserve an enormous **Thank You** for helping us find the *true* location of Grimmauld Place! Were it not for them (as well as Tara and Conny), Potterites would still be wasting time at Lincoln's Inn Fields.

Peter Mair: Thank you for *all* your London help over the years—even before the *Harry Potter Places* project.

Sarah Greene: Thanx for taking pix of the newest Platform 9¾ trolley location!

Seth Cooper: Thank you for the Chester Stevens pix and info.

Stephen Spencer: Your pix and info related to the Argyle Walk Saint Mungo's location was incredibly helpful.

Tony Sommerville of Market Porter earns a *Very Special Mention* for all his help with Borough Market Harry Potter Window info, and the marvelous manner in which he hosted Tara during her 2009 visit.

Photo Credits

Beneath each photograph in *Harry Potter Places* is the name of the person who snapped the pic. With few exceptions, permission for using these photos was granted free of charge. Some photos were obtained from **Wikipedia** or **Wikimedia**, where they were posted by photographers who generously offered the freedom of their commercial re-use.

Art Credit

The *Harry Potter Places* **Coat of Arms**—an emblem seen on the title page of every *Harry Potter Places* Supplementum and Portkey PDF, as well as in the Banner atop each HarryPotterPlaces.com webpage—was designed by two terrifically talented graphic artists, **Karen Stoehr** and **Ben Dale**. They also created our three site ratings icons. Thank you both, so very much, for all your work!

http://www.coroflot.com/kstoehr
http://bendale.daportfolio.com/

Book Cover Credits

DC Carson created all five of the original 2012 *HPP* Book Covers—free of charge! Were it not for her, the *HPP* books and website would not have had images to use while CD Miller was still broke.

All photos used for the *HPP* Book Covers were snapped by **Ms. Tara Bellers**.

From the Author, CD Miller

To Ms. Carson

I am more grateful to Ms. Carson than mere words can possibly convey.

Dina has helped me with this project from the very beginning—for more than three years—entirely free of charge! These guidebooks would be *krappe* were it not for Dina's incredible writing talent and editing instruction, as well as her invaluable assistance with getting the eBook and print versions published. Dina also was vitally important to the design of the A Novel Holiday and *Harry Potter Places* websites!

My fondest wish is to someday be able to reciprocate, and help her as significantly as she's helped me. Unfortunately, I cannot imagine what *I* could ever do that Dina can't do better! Thankfully, I anticipate being able to *financially* reward her for all her work very soon.

Then, there's Tara Bellers

I couldn't afford to visit the UK more than *once*—a measly 2 weeks in 2008—while initially working on the *Harry Potter Places* project. Thus, the information offered in all *HPP* books would be terrifically incomplete were it not for Tara's **voluntary** UK Potter Place site research and photography, as well as the Internet research she continues to freely perform. In addition to that, Tara took me to the *Wizarding World of Harry Potter* in Orlando, Florida, in 2010!

I'll *never* be able to adequately thank Tara for all her generosity and assistance. But, perhaps I'll soon be able to reward her by taking her on an all-expenses-paid UK trip!

As for My Personal Friends

Susan and Bob, Jamie, Janet, Chet, Sandy, Leeenda and Mike … these are just a *few* of the scores of people I need to thank!

I was broke and homeless. (Much like JKR was while writing *Sorcerer's Stone*, oddly enough.) Yet, each of my friends contributed—in their own way—to ensure that I had a place to live, and the means for living comfortably, during the several years it took me to complete my first *HPP* travel guidebooks. You guys have no idea how much I've appreciated your help. I swear that, someday, I'll find a way of repaying you.

Lastly, to Drew and Annabeth, Auntie Dot and Uncle Itchy

Bless You for always believing in me!

TABLE OF CONTENTS

Quick-Quill Trip: 7 of London's Best Potter Places and 1 Side-Along in one day

Kwikspell Crusade: 11 of London's Best Potter Places and 2 Side-Alongs in two days

Huffandpuff Expedition: 13 of London's Best Potter Places and 2 Side-Alongs in two rapid-paced days

Padfoot Prowl: A 3-Day Tour of *ALL* the Best London Potter Places and 4 Side-Alongs

Potter Promenade: *ALL* the Best London Potter Places and 5 Side-Alongs visited in four days

POTTER PLACES in LONDON

PRIOR INCANTATO

Welcome to the **A Novel Holiday** travel guidebook, *Harry Potter Places* **Book 1—London and London Side-Along Apparations,** the first of five guidebooks designed to help *Harry Potter* Fans (**Potterites**) visit places found in the United Kingdom of Great Britain (the **UK**) that are associated with the *Harry Potter* Universe (the **Potterverse**). In the Potterverse, you'll find:

- Real-life places mentioned within J.K. Rowling's *Harry Potter* novels.
- Real-life locations where *Harry Potter* movie filming took place.
- Real-life sites that significantly influenced *Harry Potter* movie studio set design.

The **Prior Incantato** section is the *Harry Potter Places* **Travel Guidebook Introduction.** As such, it contains important explanations of the symbols and terminology found within each of the five *Harry Potter Places* (**HPP**) travel guidebooks.

Harry Potter Places Portkeys

To assist Potterites using eBook-reading devices that don't have a web browser—devices from which you cannot apparate—or Potterites using a printed HPP travel guidebook, we've created **HPP Portkeys:** Internet-posted PDFs containing all the Internet resource links provided in each section of every HPP book.

Go to **HarryPotterPlaces.com.** Click on the link for **Book One,** then click on the **Supplementums** link. There you can access the Portkeys.

Harry Potter Places Ratings Icon Guide

It took more than three years of research, but we managed to find *sixty-eight* **(68) Potter Places in the UK**—specifically on the island of Great Britain. However, not all of these sites are places every Potterite will enjoy. Thus, we assessed each for their reasonable importance to an average Potterite's UK holiday, and created icons that provide an *at-a-glance* recognition of their rating.

👓 The **Great Site** icon indicates a Potter Place you don't want to miss. These are important sites mentioned in the books, or film locations readily recognized in real-life.

The **Might Be Fun** icon identifies places some Potterites might find disinteresting, *or* unworthy of the inconvenience required to reach them. Each Might-Be-Fun Site's entry explains why it received that rating.

The **Skip It** icon is assigned to places we strongly suggest you *avoid* visiting, and the Site's entry explains why. Although we provide SatNav/GPS coordinates and/or addresses for Skip-It-rated sites, we do not provide directions for finding them, nor are Skip-It sites included in *any* of the suggested *Harry Potter Places* itineraries. Potterites divinely inspired to visit any Skip-It site should investigate the location using the information provided in its Site entry, then create their own itineraries.

The Potterite Prime Directive

To *POLITELY* Go Where Potterites Need to Go
— without **PERTURBING** anybody —
So That Other Potterites Can *Continue* to
ENJOY GOING THERE!

It is vitally important that all Potterites be as polite as possible when visiting *any* Potter Place. This rule is even more important when visiting a Site situated within a **private Muggle neighborhood**. It only takes *one* noisy or disrespectful fan to ruin the reception experienced by *all* Potterites who visit thereafter. Please be the very best **Potterite Ambassador** you can possibly be, everywhere you go.

Terminology Used within *Harry Potter Places*

Like any other author of fiction, J.K. Rowling (JKR) exercised *artistic license* when selecting or creating names, phrases, and terms for her Potterverse. Most often, she borrowed from Latin and Greek languages or mythologies. Occasionally, JKR's Potterverse terminology was influenced by other languages, such as French, Irish, Italian—even Arabic. Below are links to two resources that comprehensively discus the origin of Potterverse names, phrases, and terms.
http://www.harrypotterfanzone.com/word-origins/
http://www.languagerealm.com/hplang/harrypotterlanguage.php

JKR also often used words that *predate* her creation of the Potterverse, such as Witch, Wizard, broomstick, and the like. Sometimes, JKR altered the previously-popular meaning of the words she used. For instance, *Time Magazine* reported in 1931 that "Muggle" was one of several slang names for a **marijuana cigarette**.
http://www.time.com/time/magazine/article/0,9171,742157,00.html

The authors of *Harry Potter Places* have similarly exercised artistic license when using Potterverse terminology within our travel guidebooks. Some names, phrases, and terms used within HPP have the same meaning as they do in the Potterverse. Others have been redefined.

For example: **Prior Incantato** is a Potterverse incantation spoken to reveal the last spell performed by a wand. JKR created this phrase from the Latin word, *prior*, meaning former or previous, in combination with *incanto*, meaning "to enchant," or *incantate*, meaning "to speak a spell." However, in the *Harry Potter Places* travel guidebooks, Prior Incantato is the title of each book's **Introduction**.

Potterverse names, phrases, and terms found within *Harry Potter Places* that may have been independently-created by J.K. Rowling are used only for the purpose of enhancing Potterites' enjoyment of the travel guidebook. The authors of *Harry Potter Places* do not claim, nor intend to imply, ownership of, or proprietary rights to, any terminology found exclusively within *Harry Potter* books.

Some Potterverse—and Potterlike—Terms Used

Ambulatus

Although **Ambulatus** *sounds* Potterlike, it isn't found anywhere within JKR's Potterverse. Ambulate is an English word derived from Latin origins, and means, "to walk from place to place" or "move about." The Latin word for navigated, traveled, or traversed, is *ambulatus*. Ambulatus is used in the title of *Harry Potter Places* sections that provide directions for walking or traveling about within the cities of Oxford and Edinburgh. (London's between-Potter-Places travel directions are found at the end of each site's entry.)

Huffandpuff

Hufflepuff is one of the four Houses of Hogwarts School of Witchcraft and Wizardry. While **Huffandpuff** sounds like Hufflepuff, it is a term created by *Harry Potter Places* authors for use as the title of any particularly arduous itinerary or walking route—indicating that you may be *huffing and puffing* when you reach the end!

Lumos

In the Potterverse, Lumos is the spell-word uttered to cause a wand to emit light from its tip. Lumos is related to *lumen*, a Latin word for light. In *Harry Potter Places*, **Lumos** is used in the title of sections that *shed a light on* a particular location, providing Potter- and Non-Potter-related information important to planning or enjoying your trek to that place.

Muggle

Every Potterite knows the Potterverse definition of a Muggle. In *Harry Potter Places*, **Muggle** is a term used when referring to any Non-Potterites one might encounter while visiting a Potter place, particularly *indigenous* Non-Potterites—those who live in the private neighborhoods that Potterites may be visiting.

NEWTs

NEWTs is a Potterverse acronym for the **Nastily Exhausting Wizarding Tests** that Hogwarts' students must pass at the end of their seventh year of school. In *Harry Potter Places*, however, **NEWTs** refers to **Northeastern England Wizarding Treks**, Potter Places that can be visited in Northeastern England.

OWLs

In the Potterverse, Hogwarts' students are subjected to **OWLs—Ordinary Wizarding Level** examinations—at the end of their fifth year of school. In *Harry Potter Places*, **OWLs** stands for **Oxford Wizarding Locations**, Potter Places found in the city of Oxford.

Parseltongue Pointers

Parseltongue is the Potterverse language spoken by a Parselmouth—someone who can communicate with snakes. In *Harry Potter Places*, **Parseltongue Pointers** are guides to correctly pronouncing place names associated with UK Potter Sites.

Specialis Revelio

A Potterverse spell invoked to reveal the ingredients of a potion or the enchantments placed upon an object, **Specialis Revelio** is a phrase created from the Latin terms *specialis*, meaning special, and *revelo*, meaning "to unveil." In *Harry Potter Places*, **Specialis Revelio** is used as the title of a section that reveals special information about visiting a particular location—including suggested itineraries.

Supplementum(s)

Another term that *sounds* Potterlike, but isn't found anywhere within JKR's Potterverse, **Supplementum** is a *Harry Potter Places* term for an Internet-posted PDF that contains extra information related to an individual Potter place. HPP Supplementums are intended to enrich a Potterite's visit to the Site they are associated with.

Please Note: Although it is more grammatically-correct to consider **Supplementum** as *both* the singular and plural version of this term, the authors of *Harry Potter Places* have elected to use **Supplementums** as the plural form of Supplementum.

Philosopher's Stone vs Sorcerer's Stone

There are a number of unconfirmed theories as to why the title of J.K. Rowling's first book, ***Harry Potter and the Philosopher's Stone***, was changed to ***Harry Potter and the Sorcerer's Stone*** for release in the USA and elsewhere. Because the authors of *Harry Potter Places* live in the USA, *Sorcerer's Stone* is used whenever we refer to the first *Harry Potter* book and movie.

We intend no disrespect to JKR—nor to Potterites living in the UK, Canada, or Australia (countries where both the book and movie are called, *Philosopher's Stone*)—by electing to use *Sorcerer's Stone* when referring to the first *Harry Potter* book and movie.

Lumos Britannia

Lumos Britannia provides general tips for Potterites planning a visit to **the United Kingdom of Great Britain**—aka **Britannia**, aka **the UK**.

UK Travel Guidebooks

Consider purchasing one or more Non-Potter (Muggle) UK travel guidebooks related to the areas where you'll be Pottering. If your holiday is solely Potter-centric, a UK Muggle travel guidebook is *not* necessary— *Harry Potter Places* will take care of you. However, Potterites also interested in visiting Non-Potter UK places will benefit from buying one *or more* Muggle travel guidebooks.

The *Harry Potter Places* Travel Store offers links to many of the Travel Guidebooks mentioned below, including several eBook versions.

HPP Recommends Rick Steves' Guidebooks
http://www.ricksteves.com

Rick Steves has been researching and writing truly excellent travel guidebooks for over 20 years, and he publishes three frequently-updated UK guides for the places you might be traveling to. Potterites only visiting London should buy *Rick Steves' London*. If you'll be visiting London and Oxford (and/or other places in England), purchase *Rick Steves' England*. If you'll be visiting England, Wales, *and* Scotland, buy *Rick Steves' Great Britain*.

Other Popular UK Muggle Travel Guidebook Companies
Fodor's Travel Guides
http://www.fodors.com

Frommer's Travel Guides
http://www.frommers.com/

Lonely Planet Guides
http://www.lonelyplanet.com/

Rough Guides
http://www.roughguides.com/

FREE UK Travel Tips Available on the Internet

Here are our favorites.

Rick Steves' Website

Whether or not you purchase a Rick Steves travel guidebook, his website offers free access to a ton of terrific European travel tip articles: packing, safety issues, health information, communicating [phone info], money matters, and other important subjects.
http://www.ricksteves.com/plan/tips/tips_menu.htm

Steves' Website also offers free travel tip articles for visiting London, England, Wales, Edinburgh, and Scotland.
http://www.ricksteves.com/plan/destinations/britain/brit_menu.htm

Reid Bramblett's Website
http://www.reidsguides.com/

In 1997, travel expert and guidebook author Reid Bramblett began what has become one of the most helpful travel planning websites on the Internet.

> "ReidsGuides.com is focused on European trip planning, with emphasis on money-saving tips and alternatives to traditional travel techniques, such as lodging options beyond hotels, no-frills airlines, short-term car leases, and sightseeing for free."

Bramblett also offers free articles about all the **traditional** UK trip planning subjects. But, he excels at making complicated money issues easy to understand. *All* of Bramblett's money articles are valuable when planning a UK trip, particularly the ones about changing money, using credit cards, and traveler's checks.

> "Here's how to get money during your [UK] travels, strategies for getting the best deals on exchange rates, how to avoid scams and rip-offs, and ways to save money every step of the way on your vacation."

http://www.reidsguides.com/t_mo/t_mo_money.html

Visit Travel Websites Related to Planning a UK Holiday

US Department of State, Bureau of Consular Affairs' Website
http://travel.state.gov/travel/cis_pa_tw/cis/cis_1052.html

Subjects include:
Entry/exit requirements for US citizens
Contact information for the **US Embassy in London** and the **US Consulate in Edinburgh.**
Medical facilities and health information

Medical insurance
The **Smart traveler enrollment program** (STEP)
Traffic safety and road conditions

The Smart Traveler Enrollment Program (STEP) is Interesting
https://travelregistration.state.gov/ibrs/ui/

STEP is a free service provided by the US Government to US citizens who are traveling to a foreign country. By registering information about your upcoming trip abroad with STEP, the US Department of State will be able to assist you better if you experience an emergency while in the UK. It also will be able to help friends and family to get in touch with you in the event of an emergency in the US.

Potterites living in countries other than the US should explore their government's website to obtain similar international travel information and assistance.

The Visit Britain Website
http://www.visitbritain.com/en/US/

Click on **Travel Tips** to reach **Customs and Immigration** information about passports and visas.
http://www.visitbritain.com/en/Travel-tips/Customs-and-immigration/

From that page, click on **Traveller Tips** for links to other important subjects.
http://www.visitbritain.com/en/Travel-tips/Traveller-tips/

Links found on Visit Britain's Traveller Tips directory page include:
Cost of daily items & tipping information
Free guides for your mobile [cell phone]
Medical & health information
Money & currency
Public holidays & time zones
Safety & security
Utilities, weights & measures

Learn About the VAT Tax Before Visiting the UK

When you pay for something in the UK, there often is a **Value Added Tax** (VAT) *included* in the purchase price. The UK VAT is *20%* of the item's commercial value *before* the tax is added—a considerable amount of additional cost.

Business Travelers are the only persons who can recover the UK VAT paid on expenses such as accommodations, car rentals, petrol, and meals.

However, persons traveling to the UK for **pleasure** *can* obtain a full re-fund of the VAT they pay on purchases of goods such as souvenirs, clothing, leather products, and the like—but only when your total purchase at an individual store equals or exceeds £30 ($48), and only if you follow the steps necessary to reclaiming the VAT paid.

The Official British Revenue & Customs VAT Webpage
http://www.hmrc.gov.uk/vat/index.htm

The Official European VAT Webpage
http://www.brvat.com/faq/index.htm

Both of these sites provide extensive information about the UK's VAT system. Unfortunately, much of the information offered is confusing.

Reid Bramblett's *"Getting the VAT Back"* Article

Mr. Bramblett provides a **clear and simple explanation of the UK VAT system**, as well as the best tips for obtaining a VAT refund.
http://www.reidsguides.com/t_mo/t_mo_vat.html

VAT Tip Highlights:
• Every time your total purchase at an individual store equals or exceeds £30, ask the sales clerk for the form needed in order to obtain a VAT refund. Sometimes, the clerk will fill it out for you. Otherwise, be sure that **you** fill out each form at the end of the purchase day—*before* your goodies get distributed throughout your luggage.

• Attach each completed VAT form to its corresponding sales receipt.

• Stash your VAT-attached sales receipts in a single envelope or Zip-bag, so that all your VAT documents are easy to present at the airport's Customs Office when you're ready to go home.

• **When leaving the UK, visit the airport's Customs Office *before* you check your luggage!** Although it rarely happens, a Customs Officer may ask to inspect your purchases when examining your sales receipts and VAT forms. If you've already checked the bag(s) containing your purchases, your VAT reclaim forms may be denied.

Peruse the Potterite UK Travel Supplementums

Harry Potter Places **Supplementums** are PDFs freely posted on the Internet, for the benefit of any Potterite planning a UK trip.

Pre-Trip Potter Preparation
http://HarryPotterPlaces.com/tips/PreTripPrep.pdf

Tips for refreshing your Potterverse knowledge before you leave (loading your Pensieve!)—such as enjoying a Potter Film Festival with your friends.

Packing Pointers
http://HarryPotterPlaces.com/tips/PackingPointers.pdf

General UK packing tips, including important methods of baggage identification and travel document copy storage, as well as *vital* personal supplies you'll not want to forget.

Supplies to Purchase *in* the UK
http://HarryPotterPlaces.com/tips/UKtripSupplies.pdf

Stuff you don't need to lug along while traveling to Great Britain, and where to cheaply purchase these items after you arrive.

UK Car Rental and Driving Tips
http://HarryPotterPlaces.com/tips/UKcarRental.pdf

Important considerations for selecting your rental car and preparing to drive in the UK.

UK Telephones
http://HarryPotterPlaces.com/tips/UKphones.pdf

How to dial from outside or inside the UK, and phone options available.

UK Internet Access
http://HarryPotterPlaces.com/tips/UKinternetAccess.pdf

The many options for connecting with the World Wide Web while in the UK, and what services to avoid.

UK Photography Issues
http://HarryPotterPlaces.com/tips/UKphotography.pdf

Railway station photography rules, the value of packing a cheap or disposable camera, and more.

UK Terminology Guide
http://HarryPotterPlaces.com/tips/UKterminology.pdf

A translation of UK English terms that have meanings *different* from the same US English terms.

Lumos London

[©2009 Tara Bellers]

Ancient and modern, exciting and exhausting, bright and beautiful, dark and dank—almost any descriptive term, *and its antonym*, can accurately be used when describing **London, England**. And, although London's status as the capital city of both **England** and the **United Kingdom** has never been officially granted by statute or decree, no one on the planet would naysay that status.

What began as a single square mile of city founded by the Romans over two thousand years ago (*Londinium*), **Greater London**—aka, **Central London**—now encompasses more than 600 square miles of land, and nine million inhabitants.

For several years, the city of London has accommodated more International visitors annually than any other city in the world. Similarly, London's Heathrow airport receives more International travelers than any other airport in the world. In 2012, London will lay claim to another world record, when it becomes the first city ever to host the modern Summer Olympic Games for a third time.

To learn more about this marvelous city's history and numerous Non-Potter attractions, consult a London Muggle travel guidebook, or peruse the following websites:

http://en.wikipedia.org/wiki/London
http://en.wikipedia.org/wiki/History_of_London
http://www.visitlondon.com/
http://www.london.gov.uk/

London Has the Most Harry Potter Places in the World

There are 18 Central London Harry Potter Sites

13 **Great Sites**

2 **Might-Be-Fun** sites

3 **Skip It** sites

There are 10 London Side-Along Apparation Sites

5 **Great Sites**

3 **Might-Be-Fun** sites

2 **Skip It** sites

London Side-Along Apparations are Potter places outside of Central London that you can quickly reach by train, visit, and then return to London—usually allowing time to also trek to several other Harry Potter sites on the same day.

In the **Specialis Revelio London** section, you'll find tips for planning your London Potter Places and Side-Along visits, as well as **Five Suggested London Potter Itineraries** for seeing the *best* of them, based on the number of days you have to visit, and the amount of energy you intend to expend.

Ready-Made Harry Potter Tours

Google "Harry Potter Tours" and you'll find loads of links to companies that offer Ready-Made Harry Potter Tours (**Potted Tours**).

Please Note: *None* of the authors of, or research contributors to, *Harry Potter Places* have ever experienced *any* of the Potted Tours offered on the Internet!

Ms. Tara Bellers is an extraordinarily thorough *Harry Potter Places* researcher who lives in the US. As of November, 2011, she has personally designed and enjoyed **three UK Potter trips**. Back in 2009, Tara penned the following comments about Ready-Made Harry Potter Tours—and her opinion hasn't changed since then:

"When planning my [first] Harry Potter trip, I looked at these [Potted Tours] and used them to start compiling a list of Potter Places I wanted to visit. I considered booking one of them for a while, but they just felt so incomplete to me—none of them included everything I wanted to see. By planning our own trip, my friends and I ended up seeing much more, and staying much longer at the best places, for less than half the cost of any [Potted Tour] package."

We wholeheartedly agree with Tara's sentiments. Potted Tours do not currently include everything an avid Potterite would wish to visit in London, or beyond. Furthermore, Potted Tours are almost always far more expensive than personally-planned Potter tours.

We suggest that Potterites *avoid* Potted Tours, unless you are blessed with a big budget. Potterites who can afford a modicum of extraneous expense *should* consider booking one (or more) of the available Potted Tours. Guided tours are almost always entertaining, and often will help you visit various Potter Places more comfortably and quickly.

Please Note: After you've booked a Potted Tour, be sure to require the Tour Company to provide you with a list of every Potter Place included. Armed with that list, you can use *Harry Potter Places* to design a **personal tour** of all the places *missed* by the Potted Tour, on one or more of your other UK visit days.

One Last Caveat!

Before booking any Potted Tour that includes **Oxford**, consider reading the **Specialis Revelio** section in *Harry Potter Places* Book Two—OWLs: Oxford Wizarding Locations. There you'll learn about the **Duke Humfrey's Library** dilemma.

Popular Ready-Made Harry Potter Tour Companies

British Tours Ltd.
http://www.britishtours.com/

Leave from London. Site Entrance fees and meals are *not* included.

"Please add £20 [$32] for collections from London Train Station."

The fee for each British Tour Ltd's Potted Tour is based on vehicle occupancy, thus the per-person cost decreases as more people are added. The fee for groups of 7 or more is available online.

London and Oxford: 8 hours; 1-2 people £420 ($662), 3-4 people £485 ($765), 5-6 people £590 ($931).

Oxford Only: 5 hours; 1-2 people £345 ($544), 3-4 people £395 ($623), 5-6 people £470 ($741).

Oxford and Gloucester: 10 hours; 1-2 people £485 ($765), 3-4 people £565 ($891), 5-6 people £655 ($1,033).

Brit Movie Tours
http://britmovietours.com/

Leave from London. Brit Movie Potted Tours are offered only on Sat, Sun, and Wed. Meals are not included.

London Locations Tour: 3 hours; Adults £25 ($40), Children under 12 £15 ($24), Family (2 Adults and 2 Children) £75 ($118).

Oxford and Lacock Tour: 10.5 hours; Adults £55 ($87), Children under 12 £40 ($63), Family (2 Adult & 2 Children) £180 ($284). Entry fees *not* included.

England Tour: 2-days; Adults £210 ($331), Children under 12 £200 ($316). Overnight accommodation not included. Site entry fees *are* included.

HP Fan Trips
http://www.hpfantrips.com/

HP Fan Trips [HPFT] tours are the closest to being ***all-inclusive*** Potted Tours.

Common HPFT tour options are 6 days/5 nights, or 9 days/8 nights.

In 2011, the 9 days/8 nights per-person, double occupancy, tour prices ranged between £1,901 ($2,999) and £2,789 ($4,399).

A 6 days/5 nights per-person, double occupancy, tour fee was £1,267 ($1,999).

An extra charge is applied to a *single* booking of any tour.

HPFT tour prices *usually* include: all UK accommodations, flight expenses between London and Scotland, a Steam Train trip, several meals (including at least one Hogwarts-style Banquet), daily services of a professional guide, and *some* site admissions fees.

HPFT tour prices *never* include Airfare to/from Britain, and most of their tours are limited to individuals 13 years old and older.

London Taxi Tours
http://www.londontaxitour.com/

This company offers the most *numerous* and *varied* Potted Tours.

London Taxi Tour (LTT) fees are based on vehicle occupancy, thus the per-person cost decreases as more people are added. The fee for groups of 7 or more is available online.

Inner London Tour: 3 hours; 1-4 people £230 ($363), 5-6 people £260 ($411).

Oxford + London Tour: 8 hours; 1-4 people £390 ($616), 5-6 people £440 ($695).

Oxford + London + Lacock Tour: 10 hours; 1-4 people £490 ($774), 5-6 people £540 ($853).

Also available on the LTT website: Extended versions of all the above Potted tours, Oxford-only Potted tours, Lacock-only Potted tours, and tours including other Potter or Non-Potter sites. LTT even offers some short *London Airport Layover* Harry Potter Tours!

Broomsticks to Portkeys: London Transportation Tips

Flying to London

Read the airfare tips published by Reid Bramblett, Rick Steves, and Lonely Planet before booking your ticket:
http://www.reidsguides.com/t_pl/t_pl_s_airfare.html
http://www.ricksteves.com/plan/tips/498fly.htm
http://www.lonelyplanet.com/england/london/transport/getting-there-around#75876

Consider using a name-your-price airline booking website such as **Priceline**:
http://www.priceline.com/

London is Served by Six International Airports

Heathrow Airport [LHR]

The UK's busiest airport, accustomed to rapidly and efficiently processing over 213,000 travelers on a busy day.
http://www.heathrowairport.com/
http://en.wikipedia.org/wiki/Heathrow_Airport

Gatwick Airport [LGW]

London's second-busiest airport.
http://www.gatwickairport.com/
http://en.wikipedia.org/wiki/Gatwick_Airport

Stansted Airport [STN]

The third-busiest London area airport.
http://www.stanstedairport.com/
http://en.wikipedia.org/wiki/London_Stansted_Airport

Luton Airport [LTN]

London's fourth-largest airport.
http://www.london-luton.co.uk/
http://en.wikipedia.org/wiki/London_Luton_Airport

Southend Airport [SEN]

This airport is primarily a regional airport, but also manages many European International flights.
http://www.southendairport.com/
http://en.wikipedia.org/wiki/London_Southend_Airport

London City Airport [LCY]

This airport has only one runway, but is the UK's leading *business* airport, principally serving wealthy International travelers visiting London's financial district.

http://www.londoncityairport.com/
http://en.wikipedia.org/wiki/London_City_Airport

Getting from the Airport to London

After your arrival at Heathrow, Gatwick, Stansted, or Luton airports, catch the airport's **Express Train** to its Central London railway station. Buy a Return (round-trip) express train ticket unless you'll be leaving London from a different airport.

Airport express train tickets can be pre-purchased via the Internet. Although Internet-purchased tickets may not be discounted, being armed with a pre-purchased express train ticket is always more convenient.

From Central London, Take a TAXI to your Lodgings

You do *not* want to lug even a single, seemingly lightweight, item of luggage through London's Tube system! When encumbered with baggage, **Murphy's Law** accurately dictates that there will be *miles* of passageways — and several *flights of steps* — to traverse in order to cheaply arrive at the Tube station closest to your London lodgings. After that, you'll have to trudge down several city blocks, dragging your increasingly-heavy burden behind you, before finally reaching your destination.

It is *well* worth the extra £/$ required to take a Taxi from the airport express train's London station to your London lodgings. Similarly, when ready to depart London, book a Taxi to pick you up and take you back to the express train's station.

🚖 Renting a Car to Travel *Outside* of London

UK car rental is best accomplished at the car rental companies that serve the airport you'll be using to reach or leave London. Read the *Harry Potter Places* **UK Car Rental Tips Supplementum**, and the **Harry Potter WB Studio Tour Itinerary Planning Supplementum**, then reserve your car.

http://HarryPotterPlaces.com/tips/UKcarRental.pdf
http://HarryPotterPlaces.com/b1/08aHPSTitineraryPlan.pdf

🚖 Do *Not* Rent a Car to Drive *in* London!

There is *no reason* to rent a car for driving in London. London's ample variety of public transportation options are by far the most inexpensive and efficient ways to travel between the airports and the city, as well as within the city. Driving within London is miserably complicated and considerably expensive.

London traffic is extremely heavy every day, all year long. And, the city's variable street systems are terrifically confusing, even for UK natives—individuals *accustomed* to driving on the left side of the road. Furthermore, for each day that you drive within Central London, you'll have to pay a "congestion charge" of £10 ($16).

http://www.direct.gov.uk/en/Diol1/DoItOnline/DG_4017688
http://www.tfl.gov.uk/assets/downloads/congestion-charging.pdf

[©2008 C.D. Miller]

Then, There's the Lousy London Parking Problems

If the lodgings you book in London offer a place to park, you'll most likely be directed to a space extremely difficult to get into, and even more difficult to get out of. If you won't be driving while in London, that won't be a problem. But, there is *no reason* to rent a car simply to reach your London lodgings! Use the efficient and inexpensive airport express train, then a taxi.

Potterites divinely inspired to drive within the city should also know that London's on- and off-street parking spaces are limited, and insanely expensive. If you can find an open on-street parking space, common London street parking fees range between £4 ($6) and £8 ($13) per hour—sometimes *more*. Fees for London Parking Garage spaces are often £10 ($16) per hour, or *more*.

We Wholeheartedly Agree with Reid Bramblett

http://www.reidsguides.com/t_au/t_au_rentals.html

> "Save a rental car for exploring the countryside and small towns—and save yourself (1) money (2) aggravation and (3) time by arranging to pick up your rented car on the final day you'll be in your first major city …

dropping it off as soon as you arrive at your last [major] city. It'll shave a few days off the rental period, and avoid [major city] parking fees ... This alone can knock several hundreds dollars off your rental costs."

Pottering in London:
Oyster Card *vs* London Travelcard *vs* London Pass

Paying cash for individual Tube or bus or train tickets while traveling in and around London is absurdly expensive. Happily, two major discount travel cards are available—the **Oyster Card** and the **London Travelcard**—and recent administrative changes have made deciding between these two cards far easier than it used to be.

The best explanation of the Oyster Card and London Travelcard differences is found *not* on the website that sells them, but on the **Trip Advisor** website.
http://www.tripadvisor.com/Travel-g186338-c75899/London:United-Kingdom:Oyster.Cards. Travelcards.And.Tickets.html

However, it's a good idea to also read the **Using Oyster** webpage that explains how to use an Oyster Card, especially the tips about Yellow and Pink card readers.
http://www.tfl.gov.uk/tickets/14839.aspx

Potterites who will be spending up to 7 days in London, *and* **visiting multiple Non-Potter Places**, are still faced with the chore of investigating the benefits of buying a **London Pass**. Good luck with that!
http://www.londonpass.com/

London Discount Travel Card Recommendations
Pre-Purchase a £50 ($80) Oyster Card

Use it on your London-based Harry Potter WB Studio Tour Day Itinerary Day, and on all but *one* of your Pottering-*in*-London days.
http://visitorshop.tfl.gov.uk/home.html

Set up the Oyster Card Auto-Top-Up Feature

Every time your Oyster Card balance falls below £8, it will automatically be reloaded with funds from your bank account, and you'll never have to queue up at a station kiosk to reload your card. When you cash-in your Oyster Card at the end of your London visit, you'll receive a full refund of any unused pre-loaded pounds, *and* the original £3 activation fee you paid.
https://oyster.tfl.gov.uk/oyster/link/0002.do

Purchase a 1-Day Anytime Travelcard for Zones 1-6

Potterites following a *Harry Potter Places* Suggested London Potter Itinerary should also purchase a 1-Day Anytime Travelcard for Zones 1-6.

Adult ticket £16 ($26), Child 11+ ticket £8 ($13). (Accompanied children under 11 years old travel for free on London's Underground and Overground transportation services.)

http://visitorshop.tfl.gov.uk/travelcards/1-day/product/day-anytime-travelcard.html

Use your London Travelcard for *all* transportation methods required to enjoy the London Potter Itinerary day that includes the *HbP* **Train Station Café (Site #20):** the Quick-Quill Trip, the Kwikspell Crusade's *POA* day, or the *SS* day of our Huffandpuff Expedition, Padfoot Prowl, and Potter Promenade itineraries.

Apart from the day you visit the *HbP* Train Station Café, a pre-loaded Oyster Card is probably the most economical way to travel in and around London.

London Hop-On-Hop-Off Tour Busses

Many major cities throughout the world are served by open-top tour bus companies that provide transportation inexpensively between each of the most famous sites found therein. These tour busses allow visitors to hop-off the bus and wander around individual locations, then hop-back-on the bus to journey to the next iconic site. If you never disembark the hop-on-hop-off (**HOHO**) bus, you can enjoy an inexpensive and scenic **drive-by tour** of the city's most famous sites.

Two major companies offer open-top HOHO tour buses that regularly travel between each of London's most famous places throughout the day.

The London Original Tour Bus Company
http://www.theoriginaltour.com/

The London Big Bus Company
http://www.bigbustours.com/eng/london/

HPP Endorses the London Original Tour Bus Company

Why? Because the London Big Bus (**BB**) route fails to travel over an extremely Potterly-important bridge that *is* included on the Original Tour Bus (**OTB**) route. Apart from that, there isn't much of a difference between the two major London HOHO tour bus companies.

FREE Thames River City Cruise Ticket

Both the London Original Tour Bus and Big Bus tickets include a FREE Thames River City Cruise ticket.

You'll not need a cruise schedule when following *Harry Potter Places* Suggested London Itineraries. However, if you wish to obtain a timetable of boat departures, visit the City Cruises' website.
http://www.citycruises.com/

Booking your HOHO bus ticket online will save you anywhere from £2 to £9 per ticket.

If you'll be visiting London during off-peak months, your HOHO bus ticket may be good for up to 48 hours. Otherwise, each HOHO ticket (and it's free river cruise ticket) is good for up to 24 hours after first-use activation.

Purchase of an OTB (or BB) tour bus ticket, with its free Thames River City Cruise ticket, is crucial to accomplishing the **Huffandpuff Expedition**, **Padfoot Prowl**, or **Potter Promenade** Suggested London Potter Itineraries.

If you'll not be following our itineraries, but have an extra day to spend Non-Pottering in London, consider buying an OTB ticket and following the information provided in the **Fly-By Bridges & Buildings (Site #4)** entry when enjoying your free Thames River cruise, and while touring overland. One way or another, you'll thoroughly enjoy your HOHO Non-Potter tour of London's most famous sites.

London Maps

Book stores and souvenir shops in all the London airports, as well as throughout the city, offer a variety of printed maps for sale. But, many Potterites may wish to become acquainted with London's layout while planning their holiday. Furthermore, it is best to be armed with a map of London before you arrive.

This Website Offers Loads of FREE London Maps and Info
http://www.visitlondon.com/maps/travel_maps/index

Separate links for the classic **London Underground (Tube) map** and **Central London Bus Routes map** are provided. However, both those maps are included in the free **Welcome to London Visitor's Guide Leaflet**. So, that would be the best Visit London document to download. Print and Pack the portions of that Leaflet that seem most important to you.

The Visit London website also offers free guides important to Potterites with special accessibility needs, such as a guide to planning step-free journeys while traveling London's Tube system.

"Whether you're on wheels, with wheels, mobility impaired or just don't fancy stairs, you can plan your step free Tube journey in advance with TfL's guide to accessible stations."

Pre-Purchased Printed Map Resources

The *Harry Potter Places* Travel Store offers links for purchasing many of the printed and eBook maps mentioned below.

Visit London has Partnered with the Collins Map Company

[Actual Map Scans; © Collins Maps]

The most portable and convenient of these maps are the **Collins London Mini Street Finder** (Collins Mini) and the **Collins Pocket Atlas London** (Collins Atlas).

Both of these maps are pocket-sized and in book form—no refolding required—with sturdy, plastic-coated covers and pages. The Collins Mini is slightly shorter, but at least three times *thicker* than the Collins Atlas. Most importantly, the Collins Mini covers a greater area of London, and its Central London map pages are larger in print and detail.

In case you purchase either of these maps, each *Harry Potter Places* London Site entry includes the page number and map coordinates for finding Potter Places on the Collins Mini and the Collins Atlas.

U.S. or Canadian Potterites can purchase either of these Collins maps from the Harry Potter Places Travel Store.

UK Potterites can purchase them from Amazon.com.co.uk:

London Mini Streetfinder Atlas (Collins Streetfinder)

http://www.amazon.co.uk/London-Mini-Streetfinder-Atlas-Collins/dp/0007303564/ref=sr_1_1?s=books&ie=UTF8&qid=1322679194&sr=1-1

London Pocket Atlas (Collins Pocket Atlas)

http://www.amazon.co.uk/London-Pocket-Atlas-Collins-UK/dp/0007452454/ref=sr_1_1?ie=UTF8&qid=1322679087&sr=8-1

Harry Potter Places Endorses Bensons MapGuides

Unfortunately, the Bensons maps are not available in the *Harry Potter Places* Travel Store. You'll have to purchase them from a Brick-and-Mortar store (such as Barnes & Noble, or the like), or from Bensons's website.
http://www.bensonsmapguides.co.uk/

[Actual Map Scans; © Bensons MapGuides]

Each *Harry Potter Places* London Site entry includes coordinates for finding Potter Places on the **Bensons London Mini Map** (Bensons Mini) and **Bensons London Street Map** (Bensons Street).

Both of these lightweight folding maps cover practically the same area of Central London. The Street Map is simply a larger-print version of the Mini Map, with large-print West End and London's Square Mile sectional maps on the back.

The reason we prefer the Bensons maps: When you open either of the Bensons folded paper maps, you can see the entire city and recognize where you are, as well as where you're going. When looking at any of the Collins map individual pages, it is almost impossible to gain a sense of your location within the city.

No matter what printed map you plan to purchase, look for 2012-updated editions that include the new Olympic Park, and other 2012 Olympic venues.

London eBook Maps

[©2011, MapsInternational.co.uk, via Amazon.com
©2010, MobileReference, via BarnesAndNoble.com]

The Kindle London Map Guides eBook—the Potter Preferred London Map eBook—is available in the *Harry Potter Places* **Travel Store**.

The Travel London MobileReference Nook eBook is available at BarnesAndNoble.com.
http://www.barnesandnoble.com/w/travel-london-england-uk-mobilereference/1021236507?e an=9781605010373

Look for editions updated in 2012 before purchasing an eBook map.

London Lodging Options

Throughout all the *Harry Potter Places* travel guidebooks, we do our best to offer tips for finding the types of lodgings you're looking for, based on your budget. Whenever possible, we provide links for finding accommodations that fall within the following three categories:
  • **Check in Cheap:** Hostels in or near the City or Village.
  • **Board at the Burrow:** City or Village Bed & Breakfast Establishments.
  • **Leaky Cauldron to Malfoy Manor:** Livable to Luxurious Hotels in or near the City or Village.

Unfortunately, when it comes to finding safe and sanitary lodgings within **major cities** such as **London**—or Oxford, or Edinburgh—if you're not able to pay big bucks (plenty o' pounds) and stay in a high-priced hotel, it's not easy to accurately assess the quality of accommodation you're looking at online. Actually, even some of the high-priced London hotels aren't particularly high-quality.

Please Note: No matter where you travel, London will always be the most expensive place to lodge during your UK holiday.

You can **Google** the type of accommodation you're looking for, such as London, England Hostels ... B&Bs ... Hotels. But, this search method is a crapshoot. Any London accommodation's Internet description may be decidedly different from its real-life appearance and quality. Furthermore, many of the really cheap London Hostel or B&B listings are barely better than skanky flophouses.

Even the **Trip Advisor** website—a website wonderfully helpful for finding quality low-cost Oxford or Edinburgh lodgings—isn't particularly helpful for finding a *safe and sanitary* place to stay in London. London is simply too huge!

Bottom Line: If a London lodging is incredibly cheap, it's probably nasty.

Book London Lodgings Recommended by a Friend

If someone you know has enjoyed staying in a particular London lodging, *that* is the place you should book. Happily, if none of your personal friends have ever lodged in London, you have some *Harry Potter Places* friends who have!

Check in Cheap: London Hostels

The only sure way to avoid skanky London flophouses is to book a safe and sanitary hostel affiliated with the **UK Youth Hostel Association** (YHA).
http://www.yha.org.uk/find-accommodation/london/

Please Note: Although they're called *Youth* hostels, Youth Hostel associations throughout Europe and the UK offer lodgings to individuals of *any* age—children, teens, adults, and seniors. Many even have a few family accommodations.

Hostelling International (HI) is another highly respected European hostel organization, and is affiliated with the YHA. HI offers safe and sanitary hostels, often situated within historic London buildings.
http://www.hihostels.com/dba/Hostels-London-list.php?lang=E&city=GB|0040

Board at the Burrow: London Bed & Breakfasts

CD Miller, has enjoyed a stay in more than one of the B&Bs located on **Sussex Gardens**, a street just north of Hyde Park, and southeast of the Paddington Railway / Tube Station.
Bensons Mini: A,B-4,5 / **Bensons Street:** C,D-4,5
Collins Mini: pg 32 / **Collins Atlas:** pg 41, E,F-5

Sussex Gardens is lined with lodgings of every quality and price on both its northern and southern sides. In fact, almost every Street, Crescent, Square, and Terrace found within the area between **Paddington Station** and **Hyde Park** is populated by rows of side-by-side Victorian townhouses that have been renovated into hotels and B&Bs.

Although this area includes some not-so-nice accommodations—as well as a few exceptionally overpriced hotels—many marvelous and inexpensive lodgings can be found here.

The following link offers a list of the most reliable Sussex Gardens lodgings options.

http://www.london-discount-hotel.com/grouped_hotels_85_Sussex+Gardens+Hotels+London

CD Miller heartily recommends the **Admiral Hotel** on Sussex Gardens.
http://www.admiral-hotel.com/

[©2002 C.D. Miller]

Don't be surprised to learn that your Sussex Gardens B&B doesn't have its own reception area. For instance, the **Berkeley Court** reception desk is located in the nearby **Seymour Hotel**. Sussex Gardens innkeepers often own several adjacent properties. Thus, it makes sense that they keep costs to a minimum by staffing a reception desk in only one location to serve all of their properties.

[©2008 C.D. Miller]

A shared dining room location is also common. But, even if your dining room is in the building next door—or two doors down—the distance you'll have to walk is rarely more than what you'd have walk within a large, high-priced hotel.

To search for cheap B&Bs or Discount Hotels in other areas of London, go to: http://www.london-discount-hotel.com/

⚓ The Leaky Cauldron to Malfoy Manor: Livable to Luxurious London Hotels

Being a business traveler, Potterite Tara Bellers has stayed in several London hotels over the years. Here are her recommendations.

The Caesar Hotel
http://www.derbyhotels.com/en/hotel-the-caesar/the-hotel/?gclid=CO2zjsKRyawCFUKo4Aod MVk-rw

> "A very cute, stylish hotel about an 8 minute walk from Paddington. Comfortable rooms, quiet street, convenient location from a transportation perspective."

Best Western Corona
http://www.bestwestern.co.uk/Hotels/Corona-London-83799/Hotel-Info/Default.aspx

> "I've stayed here 2 or 3 times. It's a budget hotel within walking distance from Paddington Station. Rates were comparable to the Caesar Hotel, but the rooms were not quite as stylish as the Caesar."

There are several Best Western Hotels in London, some more expensive, some cheaper. You can explore these possibilities on the Best Western Hotel UK website.
http://www.bestwestern.co.uk/

Hilton London Paddington Hotel
http://www.hilton.co.uk/paddington?WT.srch=1

> "Very convenient location, but also very pricey. I've only stayed here when traveling on the company's dime, or when cashing-in hotel points. I'd never personally pay their rates—not with the other less expensive options available. But, Potterites interested in a higher-end experience may want to consider this hotel."

Connected by a footbridge to the Paddington Railway Station, the Hilton London Paddington Hotel is just a few steps away from where the Heathrow Airport Express Train delivers you in London. You'll also only have to walk across the footbridge to access the London Underground system via Paddington's Tube Station.

Hilton London Euston Hotel
http://www.hilton.co.uk/euston

> "Reasonably priced hotel near Kings Cross, St. Pancras, and Euston train stations. Nothing extraordinary, but convenient to train transportation."

There are several Hilton Hotels in London, some more expensive, some cheaper. You can explore these possibilities on the Hilton Hotel UK website.
http://www.hilton.co.uk

Jolly St. Ermin Hotel
http://www.sterminshotel.co.uk/

> "I've also stayed here 2 or 3 times. It's a reasonably-priced, nice hotel near Victoria Station. Location is very convenient to Buckingham Palace, Houses of Parliament, and Westminster Abbey."

St. Ermin is a Luxury Hotel, but it has relatively low-cost business rates. You'll not have to *prove* that you're a business traveler in order to ask for a business rate here or elsewhere!

Most Hotel Chains Have More than One Property in London

Visit the website of your favorite hotel, and search for London lodging options on the dates of your visit.

Travelodge

Travelodge is likely the cheapest International hotel chain with properties in London.
http://www2.travelodge.co.uk

Sheraton Hotels in London
http://www.starwoodhotels.com

Holiday Inn (and Holiday Inn Express) Hotels in London
http://www.holidayinn.com

Marriott Hotel
http://www.marriott.com/hotel-search/london.hotels.united-kingdom.travel/

Premier Inn
http://www.premierinn.com/en/

Any international hotel chain may offer reasonable London lodgings rates, but you'll have to shop around to find them.

SPECIALIS REVELIO LONDON PART ONE

London's Harry Potter Places and Side-Along Apparations

Due to the plethora of Potter Places found in and around London, an enormous amount of information must be investigated and considered when planning a London Potter trip of any length. **Do not be dismayed!** Over the past three years, we've done the Gryffindor-Lion's share of required research.

By working your way through the following steps, *Harry Potter Places* will help you design a London Potter trip (or UK Potter trip) that perfectly suits your personal preferences, and the number of days you have to visit.

Step One

Read all of **Lumos Britannia** and **Lumos London**. Learn as much as you can about visiting the UK. Ensure that your passport is in order. Consider the pros and cons of **Potted Tours**.

Step Two

Read each of the 28 London and London Side-Along Potter Place Site Entries. You needn't worry about selecting the places you want to visit during this first read-through. Simply familiarize yourself with the many Potter Places, and the reasons for the *Might-Be-Fun* and *Skip It* site ratings.

Step Three

Read the **Harry Potter WB Studio Tour Itinerary Planning Supplementum**, the **Oxford Option** information, and the **Suggested London Potter Itineraries** found in **Specialis Revelio London Part Two**.

Step Four

Read the **General London Potter Holiday Planning Tips**, below.

Once you've perused all the Potter Place options and visiting factors, it's time to start making decisions.

Step Five

Decide on the days and dates of your Potter holiday, as well as the UK locations your trip will include. Will you only be visiting London? Will you also be renting a car to travel outside of London for a few days?

Step Six

Based on the entirety of your UK trip days, dates, and travel plans, select a *Harry Potter Places* Suggested London Potter Itinerary to follow — or use one of our itineraries as a template for creating your *own*.

Step Seven

If you'll be visiting the **Harry Potter WB Studio Tour [HPST] (Site #27)**, consider the best days for following your London Potter Itinerary, then purchase your HPST ticket. After that, design your **HPST Day Itinerary** based on instructions found in **Specialis Revelio London Part Two**.

Step Eight

Review the **Flying to London** tips segment of **Lumos London**. Book your flight. Consider also pre-booking a return (round-trip) ticket for the express train between your airport and its central London railway station. If advanced ticket purchase isn't cheaper than onsite ticket purchase, it's certainly more convenient to have your express train ticket prior to arrival.

Step Nine

If you'll be renting a car to travel outside of London, review the **Lumos London UK Car Rental Tips Supplementum**, *and* the **Harry Potter WB Studio Tour Itinerary Planning Supplementum**, then reserve your car.

Step Ten

Review the **Burrow to Malfoy Manor** lodging tips segment of **Lumos London**. Book your London lodgings, as well as all outside-London lodgings, if needed.

Last Step

Review your itinerary and begin purchasing all the *other* attraction and travel tickets or cards required to accomplish your UK Potter holiday.

General London Potter Holiday Planning Tips

Do Your Best to Avoid Visiting London on a Public Holiday

Although all London and London Side-Along Potter Places are open every day of the year except for Christmas day and Boxing Day (December 25th

and 26th), transportation delays that may adversely affect a London Potter Itinerary are more likely to occur on public holidays. A two-year schedule of London public holidays can be found at:
http://www.visitlondon.com/travel/public-holidays

Unless you plan to *attend* the 2012 Olympic Games or Paralympic Games, avoid visiting London between July 27th and August 12th, and between August 29th and September 9th, in 2012.
http://www.london2012.com/

Consider Visiting London Last

Each day of a London Pottering itinerary requires far more walking than a day spent touring any other Potter Place in the UK. If you'll be traveling to several Potter Places outside of London during your UK Potter Holiday, save your London visit for the *end* of your trip. Potterites who visit London *before* traveling to outside-London locations risk reaching those Potter Places with sore feet.

What a Difference a Day Makes!

Each of our Suggested Potter Itineraries contain a **Best Day Table** to help you schedule the most Potterly perfect trip, based on the days of the week that you'll be visiting London.

Muggle Matters

Muggles who live within London's Central City and its closest boroughs are accustomed to occasionally seeing strangers strutting about on their street. Muggles living *outside* these areas are not!

Four of the London Side-Along Apparation sites are private neighborhoods best visited on a **weekday**, when most indigenous Muggles are away at work. Visiting these sites on Saturday or Sunday is *possible*, but weekend-relaxing Muggles may be offended by your intrusion.

Do your best to avoid visiting a Muggle neighborhood Side-Along on a weekend. And, no matter what day you visit, please remember the:

Potterite Prime Directive

To **POLITELY** Go Where Potterites Need to Go
— without PERTURBING anybody —
So That Other Potterites Can **Continue** to
ENJOY GOING THERE!

🚌🚢 Hop-On-Hop-Off Tour Busses

You'll need to purchase an **Original Tour Bus** (Potter-Preferred!) or a **Big Bus** Hop-On-Hop-Off Tour Bus Ticket for one day of our Huffandpuff Expedition, Padfoot Prowl, or Potter Promenade itineraries.

All Hop-On-Hop-Off (**HOHO**) London Tour Bus tickets include a **Free River Cruise Pass**.

The three aforementioned *Harry Potter Places* Suggested London Potter Itineraries only require you to use a HOHO tour bus/cruise ticket for the two-hour Thames River **Fly-By Bridges and Buildings Tour (Site #4)**—a river cruise followed by a small portion of the HOHO overland bus tour. However, your HOHO overland bus tour ticket is good for **24 hours** (48 hours during off-season dates), to use at your leisure *before* or *after* the Fly-By Tour itinerary. Be sure to organize your HOHO tour bus ticket use so that you can complete Site #4's tour prior to the ticket's expiration time.

Please Note: You'll still need a **London Travelcard** or an **Oyster Card** for traveling to and from *other* London Potter Places when following any itinerary that includes the Fly-By Tour.

See the **Broomsticks to Portkeys** section of **Lumos London** to learn more about **London Transportation Options**, and to access links to HOHO Tour Bus websites.

Pre-Trip Transport Times Check

Two weeks before your holiday, check the transport times of each day's itinerary. Any number of events may have altered the tube or train times we investigated and employed to create the *Harry Potter Places* Suggested London Itineraries. Transportation schedule changes are most frequently caused by the ongoing renovation and repair work required to maintain London's Tube system—the oldest underground railway network in the world. If associated transport schedules have changed, site visiting times within each itinerary may need to be adjusted.

☉ **Check Tube Times** on the Transport for London website:
http://www.tfl.gov.uk/

🚆 **Check Railway Schedules** at:
http://www.nationalrail.co.uk/

Please Note: If you are following our Padfoot Prowl or Potter Promenade itineraries, do not pre-purchase your time-specific **Muggle Wax Museum (Site #14)** Madame Tussauds ticket until *after* you've performed your Pre-Trip Transport Times Check, and confirmed that day's schedule.

PART TWO

The HPST Day Itinerary Planning Supplementum

None of our Suggested London Potter Itineraries include the Harry Potter WB Studio Tour. Why? Because the HPST requires its very own itinerary day. Thus, we've created a Supplementum that provides important directions for designing your HPST Day Itinerary, based on the Studio Tour timeslot ticket you purchase, as well as the manor of travel you elect to use for reaching the Harry Potter WB Studio Tour.
http://HarryPotterPlaces.com/b1/08aHPSTitineraryPlan.pdf

Visiting Oxford During a London Potter Holiday

Busses and trains are readily available for visiting the Potter Places found in **Oxford, England**, from a London base. However, Pottering to Oxford requires at least one entire day *apart from* your HPST visit day, and *apart from* the day(s) you plan to spend touring London Potter Places and Side-Along Apparations.

Harry Potter Places **Book Two—OWLs: The Oxford Wizarding Locations** provides the in-depth information required to plan and accomplish a London-based Oxford visit that best includes all four of the Oxford City Centre OWLs, with or without also traveling to Blenheim Palace (the only outside-Oxford OWL).

Before you plan an Oxford Potter tour, or book a Potted Tour that includes Oxford, consider reading HPP Book Two's **Specialis Revelio Oxford** section. There you'll learn about the **Duke Humfrey's Library** dilemma.

Harry Potter Places Suggested London Potter Itineraries

The Best London and London Side-Along Potter Places are film locations that have retained readily recognizable features. Our Suggested London Potter Itineraries are designed to assist Potterites to visit as many of the Best Potter Places as possible, based on the number of days you'll be Pottering in London, and the amount of energy you anticipate being able to expend each day.

No Skip-It-rated Potter Places are included in *any* of our Suggested Itineraries. Potterites divinely inspired to visit one or more of the London or London Side-Along Skip-It sites should investigate each individual

Skip-It site—using the information provided in its *Harry Potter Places* Site Entry—then create your own itinerary.

Each *HPP* Suggested London Potter Itinerary Identifies:
- The most efficient order for visiting London Potter Places and Side-Alongs on any given day.
- The maximum amount of time to spend at each site.
- The approximate between-site travel time and transportation method(s).
- The Site Entry where you can find **specific** between-site travel directions.
- A bold "at" symbol [@] indicates that you must pay strict attention to the time! To keep on schedule, arrive at, or leave from, a site *no later* than the time we specify.
- A bold pound and dollar sign [£/$] indicates when shopping and/or meal time is allocated.

Beginning and Ending Each London Potter Itinerary

Each *Harry Potter Places* Suggested London Potter Itinerary identifies the Tube or Railway Station related to each itinerary day's first and last site locations.

To obtain directions from your London lodgings to the first itinerary site each morning, and directions back to your lodgings from the last itinerary site each evening, consult the **Transport for London** website.

⊖ http://www.tfl.gov.uk/

TAXI **Please Note:** Although traveling via public transportation is always cheaper for beginning or ending a London itinerary day, taking a Taxi is almost always an option—particularly at the end of a long day of sightseeing.

The Quick-Quill Trip
Only time for a ONE-DAY London Potter Place tour?
See 7 of London's Best Potter Places and 1 London Side-Along in one day.
http://HarryPotterPlaces.com/b1/08bQuickQuill.pdf

The Kwikspell Crusade
You have TWO DAYS to Potter in London, but don't want to be rushed?
See 11 of London's Best Potter Places and 2 Side-Alongs in two days.
http://HarryPotterPlaces.com/b1/08cKwikspell.pdf

The Huffandpuff Expedition

Want to cram as many London Potter Places as possible into TWO DAYS?
Visit all but 1 of London's Best Potter Places, plus 2 Side-Alongs in two days.

Please Note: We call this the *Huff*-and-*Puff* Expedition because it is an exceptionally *arduous* itinerary! The Huffandpuff Expedition may be too demanding for young children, seniors, or portly Potterites unaccustomed to frequent periods of rapid walking between sites, and being on their feet *all day long*.
http://HarryPotterPlaces.com/b1/08dHuffandpuff.pdf

The Padfoot Prowl

Have THREE DAYS to Potter in London and don't mind rushing just a bit?
Enjoy this 3-day tour of *all* the Best London Potter Places and 4 Side-Alongs. Although far less arduous than our Huffandpuff Expedition, the Padfoot Prowl does include several 10- and 15-minute rapid walks. Parties that include young children, seniors, or portly Potterites may prefer the **Potter Promenade** four-day itinerary.
http://HarryPotterPlaces.com/b1/08ePadfoot.pdf

The Potter Promenade

You have FOUR DAYS to Potter around London?
Happy You! This *almost* leisurely-paced itinerary will lead you to *all* the Best London Potter Places and 6 Side-Alongs within four days.
http://HarryPotterPlaces.com/b1/08fPromenade.pdf

Please remember that your **Harry Potter WB Studio Tour** visit must be accomplished on a day *apart from* the days you spend following our Suggested London Potter Itineraries.

1

DEATH EATERS' BRIDGE

The London Millennium Footbridge
http://en.wikipedia.org/wiki/Millennium_Bridge_(London)

Google Maps UK: 51° 30' 35" N, 0° 5' 54" W *or* 51.509722, -0.098333
Bensons Mini: K-5 / **Bensons Street:** M-5
Collins Mini: pg 51, E-1 / **Collins Atlas:** pg 16, D-4
Tube Station: Mansion House

 Original Tour Bus Saint Paul's Cathedral Red/Yellow Stops *or* Big Bus Stops 45/18

Operation Hours / Entry Fee: None

Visit Time: Schedule at least 30 minutes just to take Potter bridge pix.

Parseltongue Pointers:
- Southwark Bridge = "SUTH-uck"
- Thames River = "TEMZ"

Chapter One of *Harry Potter and the Half-Blood Prince* [*HbP*] begins with a description of the Muggle Prime Minister's outrage over his government being blamed for recent freakish murders and disasters—particularly the collapse of the **Brockdale Bridge**. Approximately a dozen motoring Muggles were dumped into a river when the Brockdale Bridge suddenly, and inexplicably, snapped cleanly in two.
http://harrypotter.wikia.com/wiki/Brockdale_Bridge

The Brockdale Bridge doesn't exist in real-life. Rather than recreate the destruction of a fictional automobile bridge, *HbP* filmmakers elected to use the iconic **London Millennium Footbridge** to dramatize the Muggle world violence perpetrated by Voldemort. A handful of Potterites have complained about this choice, because *HbP* was set in 1996, two years before Millennium Footbridge construction began. Happily, most Potterites have thoroughly enjoyed the visually exciting twisting and buckling of the Millennium Footbridge's destruction—especially in the **IMAX 3-D** version of the movie.

Stretching across the Thames River from Peter's Hill walkway (just south of **Saint Paul's Cathedral**) to the **Tate Modern** art gallery, the Millennium Footbridge is the only steel suspension bridge in London. Originally opened on June 10th, 2000, the bridge was closed that same day. When thousands of opening day *Save The Children* charity-walk participants marched over it, their passage caused the bridge to dangerously wobble from side-to-side. A one minute YouTube video shot on opening day dramatically demonstrates how serious the sway was!
http://www.youtube.com/watch?v=eAXVa__XWZ8

Thereafter nicknamed the *Wobbly Bridge*, stabilization modifications required another two years of construction. The Millennium Footbridge was finally reopened in 2002—without the wobble.

Death Eaters' Bridge Potter Pix Pointers

The order of our five Potter Pix Pointers is based on approaching the Millennium Footbridge from the north (after visiting Gringotts Bank or Saint Paul's Cathedral; or, if walking to the bridge from the Mansion House tube station). If you approach the Millennium Footbridge from the south (after visiting Borough Market), reverse the order.

Death Eaters' Bridge Potter Pic #1

[©2009 Tara Bellers]

On either side of the Millennium Footbridge's north entrance are steps leading down to **Paul's Walk**, a sidewalk that borders the north bank of the Thames, and runs beneath the bridge. From Paul's Walk, on the east side of the bridge, you can line up a pic similar to the following *HbP* screenshot. If someone else can take the pic with you standing at the top of these steps, so much the better.

[*Half-Blood Prince* screenshot (enhanced)]

Death Eaters' Bridge Potter Pic #2

[©2009 Tara Bellers]

At the central section of the Millennium Footbridge, where the support cables dip below the railing, stop and have your pic taken while dramatically grasping the railing in terror. To recreate the following *HbP* screenshot, have someone kneel down on the bridge next to you and thrust a camera out *beyond* the railing, with its lens pointed back up at you. Be sure that the camera's lanyard is securely tied to the camera operator's wrist!

[*Half-Blood Prince* screenshot (enhanced)]

Death Eaters' Bridge Potter Pic #3

Also while on the central section of the Millennium Footbridge, take a pic of the next bridge to the east (toward Tower Bridge); **Southwark Bridge** is an *Order of the Phoenix* Harry Potter **Fly-By Bridge (Site #4)**.

[©2009 Tara Bellers]

[*Order of the Phoenix* screenshot segment (enhanced)]

Between Southwark Bridge and London Bridge/King William Street is a railway bridge. So, the best place to snap this pic is while traveling on one of the Thames River Cruises (See Site #4). If you don't cruise the river, your next best chance of getting a great Southwark Bridge Potter pic is while standing on the Millennium Footbridge.

Blackfriars Bridge, another Harry Potter *Order of the Phoenix* fly-under bridge, can be seen to the west as you walk over Millennium Footbridge. Unfortunately, **Blackfriars *Railway* Bridge** is in the way. See Site #4 for Blackfriars Bridge Potter pic directions.

Death Eaters' Bridge Potter Pic #4

On the southern end of the Millennium Footbridge there is a green-tinted, transparent Plexiglas-like barrier lining the interior edge of the two ramps leading up to it. Stand on the bridge with your back at the center of this southern barrier. Hold your camera as high overhead as possible to take a pic of the length of the Millennium Footbridge, with Saint Paul's Cathedral in the background.

[*Half-Blood Prince* screenshot (enhanced)]

Even with few people on the bridge, you still can snag a great Potter pic.

[©2009 Tara Bellers]

Death Eaters' Bridge Potter Pic #5

[©2009 Tara Bellers]

Finally, get a few pix of yourself standing on the south bank of the Thames, with the Millennium Footbridge and Saint Paul's Cathedral in the background. No, there isn't a corresponding Harry Potter screenshot for this. But who cares? This view makes for a great photo.

One More Death Eaters' Bridge Potter Pic Remains

[*Half-Blood Prince* screenshot (enhanced)]

This shot is best snapped from the top of an **Original Tour Bus**, while riding over **Blackfriars Bridge**. (The Big Bus doesn't drive over Blackfriars Bridge.) See Site #4 for other options.

Nearby Non-Potter Places

The following three Non-Potter Places lie between the south bank of the Millennium Footbridge and **Borough Market** [Leaky Cauldron, *Prisoner of Azkaban* (Site #7)].

The Tate Modern Art Museum
http://www.tate.org.uk/modern/

Located at the southern entrance to the Millennium Footbridge and housed within a spectacular building renovated from a disused power station, the Tate Modern is Britain's premier gallery of international modern art. All the major modern art movements are represented here, from Fauvism onwards: Turner, Picasso, Monet, Matisse, and Dali; Pollock, Naum Gabo, Giacometti, and Rothko. Works of Pop Art artists such as Lichtenstein and Warhol can be found here, as well as those defined as Minimal and Conceptual artists.

Open Sun to Thurs, 10am-6pm; Fri and Sat, 10am-10pm. **Closed** Dec 24, 25, 26. Open on Jan 1.

Admission is free except for major exhibitions.

London Pass holders are entitled to a free audio-guide.

[©2009 Tara Bellers]

Shakespeare's Globe Theater
http://www.shakespeares-globe.org/

The original **Globe Theater** opened in 1599, only four years before the end of Queen Elizabeth I's 45-year reign. Built by a company in which Shakespeare owned a stake, it is famously referred to as The Shakespearean Globe. The original Globe Theater was destroyed by fire in 1613, rebuilt in

1614, and finally closed in 1642. Only a block or so east of the Millennium Footbridge's south entrance, today's Globe Theater is an exact replica of the 1614 Shakespearean structure. Built in 1997 approximately 200 yards from the original Globe's location, the modern Globe Theatre was the first building in London allowed to have a thatched roof since the Great Fire of 1666.

The Globe Shop is located just inside the theatre foyer, and is open year-round; Mon-Sun, 10am-6pm. If you're a theater fan (or someone on your gift list is a theater fan), schedule at least 30 minutes to shop at the Globe. You can see a preview of its products online.
http://www.shakespearesglobe.com/shop/

The Globe Exhibition and Theater Tour is offered year-round, Monday through Sunday. Check the Globe's website for opening times during the dates of your visit, and allow at least 2 to 3 hours to enjoy this Non-Potter Place.

London Pass holders are entitled to free entry and a 10% Globe Shop discount.

The Globe Exhibition is a museum located beneath the theater. Your all-day ticket allows you to wander leisurely through static and *interactive* displays—as well as live demonstrations—related to Shakespeare, the London where he lived and the theatre for which he wrote.

The 30 to 40 minute guided Globe Theater Tour appointment included in your ticket will take you throughout the building, revealing the story of its reconstruction and offering insight into the working life of an Elizabethan theater.

The Globe Theater Tour is not offered during matinee performances. Instead, tour ticket-holders are taken to the nearby site of Bankside's very first theatre, **The Rose**. This is the theater for which Christopher Marlowe and Ben Jonson wrote their greatest plays, and where William Shakespeare learned his trade. The Rose is the only Elizabethan playhouse that has been thoroughly excavated by archaeologists.
http://www.rosetheatre.org.uk/

2011 Globe Exhibition & Theatre Tour Tickets: Adults £12.50 ($19); Seniors (60+) and Students (with valid ID) £11 ($17); Children (5-15) £8 ($12); Children under 5 free. See the Globe's website for family, group, and other discounts.

2011 Globe Exhibition & Rose Theatre Tour Tickets: Adults £10 ($16); Seniors (60+) and Students (with valid ID) £8.50 ($13); Children (5-15) £7 ($11); Children under 5 free. See the Globe's website for family, group, and other discounts.

A ttending a Globe Theater Performance is Highly Recommended

Ringed by three levels of covered seats, the center of the theater's structure is **open to the elements**. Thus, winter temperatures limit the Globe's performance season. To attend a performance, you'll need to visit between late April and early October.

Covered Seat Tickets are priced according to degree of visibility and proximity to the stage. Seat tickets range from £15 ($23) to £37.50 ($58). However, due to the many pillars that support the upper seating levels and roof, almost every seat in the theatre occasionally suffers an obscured view.

Oddly enough, the cheapest Globe Theater tickets offer the best, entirely unobstructed, view of the stage, the **Standing Tickets**. Tickets to stand in the large, circular **Yard** in front of the stage cost only £5 ($8). But, you literally must STAND for the entire performance, and many plays last up to 3 hours. Furthermore, because *700* standing tickets are available per show, the Yard may be incredibly crowded. Unless you're very tall *and* have loads of stamina, pay the extra pounds to buy a covered seat ticket.

[©2008 C.D. Miller]

The Clink Prison Museum
http://www.clink.co.uk/

This museum occupies the original site of the **Clink Prison**, a notoriously brutal London prison that operated from 1144 to 1780, when it was burned to the ground by rioting Protestants. The prison's name was derived from the *clinking* noise made by the various manacles, fetters, and chains worn by its prisoners. In fact, Clink Prison is the origin of the phrase, *"in the clink."*

Plan to spend at least 30 to 45 minutes here.

Open 7 days a week at 10am. Check the website for closing times during your visit.

2011 Admission: Adults £7 ($11); Children under 16, Seniors over 60, and Students with an ID, £5.50 ($9).

[**TIP:** See the **Leaky Cauldron;** *Prisoner of Azkaban* **(Site #7)** for a comparison of the Clink Prison Museum, the London Bridge and Tombs Experience (London Pass free entry), and the London Dungeon.]

Nearby Potter Places

Gringotts Bank (Site #5), a 15 minute walk or a 20 minute ride/walk.

Hogwarts Staircase (Site #6), a 4 to 5 minute walk.

Leaky Cauldron, *Prisoner of Azkaban*: **Borough Market (Site #7)**, a 10 minute walk.

Going to The Death Eaters' Bridge

From Hogwarts Staircase (Site #6)
A 4 to 5 minute walk.

If you exit Saint Paul's Cathedral from the South Churchyard entrance, you'll see the Millennium Footbridge directly to the south. If you exit from Saint Paul's Great West Door entrance, turn left and walk around the cathedral to the crosswalk in front of the South Churchyard entrance. ♦ Cross the street to Peter's Hill walkway and continue south to the north bank of the Millennium Footbridge.

From Original Tour Bus Saint Paul's Cathedral Red/Yellow Stops, *or* Big Bus Stops 45/18
A 6 minute walk.

You'll be on the north side of Ludgate Hill when you disembark the bus. Head east toward Saint Paul's Cathedral. [Consider following the **Hogwarts Staircase (Site #6)** directions for popping into the Saint Paul's Cathedral Shop before heading to the Death Eaters' Bridge.] ♦ At the next crosswalk, turn right and cross to the south side of the street. ♦ Turn left and head southeast to Peter's Hill walkway (directly across the street from the cathedral's South Churchyard entrance). ♦ Turn right and walk south to the north bank of the Millennium Footbridge.

⊖ From Mansion House Tube Station
A 9 minute walk.

🔥 Follow station signs to **Queen Victoria Street & Cannon Street (South Side) Exit #1A.** ♦ From the exit, turn left and walk west on the south side of Queen Victoria Street, to Peter's Hill. You'll know you've reached Peter's Hill when you can see Saint Paul's Cathedral one block north (on your right). ♦ Turn left and you'll see the Millennium Footbridge ahead.

From the Leaky Cauldron, *Prisoner of Azkaban*: Borough Market (Site #7)
A 10 minute walk.

🔥 Head north on Stoney Street to its end. ♦ Turn left and walk west on Clink Street, past the **Clink Prison Museum** and under the railway bridge. ♦ At Bank End, turn right and walk north to its end. ♦ At Bankside, turn left and walk northwest until it reaches the river and becomes Thames Path. ♦ Follow Thames Path as it goes northwest along the river. ♦ At the end of Thames Path, turn left and walk south. ♦ At the next street, turn right and walk west under Southwark Bridge. ♦ On the other side of the bridge, turn slightly right and head northwest on Bankside (yes, it reappears). ♦ At the river, follow Bankside as it heads northwest again and becomes the Bankside Jetty. ♦ As you are passing the **Globe Theater**, head right and continue west along the Thames River until you reach the south bank of the Millennium Footbridge (and the north entrance of the **Tate Modern Art Museum**).

From Gringotts Bank (Site #5)
A 15 minute walk *or* a 20 minute walk/ride/walk.

🔥 Walk to the Millennium Footbridge along the Thames River.

From the east entrance of Australia House, cross to the south side of the Strand and walk southwest on Arundel Street to its end. ♦ At Temple Place, cross to the south side and turn left. Walk east on Temple Place, continuing as it curves south toward the Thames river. ♦ Cross Victoria Embankment and turn left. Walk east along the path that follows the Thames river, which becomes Paul's Walk as you near the Millennium Footbridge. [**TIP:** Stay on Paul's Walk and cross under the Millennium Footbridge to its east side. There, you can take **Death Eaters' Bridge Potter Pic #1** before climbing the steps up to Peter's Hill walkway and the north entrance of the Millennium Footbridge.]

Ride a Tour Bus to the Millennium Footbridge.

Walk east from the main entrance of Australia House and cross the island to the east side of Aldwych in front of Saint Clement Danes Church ♦ Turn left to walk north and then west as Aldwych curves around to the Tour Bus stop. ♦ Board the next tour bus and ride to the next stop on Ludgate Hill, a block west of the Great West Door entrance to Saint Paul's Cathedral. (You'll see the Cathedral as you approach the stop.) [Consider following the **Hogwarts Staircase (Site #6)** directions for popping into the Saint Paul's Cathedral Shop before heading to the Death Eaters' Bridge.] ♦ Walk east toward the Cathedral's western entrance. ♦ Cross to the south side of Ludgate Hill or Saint Paul's Churchyard. ♦ Watch on your right for the entrance to Peter's Hill walkway. ♦ Turn right and head south on Peter's Hill walkway to the north entrance of the Millennium Footbridge.

⊖ From Piccadilly Circus Station

A 15 min Underground journey, followed by a 9 min walk.

Take the **Bakerloo Line** toward **Elephant & Castle** to reach **Embankment Tube Station**. Then take the **District Line** toward **Upminster, Barking, Dagenham East**, or **Tower Hill** to reach **Mansion House Tube Station**.

OR, take the **Bakerloo Line** toward **Elephant & Castle** to reach **Embankment Tube Station**. Then take the **Circle Line** toward **Liverpool Street** to reach **Mansion House Tube Station**.

🕺 Follow Mansion House station signs to **Queen Victoria Street & Cannon Street (South Side) Exit #1A**. ♦ From the exit, turn left and walk west on the south side of Queen Victoria Street, to Peter's Hill. You'll know you've reached Peter's Hill when you can see Saint Paul's Cathedral one block north (on your right). ♦ Turn left and you'll see the Millennium Footbridge ahead.

2

DEATHLY HALLOWS
PART ONE

CAFÉ-RELATED FILM SITES

Piccadilly Circus; Shaftesbury Avenue & The Trocadero
http://en.wikipedia.org/wiki/Piccadilly_Circus

Google Maps UK: 1 Shaftesbury Avenue, London W1D 7EA
Bensons Mini: F-5 / **Bensons Street:** W-3
Collins Mini: pg 47, F-1; pg 48, A-1 / **Collins Atlas:** pg 14, C-4

Tube Station: Piccadilly Circus

Original Tour Bus Piccadilly Circus Red or **Yellow Stops** *or* Big Bus Stop 35/8

Operation Hours: Being *exterior* film sites, no operation hours apply. However, the best time to visit this area is between 1pm and 7pm on Thursdays through Sundays, when the Crest of London Bear is available for pic-taking.

Entry Fee: None

Visit Time: Schedule at least 45 minutes to take pix at both film sites. Schedule at least 90 minutes to allow time for shopping at the Crest of London store after snapping Potter Pix.

Parseltongue Pointer:
• Shaftesbury = "SHAFTS-bree"

☙❧

In Chapter Nine of *Deathly Hallows*, Harry, Ron, and Hermione (HR&H) performed an emergency disapparation from Bill and Fleur's wedding to **Tottenham Court Road**—a real-life place in London, but *not* a film site. Once there, they scurried into an alley to change clothes, and then walked to a small and shabby all-night Muggle café.

Due to the pyrotechnics associated with filming the Death Eaters battle inside the café, a **Leavesden Studios set** was built to shoot *Deathly Hallows Part One* Muggle café interior scenes. Happily, exterior scenes seen before and after interior café footage were shot in two **Piccadilly Circus** locations. And, both of these film sites are easy to find.

Go to Piccadilly Circus and head for the iconic **SANYO** sign above the **GAP** store. When facing it, look to your right (northeast) and you'll see the **Crest of London** store on **Shaftesbury Avenue**.

[*Deathly Hallows Part 1* screenshot (enhanced)]
(Note that the "A" in **SANYO** was burned-out when this *DHp1* aerial footage was shot.)

The Shaftsbury Avenue *DHp1* Film Site

In Chapter Nine of *Deathly Hallows*, HR&H were described as half-walking, half-running, up a wide street that was lined with shops and thronged with late-night revelers, while enroute to a Tottenham Court Road Muggle café. This is precisely the kind of activity that was filmed along London's **Shaftesbury Avenue** in April of 2009.

In the *Deathly Hallows Part One* movie, the Trio is seen arriving at the Piccadilly Circus entrance to Shaftesbury Avenue (barely avoiding being hit by a double-decker bus), then rapidly striding northeast on Shaftesbury Avenue from the **Crest of London** store toward **Denman Street**, threading their way through scores of oncoming pedestrians. They are seen passing the **NatWest Bank** and the **Piazza Italiano Espresso Bar**, with the scene ending when they reach the last window of the **Churchill Gifts** store, just before Denman Street.

Shaftesbury Avenue Potter Pic #1

While passing the NatWest Bank building, the Trio had to dodge the famous **Crest of London Bear** character, wearing his Queen's Foot Guards uniform. Oddly enough, the Crest Bear was **wielding a *wand***—something we didn't notice until after snagging *DHp1* screenshots!

[©2009 Tara Bellers] [*Deathly Hallows Part 1* screenshot segment (enhanced)]

If he's out and about when you arrive, have your photo taken with the Crest Bear character before doing anything else, to ensure that you don't miss this opportunity. If you have an extra wand with you, ask the Bear to hold it while taking your pix.

http://www.crestoflondon.co.uk/crest-bear/

> The Crest of London Bear "can be seen welcoming guests and posing for photos at our Piccadilly Circus store each Thursday, Friday, Saturday and Sunday … from 1pm to 7pm."

We highly recommend souvenir shopping at the Crest of London store. However, Crest of London shopping is best delayed until *after* your Piccadilly Circus Potter pic-taking trek, so that you'll not be juggling packages while snapping Shaftesbury Avenue and Trocadero Potter pix.

Shaftesbury Avenue Potter Pic #2

[*Deathly Hallows Part 1* screenshot (enhanced)]

After accidentally apparating into the middle of Shaftesbury Avenue, HR&H barely managed to avoid being run over by a double-decker bus. They leapt onto the nearest curb and pressed themselves against the iron railing found directly in front of the Crest of London store.

For obvious safety reasons, do *not* attempt to recreate this scene with your Trio-stand-ins positioned on the **street-side** of the Crest of London curb iron railing. Instead, take your pix with them standing on the **store-side** of the iron railing.

If you happen to snap pix while a red bus is passing in front of your stand-ins, your recreation pic will be perfect—no one will notice that your stand-ins are on the *inside* of the iron railing!

Shaftesbury Avenue Potter Pic #3

[*Deathly Hallows Part 1* screenshot (enhanced)]

To recreate this screenshot, your photographer should be standing near the last NatWest bank column northeast of Piccadilly Circus, while you stand where Ron is, just *before* the first NatWest bank column. In this screenshot, the GAP store sign is seen between Ron's head and the Crest of London coat-of-arms sign.

Shaftesbury Avenue Potter Pic #4

[*Deathly Hallows Part 1* screenshot (enhanced)]

This pic should be taken while your Trio-stand-ins are passing by the tables on the sidewalk in front of the Piazza Italiano Espresso Bar.

Shaftesbury Avenue Potter Pic #5

Your last Shaftesbury Avenue Potter pix should be taken as your Trio-stand-ins pass the sales displays on the sidewalk in front of the Churchill Gifts store. Hopefully, there'll be a **2 for £5** sign above one of the display racks you find here.

[*Deathly Hallows Part 1* screenshot (enhanced)]

BOLO

While Pottering around the Piccadilly Circus area, **Be On the Look Out** for the alley that the Trio darted into to change clothes before heading to the Muggle café. Finding this alley is a long shot, especially since it may have been filmed on an **alley set** with a green-screen at the end. Still, even if it was filmed on a set, the image seen at the alley's end *should* exist **somewhere**.

[*Deathly Hallows Part 1* screenshots (enhanced), above and below.]

Location Clues:

- Overlapping half of the alley entrance is a large circular canopy — perhaps that of a hotel or theatre marquee. The canopy's lower border is festooned with large light bulbs, or a large light ring.
- Just inside the alley's entrance is a pole bearing a closed-circuit television (**CCTV**) camera.

If you find an alley containing these features, please blog about its location on the *Harry Potter Places* website.

The Trocadero Walkway *DHp1* Film Site

[©2011 Tara Bellers]

When you've finished snapping sidewalk pix in front of the Churchill Gifts store you'll reach **Denman Street**. Turn right and cross Shaftesbury Avenue to the north corner of the triangular **Ripley's Believe It or Not** building (seen at center, above). Then, cross **Great Windmill Street** to reach the **London Trocadero** walkway's northern entrance. When you enter, you'll be walking south, toward **Coventry Street**.

The London Trocadero is a super-sized shopping center and entertainment complex, consisting of several adjacent buildings with store fronts on Piccadilly Circus and the surrounding streets.
http://www.londontrocadero.com/

[©2009 Tara Bellers]

Footage of HR&H walking through a shopping center appears after the café battle. Although it looks as though the Trio is traversing an interior corridor, the April of 2009 film site is actually an *exterior* walkway tucked under the second floor of the Trocadero building on the east side of Great Windmill Street, between Shaftesbury Avenue and Coventry Street. Open to the street on the west side, railings between the columns prevent entrance to the Trocadero walkway, except at the northern and southern ends. In all of the following *DHp1* screenshots, HR&H are walking south from the northern entrance, toward the Coventry Street entrance.

Trocadero Potter Pic #1

After entering the walkway's north end, send your photographer ahead to stand beneath the overhead **CINEMAS** sign located approximately halfway between Shaftesbury Avenue and Coventry Street, and have pix taken of you with the northern entrance to this Trocadero walkway seen just behind you.

[*Deathly Hallows Part 1* screenshot (enhanced)]

The neon sign seen behind the Trio in this screenshot doesn't exist in this real-life location. The building directly across the street from the Trocadero walkway's northern entrance is a **McDonalds**. Happily, everything else seen in this screenshot does.

Trocadero Potter Pic #2

[*Deathly Hallows Part 1* screenshot (enhanced)]

This screenshot was filmed between the heads of Ron and Harry, while the Trio were passing under the CINEMAS sign, enroute to the southern Coventry Street exit of this Trocadero walkway.

Stand beneath the CINEMAS sign. Have your photographer dash to a position several feet *behind* you, then turn and take pix of the backs of your head, with the southern Coventry Street exit seen in front of you.

Trocadero Potter Pic #3

[*Deathly Hallows Part 1* screenshot (enhanced)]

Although seen on screen for less than a second, the CINEMAS overhead neon sign makes for a great *DHp1* screenshot recreation opportunity. Send your photographer ahead of you again, and have pix taken while you're striding just south of the CINEMAS sign.

[©2011 Tara Bellers]

During April of 2009 *DHp1* filming, the "MAS" portion of the CINEMAS neon sign was **burned-out**. It was *still* burned-out when Tara revisited this site in July of 2011. If the sign has been repaired before your visit, consider using a photo-editing program to black-out the "MAS" portion.

[©2011 Tara Bellers]

When you emerge from under the arch at the southern end of the Trocadero walkway (seen beneath the **LONDON** sign in the lower right corner of the pic above), you'll be on Coventry Street at Piccadilly Circus. To find the nearest underground entrance, turn right, cross Great Windmill Street, and walk west. The Piccadilly Circus Tube Station entrance is in the short block found in front of the Ripley's Believe It or Not building, just before reaching the SANYO sign and Shaftesbury Avenue.

Time to Shop?

Pass by the Piccadilly Circus Tube Station entrance and return to the Crest of London store on Shaftesbury Avenue. Yes, this is a non-Potter souvenir store. But, it offers loads of inexpensive London trip gifts.

Crest of London's Piccadilly Store
http://www.crestoflondon.co.uk/stores/piccadilly-circus/

Open Mon to Thurs, 9am-11:30pm; Fri & Sat, 9am-Midnight; Sun, 10am-11pm.

London Free Pass purchasers are entitled to an "Exclusive free gift" from Crest of London.

Nearby Non-Potter Places

Piccadilly Circus is jam-packed full of non-Potter tourist attractions, cafés and restaurants, nightclubs, souvenir and gift shops, retail stores, cinemas and theaters. The best business directory for this area is the **All in London** website's Piccadilly Circus Tube Station page.
http://www.allinlondon.co.uk/tube-piccadilly-circus.php

Nearby Potter Places

Diagon Alley Wizard Entrance (Site #3), a 10 minute walk.

Ministry of Magic Film Sites (Site #10), a 15 minute walk.

Muggle Portrait Gallery (Site #12), a 10 minute walk.

Going to The *DHp1* Café-Related Film Sites

From the Piccadilly Tube Station
A 30 second walk from the exit.

Follow station signs to the **Shaftesbury Avenue #4A** exit on Coventry Street. ♦ After reaching street level, make a U-turn to the left and walk west toward the SANYO sign. When facing the sign, look to your right for the Crest of London store.

From Big Bus Stop 35/8
A 2 minute walk.

Walk east to Piccadilly Circus, look to your left and walk to the SANYO sign. When facing the sign, look to your right for the Crest of London store.

From the Original Tour Bus Red Route Stop
A 4 minute walk.

Walk north on Haymarket to Coventry Street. ♦ Turn left and walk west to the SANYO sign. When facing the sign, look to your right for the Crest of London store.

From the Original Tour Bus Yellow Route Stop
A 5 minute walk.

Walk west on Coventry Street to the SANYO sign. When facing the sign, look to your right for the Crest of London store.

From the Diagon Alley Wizard Entrance (Site #3)
A 10 minute walk.

🚶 Cross to the west side of Charing Cross Road, turn left and walk south to Cranbourn Street. ♦ Turn right and walk southwest as Cranbourn Street becomes Leicester Square, then Swiss Court, then Coventry Street. ♦ Continue west on Coventry Street until you reach the Piccadilly Circus SANYO sign. When facing the sign, look to your right for the Crest of London store.

From the Muggle Portrait Gallery (Site #12)
A 10 minute walk.

🚶 If leaving from the National Portrait Gallery's main entrance, turn left and walk north on Saint Martin's Place, continuing as it curves northwest to Irving Street.

If leaving from the National Portrait Gallery's Orange Street entrance, turn right and walk east until the street curves north to Irving Street.

Turn left and walk west on Irving Street, continuing as it curves northwest and ends at the southeast corner of Leicester Square. ♦ Cross to the park and walk northwest on the diagonal path leading through the park to Leicester Square's northwest corner. ♦ Turn left and walk southwest on Swiss Court, continuing as it becomes Coventry Street. ♦ When you reach the Piccadilly Circus SANYO sign, look to your right for the Crest of London store.

⊖ From the Muggle Underground Station (Site #13)
An 11 min journey.

Take the Jubilee Line towards Stanmore or Wembley Park to Green Park Tube Station. ♦ Then take the Piccadilly Line towards Cockfosters or Arnos Grove to Piccadilly Circus Tube Station.

Or, take the District Line towards Upminster or Tower Hill to Embankment Tube Station. ♦ Then take the Bakerloo Line towards Queen's Park, Harrow & Wealdstone, or Stonebridge Park to Piccadilly Circus Tube Station.

From the Ministry of Magic Film Sites (Site #10)
A 15 minute walk.

Please Note: Consider heading to the **Muggle Portrait Gallery (Site #12)** first and popping into the National Portrait Gallery *Shop* while on your way to Piccadilly Circus. It's about a 10 minute walk to the gallery, then a 10 minute walk from the gallery to Piccadilly Circus. See Site #12 for directions.

🚶 Walk southwest on Great Scotland Yard—or Whitehall Place, or Horse Guards Avenue—to Whitehall (street). ♦ Turn right and walk north on Whitehall to its end at **King Charles I Island** (a large, circular island directly south of **Trafalgar Square**, containing a bronze statue of King Charles I on a horse). Several streets intersect here, making this a very confusing area. ♦ Turn left and walk west across the mouth of Whitehall. Continue as the street curves northward around King Charles I Island, past The Mall (street), to the next corner. ♦ Keep left to walk west along Cockspur Street, past Warwick House Street. [There's a small Crest of London store on the southwest corner of Cockspur and Warwick House Streets.]

Continue west along Cockspur Street until you reach the crosswalk just past the Bank of Scotland building. ♦ Turn right and cross to the north side of Pall Mall. ♦ Turn left and cross to the west side of Haymarket. ♦ Turn right and walk north on the west side of Haymarket to its end at Coventry Street. ♦ When you reach the four **Horses of Helios** fountain, keep left, walking west around the fountain to the next crosswalk. ♦ Turn right and cross to the north side of Coventry Street (at the northwest corner of Great Windmill Street). ♦ Turn left and walk west on Coventry Street to the SANYO sign. When facing the SANYO sign, look to your right for the Crest of London store.

⇌⊖ From Euston Railway and Underground Station (HPST Itinerary)
A 10 min journey.

Make your way to the Euston Tube Station. ♦ Take the next Victoria Line train towards Brixton to Oxford Circus Tube Station. ♦ Then take the Bakerloo Line towards Elephant & Castle to Piccadilly Circus Tube Station.

⊖From Victoria Underground Station (HPST Golden Tours Itinerary)
A 10 min journey.

Walk a block northeast to the Victoria Tube Station. ♦ Catch the Victoria Line towards Seven Sisters or Walthamstow Central to Green Park Tube Station. ♦ Then take the Piccadilly Line towards Cockfosters or Arnos Grove to Piccadilly Circus Tube Station.

⇌⊖ From Liverpool Street Railway and Underground Station (Potter Promenade Itinerary)
A 17 min journey.

Make your way to the Liverpool Tube Station. ♦ Take the Central Line towards Ealing Broadway, West Ruislip, Northolt, or White City to Holborn Underground Station. ♦ Then take the Piccadilly Line towards Uxbridge, Heathrow Terminal 4, Heathrow Terminal 5, Rayners Lane, or Northfields to Piccadilly Circus Tube Station.

If you miss Holborn Underground Station, get off at Oxford Circus and take the Bakerloo Line towards Elephant & Castle to Piccadilly Circus.

THE DIAGON ALLEY WIZARD ENTRANCE

Charing Cross Road
http://en.wikipedia.org/wiki/Charing_Cross_Road
http://harrypotter.wikia.com/wiki/Charing_Cross_Road

Google Maps UK: 48 Charing Cross Road, London WC2H 0BS
Bensons Mini: G-5 / **Bensons Street:** J-5
Collins Mini: pg 36, B-4 / **Collins Atlas:** pg 14, D-3

⊖ **Tube Station:** Leicester Square

🚌 **Original Tour Bus Loop Line** Start/End point at Leicester Square Station.

🚌 **Original Tour Bus Trafalgar Square** Red/Yellow Stops or **Big Bus Stops** 37/10/77

Operation Hours and **Entry Fee:** None

Visit Time: You'll only need about 15 minutes to take your Potter pix here, 30 to 45 minutes if you visit the two surprise sites. However, Potterite Bibliophiles will want to schedule two hours or more when visiting the most famous literary street in the world.

Parseltongue Pointers:
- Charing = "CHAR-ing" (like CHARcoal, not "CHAIR-ing")
- Leicester = "LES-ter"

ભ્ર૪ૐ

Charing Cross Road is a London street that runs north from the **National Portrait Gallery (Site #12)**, past **Leicester Square Tube Station**, until it reaches **Saint Giles Circus**. Charing Cross Road is Internationally renowned for the specialist, antiquarian, and second-hand bookshops that have long lined its length. In modern times, many sellers of new books have obtained space here, bookstores such as Borders and Foyles.

In JK Rowling's novels, Muggles could only access Diagon Alley by passing through the **Leaky Cauldron**, which is found on Charing Cross Road. However, movie scenes featuring the Leaky Cauldron's Muggle entrance were filmed in **Leadenhall Market (Site #8)** for *Sorcerer's Stone*, and in **Borough Market (Site #7)** for *Prisoner of Azkaban*.

Prisoner of Azkaban footage was shot of the Knight Bus careening along the real-life Charing Cross Road while delivering Harry to the Leaky Cauldron. Unfortunately, not a single Charing Cross Road building can be recognized during those rapid and blurry *POA* scenes. In fact, throughout all of the *POA* Knight Bus street-careening footage, only one building can be recognized with certainty—the **Chester Stevens Estate Agents** office building.

[*Prisoner of Azkaban* screenshot (enhanced)]

This building and street exist exactly as they appear on screen, but they're nowhere near Charing Cross Road. The Chester Stevens building is on the northeast corner of **Green Lanes** and **Park Avenue** in **Palmers Green**, an intersection found within the northern **London Borough of Enfield**. Additionally, film footage of the Knight Bus almost running into an elderly woman slowly crossing the street with her walker was shot on Park Avenue, just around the corner from the Chester Stevens building. Because these two film sites are not within Central London, the **Knight Bus Streets (Site #23)** entry can be found in the **London Side-Along** section.

The Diagon Alley Wizard Entrance

After destroying the Millennium Bridge in the opening scenes of *Half-Blood Prince*, a group of Voldemort's Death Eaters head for Diagon Alley to kidnap Mr. Ollivander. Their oily-black flight trails track them zooming down into

Trafalgar Square and past the National Portrait Gallery, before swooping north along Charing Cross Road to the Diagon Alley *Wizard* Entrance—an entrance that doesn't require passage through the Leaky Cauldron's common room.

A *Harry Potter Places* **Wizard Entrance Supplementum** contains the entire sequence of screenshots showing the Death Eaters' route from Trafalgar Square to the Diagon Alley Wizard Entrance.
http://HarryPotterPlaces.com/b1/WizardEntranceSupplementum.pdf

[*Half-Blood Prince* screenshot (enhanced)]

The Diagon Alley Wizard Entrance seen in *HbP* is found near the intersection of **Charing Cross Road** and **Great Newport Street**. At the time of *HbP* filming, the brown brick building on the northeast corner was home to the **Quinto/Francis Edwards** bookshop, established in 1855.
http://www.francisedwards.co.uk/

Since then, the bookshop moved to a new location, and this space is now occupied by a **Patisserie Valerie Café**.

> "A haven for self- indulgence in the most exquisite cakes and patisseries you will ever feast your eyes upon."

http://www.patisserie-valerie.co.uk/charingcross.aspx

The white stone building just east of the patisserie looks the same as it did during *HbP* filming, and houses several business offices. **#12 Great Newport Street** has a gigantic bank of windows and a stone arch above its entrance.

The gated gap *between* these two buildings is where the *HbP* Diagon Alley Wizard Entrance is located.

[*Half-Blood Prince* screenshot (enhanced)]

Diagon Alley Wizard Entrance Potter Pix

[©2011 Tara Bellers]

Only about four feet wide, this gated real-life alley serves as the fire escape route from a private courtyard surrounded by several tall buildings containing numerous flats and offices. There are no screenshots showing Potter characters in front of this entrance, or approaching it. Thus, feel free to snap several Potter pix of your own design, using the screenshots above as inspiration.

A Surprise Diagon Alley Wizard Entrance Potter Pic Op

Soon after their emergency disapparation from Bill and Fleur's wedding in *Deathly Hallows Part One*, Harry, Ron, and Hermione went to an all-night Muggle Café. Exterior footage of the trio reaching this café was shot in **Piccadilly Circus**, on **Shaftesbury Avenue** (see **Site #2**). However, due to the pyrotechnics associated with the Death Eaters battle that ensued, a Leavesden Studios **set** was built to film interior café scenes for *DHp1*.

[*Deathly Hallows Part 1* screenshot (enhanced)]

The window of the *DHp1* Muggle Café set was a green-screen. The real-life street images that were digitally inserted into the movie's café window were shot from across the street of a building located on the northeast corner of **Charing Cross Road** and **Denmark Street**.

[©2011 Tara Bellers]

Chris Bryant's Musical Instruments store is about 6 blocks north of the Diagon Alley Wizard Entrance intersection of Charing Cross Road and Great Newport Street, and only 3 blocks south of **Saint Giles Circus**—the junction of Tottenham Court Road, Charing Cross Road, Oxford Street, and New Oxford Street.

Google Maps UK: 126 Charing Cross Road, London, WC2H 0LA

If you have time to walk north of the Diagon Alley Wizard Entrance—perhaps while walking to the **British Museum (Site #18)**—snap *DHp1* Café-Related Potter Pix here.

Another Surprise Potter Pic Op on Charing Cross Road

On the south side of Denmark Street, directly across from Chris Bryant's Musical Instruments store, you'll find another interesting Potter-related surprise—something we'll let you discover on your own.

Nearby Non-Potter Places

Charing Cross Road is considered the hub of literary London. What follows is only a small sampling of the bookstores found there.

Blackwell's Bookstore
http://bookshop.blackwell.co.uk/jsp/editorial/shops/SHOP36.jsp

100 Charing Cross Road, London, WC2H 0JG

"One of the biggest stores in Blackwells, we are situated in the heart of the world-famous Charing Cross Road. Open since 1995 we have built a great team of experienced, dedicated Booksellers. Although focusing on Academic books we also have a wide range of general topics plus stationary & an eclectic mix of DVDS."

Bloomsbury Publishers
http://www.bloomsbury.com/
http://en.wikipedia.org/wiki/Bloomsbury_Publishing

36 Soho Square, London W1D 3QY
Located about four blocks south and west of Charing Cross Road's northern end, this is an *office* building, not a book store. As home to the publisher of JK Rowling's Harry Potter novels, it may be of interest to Potterites. But, because it doesn't have a Potter-pic-worthy company sign outside (at least not according to the Google Maps UK streetview), Bloomsbury Publishers does not offer Potter Pix opportunities.

Foyles Bookstore
http://www.foyles.co.uk/Public/Stores/Detail.aspx?storeid=1011

113-119 Charing Cross Road, London WC2H 0EB

"**Our flagship store** is Europe's largest bookshop with 5 floors and more than 200,000 titles in stock plus a wide range of gifts and stationery, printed music and second-hand and rare books, as well [as] Ray's Jazz Music and Books, the Cafe and a Gallery and events space."

Orbital Comics & Collectibles
http://www.orbitalcomics.com/
http://www.qype.co.uk/place/96985-Orbital-Comics-Collectibles-London

8 Great Newport Street, London WC2H 7JA
Located just a few doors east of the Diagon Alley Wizard Entrance.

"We have the UK's largest selection of back issue comics and graphic novels, with comics from the Modern Age to the Golden Age. ... Our comic shop has a full range of mostly American comics from the 1940s onwards. We specialize in back issues but have all the recent comics, graphic novels and related merchandise as well. We also have tons of independently published comics."

Quinto Bookshop / Francis Edwards Antiquarian Booksellers
http://quintobookshop.co.uk/
http://www.francisedwards.co.uk/

"Francis Edwards is pleased to announce that our London shop has relocated 50 yards up the road to 72 Charing Cross Road, London."

Nearby Potter Places

😎 Muggle Portrait Gallery (Site 12): An 8 minute walk.

😃 *DHp1* Café-Related Film Sites (Site #2): A 9 minute walk.

😃 Wizard Chessmen (Site #18): A 10 minute walk.

😃 Ministry of Magic Area (Site#10): A 15 minute walk.

Going to the Diagon Alley Wizard Entrance

[After snapping Wizard Entrance pix, consider returning to Charing Cross Road, turning right, and heading north to the Denmark Street intersection and **Chris Bryant's Musical Instruments** store.]

☻ From Leicester Square Tube Station Exit #3
A 30 second walk from the street exit.

🚶 Follow station signs to **Exit #3** so that you emerge on the east side of Charing Cross Road, just south of Great Newport Street. ♦ Turn right and go north to the intersection. You'll see the Diagon Alley Wizard Entrance gap across the street to your right.

🚌 From the Original Tour Bus Loop Line Start/End Point
A 1 minute walk.

🚶 The Loop Line's Start/End point is on Charing Cross Road in the vicinity of the Leicester Square Tube Station's Exit #2. If you board an Original Tour Bus elsewhere, ask bus personnel to help you transfer to a Loop Line bus so you can ride to this location. ♦ After disembarking, cross to the east side of Charing Cross Road. ♦ Turn left and walk north to Great Newport Street, where you'll see the Diagon Alley Wizard Entrance gap across the street to your right.

From the Muggle Portrait Gallery (Site #12)
A 5 minute walk.

🚶 Exit the National Portrait Gallery from the main entrance on Saint Martin's Place. Turn left and walk north on Saint Martin's Place, keeping left until you're walking north on the west side of Charing Cross Road. ♦ Turn right at the Cranbourn Street intersection and cross to the east side of Charing Cross Road. ♦ Turn left and continue north to Great Newport Street. You'll see the Diagon Alley Wizard Entrance gap across the street to your right.

From the Trafalgar Square Original Tour Bus Red/Yellow Stops *or* Big Bus Stops 37/10/77
A 7 minute walk.

Disembark the tour bus near the northwestern corner of Trafalgar Square. Walk east across Trafalgar Square, until you reach its northeastern corner. ♦ Turn left and walk north on Saint Martin's Place. You'll pass the **National Portrait Gallery (Site #12)** on your left. [Consider popping into the gallery's Shop to buy two postcards before continuing your trek to the Diagon Alley Wizard Entrance.] ♦ Continue north along Saint Martin's Place, keeping left until you're walking north on the west side of Charing Cross Road. ♦ At the Cranbourn Street intersection, turn right and cross to the east side of Charing Cross Road. ♦ Turn left and continue north to Great Newport Street. You'll see the Diagon Alley Wizard Entrance gap across the street to your right.

From the *DHp1* Café-Related Film Sites (Site #2)
A 10 minute walk.

From Piccadilly Circus, walk east on Coventry Street as it turns northeast and becomes Swiss Court, then Leicester Square, then Cranbourn Street. ♦ Continue east on Cranbourn Street until you reach Charing Cross Road. ♦ Cross to the east side and turn left, to walk north on Charing Cross Road to Great Newport Street. You'll see the Diagon Alley Wizard Entrance gap across the street to your right.

From the Wizard Chessmen (Site #18)
A 10 minute walk.

Exit from the British Museum's main entrance to Great Russell Street and cross to the south side. ♦ Turn right and walk southwest for approximately 3 blocks to Tottenham Court Road. [**TIP:** Snap a Tottenham Court Road street sign pic. The *Deathly Hallows* Café was on this street in the book.] ♦ Turn left and walk southeast to **Saint Giles Circus** (the junction of Tottenham Court Road, Charing Cross Road, Oxford Street, and New Oxford Street). ♦ Cross to the east side of Charing Cross Road and continue south 3 blocks to Denmark Street. On your left will be the **Chris Bryant's Musical Instruments** store.

After snapping pix, return to Charing Cross Road. ♦ Turn left and walk approximately 6 blocks south to Great Newport Street. ♦ Turn left. The Diagon Alley Wizard Entrance gap is a few steps east, on your left.

From the Ministry of Magic Film Sites (Site #10)

A 15 minute walk.

🚶 Walk southwest on Great Scotland Yard or Whitehall Place to Whitehall. ♦ Turn right and walk north on Whitehall to its end at **King Charles I Island** (a large, circular island directly south of **Trafalgar Square**, containing a bronze statue of King Charles I on a horse). Several streets intersect here, making this a very confusing area. Your goal is to cross to King Charles I Island, then cross to the southeast corner of Trafalgar Square. ♦ Once there, walk north along the eastern border of Trafalgar Square, continuing north as you begin walking along Saint Martin's Place. You'll pass the **National Portrait Gallery (Site #12)** on your left. [Consider popping into the gallery's Shop to buy two postcards before continuing your trek to the Diagon Alley Wizard Entrance.] ♦ Continue north along Saint Martin's Place, keeping left until you're walking north on the west side of Charing Cross Road. ♦ At the Cranbourn Street intersection, turn right and cross to the east side of Charing Cross Road. ♦ Turn left and continue north to Great Newport Street. You'll see the Diagon Alley Wizard Entrance gap across the street to your right.

From the Leaky Cauldron, *Sorcerer's Stone*: Leadenhall Market (Site #8)

A 4 min walk to the Tube station entrance, a 5 min walk to your platform, then a 16-18 min tube trip; **a total journey of 25-27 minutes**.

🚶 Head west from any point in Leadenhall Market to Gracechurch Street. ♦ Turn left and walk south, crossing to the west side when convenient. ♦ Keep right at the southern end of Gracechurch Street, following the curve to walk west. You'll see an entrance to the **Monument** Tube station ahead of you—take the stairs down to the station.

⊖ Follow station signs to the **Circle & District Lines Booking Hall**. ♦ Follow signs to the **Circle Line** towards **Embankment** platform. ♦ Take the next train to **Embankment**. ♦ Follow station signs to a **Northern Line** platform towards **Edgware**, **High Barnet**, or **Mill Hill East**. ♦ Take the next train to **Leicester Square**.

Follow station signs to **Exit #3** so that you emerge on the east side of Charing Cross Road, south of Great Newport Street. ♦ Turn right and take a few steps north to the intersection. You'll see the Diagon Alley Wizard Entrance gap across the street to your right.

FLY-BY BRIDGES & BUILDINGS

Thames Bridges & Buildings Seen in *Harry Potter* Films

Westminster Pier Original Tour Bus Red/Green Stop or **Big Bus** Stop 49/22

Westminster Millennium Pier [51.501901, -0.123223]
http://en.wikipedia.org/wiki/Westminster_Millennium_Pier

Bensons Mini: J-7 / **Bensons Street:** G-7
Collins Mini: pg 49, D-4 / **Collins Atlas:** pg 21, F-1

Operation Hours: Visit the tour bus websites to obtain the schedules during your holiday, and to purchase discounted tickets online.

The London Original Tour Bus Company (OTB): Potter-Preferred
http://www.theoriginaltour.com/

The London Big Bus Company (BB)
http://www.bigbustours.com/eng/london/

To obtain a timetable of boat departures, visit the City Cruises' website.
http://www.citycruises.com/

Entry Fee: The cheapest Hop-On-Hop-Off (HOHO) tickets are those purchased online. The fare for a Thames River City Cruise is *included* in the HOHO ticket offered by both OTB and BB. 2011 online Adult HOHO tickets range from £18 to £23 ($28 to $36). Online tickets for Children 5-15 years old range from £10 to £11 ($16 to $17).

Fly-By Bridges Tour Time: Two hours, with options for more lengthy versions of this tour explained below.

Parseltongue Pointers:
- Greenwich = "GREN-itch"
- Southwark = "SUTH-uck"
- Thames River = "TEMZ"
- Vauxhall = "VOX-hall" (*not* "VO-hall")
- Westminster = "WEST-min-stah"

CRED

Many of London's bridges and Thames-River-related buildings have appeared in Harry Potter movies. All of them can be viewed and photographed while riding in a taxi or a conventional city bus. But, the best possible bridge and building screenshot recreation pix are those taken from the open top of a Hop-On-Hop-Off (HOHO) tour bus, and from the open deck of a Thames River cruise ship.

Our efficient, two hour **Fly-By Bridges & Buildings Tour** (Fly-By Tour) coordinates a one-way Thames River cruise with the river-related section of an overland HOHO bus trip. It's designed to ensure that you catch the most river-related screenshot pix from the best possible vantage points, in the least amount of time.

In *Prisoner of Azkaban*, footage of the **Knight Bus** was filmed while crossing over **Lambeth Bridge**. In *Order of the Phoenix*, Harry et al were seen flying from **Tower Bridge** to **Westminster Bridge**, on their way to #12 Grimmauld Place.

City Cruise ships travel both directions between **Westminster Millennium Pier** (located just north of Westminster Bridge) and **Tower Millennium Pier** (located just west of Tower Bridge), but do not cruise *under* Westminster Bridge.

Two *OOTP* screenshots were filmed facing west, showing the group approaching the east side of London Bridge and Southwark Bridge. Two were filmed facing east, while the group passed by the HMS Belfast, and after flying under Blackfriars Bridge. Whatever direction you cruise between Tower Bridge and Westminster Bridge, you'll occasionally have to face *backwards* on the ship's viewing deck to snap your screenshot recreation pix.

Our two-hour tour begins by cruising from Westminster Pier to Tower Pier because Tower Hill (near to Tower Pier) is the best place to board the river-related overland HOHO bus trip.

If you elect to cruise in reverse order—from Tower Pier to Westminster Pier—you'll have to ride the HOHO bus from Westminster all the way back to Tower Hill before being able to travel the overland route that allows you to take the best surface-snapped Potter Bridge pix, adding at least an additional hour of travel to your schedule.

Alternatively, you could *cruise back* to Tower Pier and board the Tower Hill HOHO bus. That travel method will add only 45 minutes to your schedule.

Please Note: *OOTP* and *POA* bridge screenshots were filmed in the dark of night, when bridge lights were blazing. Unfortunately, London HOHO busses and Thames River cruise ships don't usually run late enough to snap bridge pix while they're illuminated. *Never fear!* The daytime pix you'll capture will not disappoint.

If riding the Original Tour Bus, only *one* river-related Bridge & Building screenshot recreation pic is missed by our Fly-By Tour, because it must be snapped while traveling *over* **Vauxhall Bridge**—the bridge immediately southwest of Lambeth Bridge. None of the OTB or BB tour busses travel over Vauxhall Bridge. You'll have to snag that screenshot while riding in a taxi or a conventional city bus.

The **Millennium Footbridge** was featured in *Half-Blood Prince*, and has a separate entry all of its own. [**Death Eaters' Bridge (Site #1)**] There we provide directions for obtaining screenshot pix of both the footbridge and **Saint Paul's Cathedral**.

Screenshot directions involving iconic London buildings *unrelated* to the Thames River and its bridges are provided in other of our London Potter Places entries.

The Thames River Bridges

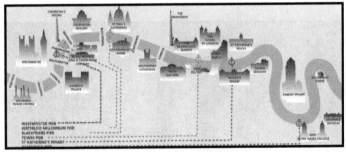

[Scanned Image, ©2010 City Cruises]

The City Cruises website offers a wonderful Thames River map that identifies almost all the bridges between Westminster and Tower piers, as well as both of the Potterly-important bridges found southwest of Westminster Bridge.
http://www.citycruises.com/thames.htm

Thames River Bridge List

Here is a list of *all* Thames River Bridges, in order of their appearance when traveling from Westminster Pier to Tower Pier:

- Westminster Bridge
- Hungerford Bridge
- Waterloo Bridge
- Blackfriars Bridge
- Blackfriars Railway Bridge
- The Millennium Footbridge
- Southwark Bridge
- Cannon Street Railway Bridge
- London Bridge
- Tower Bridge

Potterly-Important Bridges Southwest of Westminster Bridge:
- Lambeth Bridge
- Vauxhall Bridge

Begin at Westminster Millennium Pier

The *Harry Potter Places* Fly-by Bridges & Buildings Tour begins at Westminster Millennium Pier. The following tips for taking *eleven* (11) Fly-By Tour screenshots are presented in the order they are encountered during our two-hour tour. We also include suggestions for snapping great, non-Potter, London tourist pix.

Fly-By Tour Screenshot #1: Westminster Bridge

[*Order of the Phoenix* screenshot (enhanced)]

Screenshot #1 shows Harry and Order Members emerging from beneath Westminster Bridge to fly south, past the **Houses of Parliament**. (**Big Ben** is hidden behind the bridge support.) This screenshot is somewhat difficult to recreate because the City Cruise ship doesn't travel *beneath* Westminster Bridge.

[©2009 Tara Bellers]

Arrive at least 10 or 15 minutes before your cruise departure to have time to snap some under-Westminster-Bridge pix from the southernmost point of Westminster Millennium Pier before boarding the ship.

[©2009 Tara Bellers]

Once aboard, position yourself to snag potentially better Screenshot #1 under-Westminster-Bridge pix as the ship departs Westminster Pier and swings out into the river before heading away from Westminster Bridge.

[©2009 Tara Bellers]

Face backwards on the ship as you journey farther away from Westminster Pier to take some fabulous tourist pix of the Houses of Parliament that include Big Ben. **Please Note:** photos like this cannot be snapped from the street because other buildings are in the way.

Next, you'll travel under **Hungerford Bridge** (a side-by-side Footbridge and Railway Bridge) and **Waterloo Bridge**. Since they aren't Potter bridges, you'll have a little time to sit back, relax, and enjoy the cruise.

As you emerge from beneath Waterloo Bridge, prepare for your next Fly-By Tour pic—one that should be taken while facing forward, *before* sailing under **Blackfriars Bridge**.

[©2009 Tara Bellers]

The tapered building seen at the right of Tara Bellers' photo above is the **Swiss Re Building**, an iconic London financial district skyscraper commonly known as the **Gherkin**, due to its green color and pickle-like shape.
http://en.wikipedia.org/wiki/30_St_Mary_Axe

Seen just barely in Fly-By Tour Screenshot #2, the Gherkin is prominently featured in Screenshot #5.

Fly-By Tour Screenshot #2: Blackfriars Bridge

[*Order of the Phoenix* screenshot (enhanced)]

Screenshot #2 shows Harry emerging on the west side of Blackfriars Bridge. The tippy-top of the Gherkin is seen just above his fluttering cloak.

Please Note: If you cannot take the City Cruise river tour, your next best bet for getting a Blackfriars Bridge pic like Screenshot #2 is while looking *right* as you travel over **Waterloo Bridge** on an open-top tour bus.

After taking pix of Blackfriars Bridge's west side on your approach, you can sit back and relax until after you've passed under **Blackfriars Railway Bridge.**

The **Millennium Footbridge** is next. Although pix snapped from a river-viewpoint won't correspond to any Harry Potter screenshots, you can take some great tourist photos before, during, and after you pass beneath it. See the **Death Eaters' Bridge (Site #1)** entry for more information about the Millennium Footbridge.

Fly-By Tour Screenshot #3: Riverside House

[*Half-Blood Prince* screenshot (enhanced)]

After snapping river views of the Millennium Footbridge, face forward and look to your right for **Riverside House**, an office building located on the South Bank of the Thames, immediately *before* Southwark Bridge. The architecturally distinctive curved face of Riverside House clearly identifies it as the location wherein *HbP* scenes were filmed of stunned Muggles watching the Millennium Footbridge buckle and twist before falling into the Thames.

[©2009 Tara Bellers; Riverside House at right.]

Since you cannot go inside Riverside House, take exterior pix of its rounded window section that faces the Thames.

After taking Riverside House pix, you'll cruise under **Southwark Bridge**. Turn to face backwards as you emerge on its east side and take turns snapping tourist pix of you and your companions with Southwark Bridge in the close background.

[©2009 Tara Bellers]

If you're traveling alone, ask a fellow cruiser to take a few pix of you with the bridge close behind. Since she/he cannot leave the boat, it's probably safe to hand your digital camera to a helpful stranger.

By the time you've finished taking tourist pix, you'll have enough distance to shoot your backward-facing Screenshot #4 pix of Harry et al approaching the east side of Southwark Bridge.

Fly-By Tour Screenshot #4: Southwark Bridge

[*Order of the Phoenix* screenshot (enhanced)]

To recreate the screenshot's slant, tilt your camera to the **left** while snapping Southwark Bridge. Yes, this may seem counterintuitive, but it's true. To capture a view that slants down on the right, you must tilt your camera to the left—and vice versa.

Next Up, London Bridge

[©2009 Tara Bellers]

Although only seen on screen for a couple seconds (Screenshot #6), London Bridge is another *OOTP* Fly-Under bridge, and good for tourist pix.

Please Note: The following **five** photo opportunities (including three screenshots) are *all* encountered between London Bridge and Tower Bridge—a distance of approximately 3500 feet. Thus, they must be accomplished quite quickly! In fact, it takes longer to explain the shots than the time you have to snap them.

Fly-By Tour Screenshot #5: Gherkin Reflection

[*Half-Blood Prince* screenshot (enhanced)]

A reflection of the iconic Gherkin skyscraper is quite prominently seen at the far right of Screenshot #5. This screenshot's order of appearance in *HbP* seems to imply that these reflections were observed in the glass front of the **Riverside House**. They were not. The Gherkin is located almost a mile north of the Thames River, between London Bridge and Tower Bridge—*far east* of the Millennium Footbridge.

[**bing** map Bird's Eye segment (cropped and enhanced)]

Face forward as you emerge on the east side of London Bridge and look *right* to see the first office building on the South Bank—the one with a **triangular section of angled flat glass** approximately **50 feet east** of London Bridge.

We believe that the reflections seen in Screenshot #5 were filmed in this building's glass, *OR*, that the glass was filmed as a *background plate* for CGI-created reflections. Whatever was or wasn't filmed here, this is the only building found between Westminster and Tower Piers with the same kind of glass seen in Screenshot #5.

You only have a few *seconds* to snap pix of the glass section. After that, turn to face backwards on the ship and quickly take tourist pix of you and your companions with the east side of London Bridge in the close background.

Fly-By Tour Screenshot #6: London Bridge

[*Order of the Phoenix* screenshot (enhanced)]

Within a minute of shooting your tourist pix, you'll have gained a greater distance from the bridge and will be in position to take backward-facing pix of London Bridge's east side as seen in Screenshot #6. Tilt your camera to the **right** (so that the bridge tilts down to the left) when taking them.

The moment you've accomplished a few Screenshot #6 pix, face forward and look to your *right*.

Fly-By Tour Screenshot #7: The HMS Belfast

[*Order of the Phoenix* screenshot (enhanced)]

Begin snapping Screenshot #7 pix as you approach the **HMS Belfast**, with Tower Bridge in the background.

[©2009 Tara Bellers]

Among the most powerful large light cruisers ever built, the HMS Belfast is the only surviving vessel of her type to have seen active service during WWII. If you're interested, touring the HMS Belfast takes 1 ½ to 2 hours.
http://www.iwm.org.uk/visits/hms-belfast

Accompanied Children 1-15 years old enter free.
Adult (16-59 years old) entry fee is £13 [$20]
Senior (60+) entry fee is £10.40 [$16]

Tower Bridge

[©2009 Tara Bellers]

After taking HMS Belfast pix, quickly shoot tourist pix of **Tower Bridge** before the ship turns left to dock at the Tower Millennium Pier.

Please Note: If you want to enjoy the full Thames River cruise, remain on the ship while it's docked at Tower Pier, and continue cruising east to **Greenwich Pier.** From there, cruise back to Tower Pier. This will add **1 hour and 10 minutes** to your tour.

Disembark the Cruise Ship at Tower Millennium Pier

Walk northwest from Tower Pier to Tower Hill, the first cross street. ♦ Turn right and walk a block east to the **Original Tour Bus** (or Big Bus) **Red Route** Tower Hill bus stop plaza. ♦ Board the Red Route Tour Bus that travels west along the Thames' North Bank.

Fly-By Tour Screenshot #8: Millennium Footbridge

Only the Original Tour Bus Red Route diverts from the north bank and takes you south over Southwark Bridge, west on Southwark Street, then north again—crossing over Blackfriars Bridge. This is the reason the OTB is preferred for our two-hour Thames River Bridges & Buildings Tour.

[*Half-Blood Prince* screenshot (enhanced)]

Look to your right while riding over Blackfriars Bridge to snap Screenshot #8. Being in the open-top of an OTB tour bus gives you the height required to photograph the Millennium Footbridge's west side without Blackfriars Railway Bridge in the way

At the end of Blackfriars Bridge, the OTB tour bus will rejoin the BB route and travel west along Victoria Embankment. While passing Waterloo Bridge, Victoria Embankment curves south and the bus will take you past Hungerford Bridge and Westminster Pier. Next it will turn east and take you over Westminster Bridge—giving you another opportunity to take unique tourist pix of the Houses of Parliament and Big Ben.

Once on the opposite bank of the Thames, the tour bus will make its way south and then turn back west to take you over **Lambeth Bridge.** The moment you begin crossing Lambeth Bridge, begin taking your *POA* **Knight Bus Bridge** screenshots.

Fly-By Tour Screenshot #9: The Knight Bus on Lambeth Bridge

[*Prisoner of Azkaban* screenshot (enhanced)]

Screenshot #9 shows the Knight Bus continuing west over Lambeth Bridge *after* squeezing between two city busses. Snap your version of this screenshot as you first begin traveling over Lambeth Bridge, from its eastern end.

[©2009 Tara Bellers; Screenshot #9 at left, Screenshot #10 at right.]

Fly-By Tour Screenshot #10: City Busses on Lambeth Bridge

[*Prisoner of Azkaban* screenshot (enhanced)]

Screenshot #10 shows two red city busses *approaching* the Knight Bus (before the squeeze). Snap your version of this screenshot when approximately halfway across Lambeth Bridge.

Ending the Fly-By Bridges & Buildings Tour

Our two-hour Fly-by Bridges & Buildings Tour ends once you've crossed over Lambeth Bridge. At that time, you have three options:

(1) If you have more time to tour, stay on the bus.

You can spend another hour or so simply riding the bus and driving by several famous non-Potter London landmarks, snapping Muggle tourist pix galore. If you have several hours to spare, you can hop-off to visit one or more of the locations you encounter, then hop-back-on the tour bus and travel to the next site that interests you.

(2) Get off at the next bus stop and walk to Westminster Underground Station.

The first Original Tour Bus stop is just a block beyond the western end of Lambeth Bridge, a 15 minute walk to the Westminster Tube Station.

Walk back toward the river and turn left to head north on Milbank. ♦ Continue north as it becomes Abingdon Street. As you pass between Westminster Abbey and the Houses of Parliament, Abingdon Street becomes Saint Margaret Street. ♦ Continue north until you can cross to the northeast corner of Bridge Street. ♦ Turn right to walk to the Bridge Street Westminster Underground Station entrance.

The first Big Bus stop is a couple blocks north from the end of Lambeth Bridge, on Abingdon Street just before it becomes Saint Margaret Street (between Westminster Abbey and the Houses of Parliament). It is only a 7 minute walk from BB stop 52/25 to the Westminster Tube Station.

Walk north on Abingdon Street. ♦ Continue north as it becomes Saint Margaret Street, until you can cross to the northeast corner of Bridge Street. ♦ Turn right to walk to the Bridge Street Westminster Underground Station entrance.

(3) Stay on the bus until you reach the next underground station bus stop.

If riding the Original Tour Bus, the first Tube Station you'll reach is Victoria Station, about a 20 minute ride beyond the end of Lambeth Bridge. (You'll pass by Buckingham Palace.)

If riding the Big Bus, the first Tube Station you'll reach is Saint James Park (BB stop 53/26), about a 10 minute ride beyond the end of Lambeth Bridge. (You'll pass by Westminster Abbey and the Houses of Parliament, but won't be allowed off the bus to go to Westminster Tube Station.)

As previously mentioned, if you ride the **Original Tour Bus Red Route**, only **one** Potter Bridge and Building screenshot is missed by our two-hour tour. Screenshot #11 must be snapped while **riding over Vauxhall Bridge**—the next bridge southwest of Lambeth Bridge. Because HOHO busses travel over it, Screenshot #11 must be snapped while riding over Vauxhall Bridge in a taxi or conventional city bus. Happily, this shot can be accomplished on any day of your London visit, at any time.

Fly-By Tour Screenshot #11: Lambeth Bridge, Houses of Parliament, & Big Ben

[*Sorcerer's Stone* screenshot (enhanced)]

Nearby Non-Potter Places
The Tower of London
http://www.hrp.org.uk/TowerOfLondon/

If you can afford to add 1, 2, or 3 hours to your two-hour Thames River Bridges & Buildings Tour, we highly recommend that you enjoy a Tower of London tour after finishing the river cruise, before boarding an OTB (or BB) tour bus.

Founded by William the Conqueror in 1066, the Tower of London has generated remarkable stories across the centuries. Despite its grim reputation as a prison and a place of torture and execution, this fortress stronghold has also served as a royal residence, a coronation site, an armory, and a barracks—it even housed a Zoo for many years. The modern day Tower of London contains the vault that protects the **English Crown Jewels**, and is still guarded by the **Yeoman Warders** (nicknamed **Beefeaters**).

Opening Times: Except for December 24-26 and January 1, the Tower is open year-round at 9am on Tues through Sat, at 10am on Sun & Mon. In the

Winter (Nov 1 to Feb 28), the tower closes daily at 5pm. In the Summer (Mar 1 to Oct 31), the Tower is open until 6pm daily.

Entry Fees: Children under 5 enter FREE. Children 5 to 15 years old £9.50 [$14]. Adults (16 to 59 years old) £17 [$26]. Students with a valid ID card or Seniors 60+ (Concessions tickets) £14.50 [$22]. Discounted Family and On-line-Purchased tickets are also available.

The Tours: Each Entry Fee allows you the option of enjoying Tower of London tours lasting 1, 2, or 3 hours.

http://www.hrp.org.uk/TowerOfLondon/planyourvisit/suggesteditineraries.aspx

Nearby Potter Places
⁣👓 The Muggle Underground Station (Site #13)

If you'll be traveling the underground to Westminster Millennium Pier, consider arriving at **Westminster Tube Station** at least an hour and 15 minutes before your cruise ship is scheduled to leave. This will allow time to leisurely accomplish a Muggle Underground Station visit, as well as your pre-cruise pier pix.

Going to the Fly-By Bridges & Buildings Tour

Please Note: The tour starts at Westminster Millennium Pier. No matter how you arrive, you must obtain your free Thames River Cruise pass from OTB or BB personnel *before* walking down to the pier. If you travel to Westminster Pier via OTB/BB bus, get your pass wherever you board. If you travel to Westminster Pier via Taxi or Tube, get your pass at the bus stop nearest the Pier entrance: **Westminster Pier Bus Stop M**, aka **Westminster Pier Original Tour Bus Red/Green Stops**, aka **Big Bus stops 49/22.**

🚌 From Westminster Pier Bus Stop M
A 2 minute walk.

🚶 Walk down the closest steps leading to the sunken sidewalk along Westminster Pier. ♦ Turn right and walk to the City Cruise Ship boarding area.

⊖ From Westminster Underground Station
A 5 minute walk.

Option One:

🚶 Follow station signs to an underground passageway that leads to the **Westminster Millennium Pier** or the **Victoria Embankment #2** exit. You'll emerge on the east side of Victoria Embankment—the same side the pier is on—just north of Westminster Bridge and south of the pier entrance. ♦ Walk straight ahead for nearly two blocks, passing the main steps leading down to Westminster Millennium Pier, to the first **Westminster Pier Bus Stop**.

Option Two:

🚶 Follow station signs to the **Bridge Street** exit. ♦ Turn left and walk east to the next street, Victoria Embankment, crossing to its eastern side. ♦ Turn left and walk north for almost two blocks, passing the main steps leading down to Westminster Millennium Pier, to the first **Westminster Pier Bus Stop**.

From the Ministry of Magic Area (Site #10): Huffandpuff Expedition POA Day
A 5 minute walk.

🚶 Walk east on **Horse Guards Avenue** to Victoria Embankment and cross to the river side. ♦ Turn right and walk south to **Westminster Pier Bus Stop M**.

From Westminster Parliament Street (Big Ben) Original Tour Bus Red/Yellow/Green Stops *or* Big Bus Stop 40/13
A 7 minute walk.

🚶 Disembark the bus and head south on Parliament Street, toward Big Ben. ♦ Turn left at Bridge Street and walk east to the next street, Victoria Embankment, crossing to its eastern side. ♦ Turn left and walk north, watching on your right for the first steps leading down to **Westminster Millennium Pier**.

From Camden Town Underground Station: Padfoot Prowl or Potter Promenade Zoo Day
A 19 minute underground journey, then a 5 minute walk.
You need to hustle! Your cruise leaves the pier at **2:45 pm**.

From **Camden Town** Tube Station, take the **Northern Line** towards **Kennington** to reach **Embankment** Underground Station. ♦ Take the **Circle Line** towards **Victoria**, or take the **District Line** towards **Wimbledon**, **Richmond**, or **Ealing Broadway**, to reach **Westminster** Tube Station.

🚶 Follow station signs to an underground passageway that leads to the **Westminster Millennium Pier** or the **Victoria Embankment #2** exit. You'll emerge on the east side of Victoria Embankment—the same side the pier is on—just north of Westminster Bridge and south of the pier entrance. ♦ Walk straight ahead for nearly two blocks, passing the main steps leading down to Westminster Millennium Pier, to the first **Westminster Pier Bus Stop**.

5

GRINGOTTS BANK

The Australia House
http://www.uk.embassy.gov.au/
http://harrypotter.wikia.com/wiki/Gringotts_Wizarding_Bank

Google Maps UK: Australia House, Strand, Westminster, London WC2B 4LA
Bensons Mini: H-5 / **Bensons Street:** K-5
Collins Mini: pg 37, F-3,4 / **Collins Atlas:** pg 15, H-2,3

⊖**Tube Station:** Temple

🚌 **Original Tour Bus** Aldwych Red/Yellow Stops *or* **Big Bus Stops** 44/17

⊖**Transport For London:** Use "Saint Clement Danes R A F Church" as your destination

Operation Hours or **Entry Fee:** None

Visit Time: Schedule at least 30 to 45 minutes here

☙❧

Opened by England's King Edward V in 1918, the **Australia House** is London's **Australian Embassy**. The crown jewel of Australia House's interior architecture is the magnificent **Exhibition Hall**. Its distinctive mosaic floor is composed of black and white Australian marble. The hall's central area is illuminated by Empire-style, Italian crystal chandeliers.

[©2003 Wolfgang Mletzko]

For *Harry Potter and the Sorcerer's Stone* filming in November of 2000, the Exhibition Hall was embellished by a multitude of set pieces, props, cobwebs and other accoutrements—transforming it into **the lobby of Gringotts Bank**.

[*Sorcerer's Stone* screenshot (enhanced)]

Due to the destruction caused by a Dragon escaping the vaults below it, a Leavesden Studios **set** was built to film the *Deathly Hallows Part Two* Gringotts Bank lobby scenes. The set nearly reproduced the Australia House Exhibition Hall as seen in *Sorcerer's Stone*.

[*DHp2* screenshot (enhanced)]

Unfortunately, due to global security concerns following September 11th, 2001, the Australia House has been **permanently closed to the general public**. Even visiting Australian citizens are allowed entry only to the visa and passport business areas. These days, entrance to the Exhibition Hall is limited to VIPs with personal invitations to the Australian High Commission galas occasionally held here.

The Exhibition Hall runs from east to west through the center of this triangular-shaped building. The eastern Australia House entrance is topped by columns supporting several statues, and opens to a small lobby containing a security desk. Anyone can enter this lobby. But, peering through the opaque glass door that leads into the Exhibition Hall will not gain you a clear view of it.

At the Exhibition Hall's western end on **Melbourne Place** there is a tall pair of glass doors, surrounded by banks of windows. It was through this glass that Wolfgang Mletzko snapped his Exhibition Hall photo (above) in May of 2003.

[©2009 Tara Bellers]

Beware of tour companies that promise you a view of the Exhibition Hall from the Melbourne Place windows! According to Australian High Commission Public Affairs personnel, the curtains surrounding these windows and glass doors have routinely been kept *closed* since 2005. But, as long as you're in the area, it wouldn't hurt to pop around to Melbourne Place, just in case the curtains might be open.

The Australia House merits a **Might-Be-Fun** rating (rather than a **Skip It** rating), because even though the Melbourne Place curtains will probably be closed and you'll not be able to snap Exhibition Hall pix, you might enjoy having your photo taken in front of the Australia House's Gringotts-Bank-like main entrance.

[©2009 Tara Bellers] [*Sorcerer's Stone* screenshot segments morphed (enhanced)]

The Australia House and Gringotts Bank are unusually similar in that both are *triangular*-shaped buildings. Upon closer inspection, it is pretty clear that a great deal of Australia House's architecture inspired the CGI artists who designed Gringotts Bank's exterior for *Sorcerer's Stone, Half-Blood Prince,* and both *Deathly Hallows* movies.

The best spot for the camera operator to stand when snapping a photo of you standing in front of Gringotts Bank is in the plaza of **Saint Clement Danes Church**, across the island directly east of the Australia House's main entrance.

TIP: Bring a *disposable camera* with you on your Harry Potter Holiday. Whenever you need to ask a stranger to take a photo for you from a distance, giving her or him a disposable camera minimizes the risk that she/he will abscond with your camera. Remember to ask the photographer to take at least three shots, so that you'll be sure to get at least one good shot.

Warwick Davis and Gringotts Bank

[*DHp2* screenshot (enhanced)]

Throughout all eight Harry Potter films, the primary role of actor **Warwick Davis** has been that of **Professor Filius Flitwick**, the kindly and loveable Hogwarts' Charms Instructor. However, Warwick's very first Harry Potter appearance was as a **Gringotts Goblin Bank Teller** in *Sorcerer's Stone*.

Because we discovered so many interesting facts about the **five** Harry Potter characters Warwick has portrayed, and his relationship(s) to Gringotts Bank, we created a **Warwick Davis Revelio Supplementum**.
http://HarryPotterPlaces.com/b1/WarwickDavisRevelio.pdf

This Supplementum also reveals the secret identities of the two very small Goblins seen moving a wagon in the *DHp2* screenshot above—as well as the identity of another uncredited *DHp2* Gringotts Goblin!

Nearby Non-Potter Places

Home of Twinings Tea
http://www.twinings.co.uk/about-twinings/our-stores/twinings,-216,-strand,-london

Prince Henry's Room
http://www.cityoflondon.gov.uk/Corporation/LGNL_Services/Leisure_and_culture/Local_history_and_heritage/Buildings_within_the_City/prince_henrys.htm

Saint Clement Danes Royal Air Force Chapel
http://www.raf.mod.uk/stclementdanes/

Temple Church
http://www.templechurch.com/

Nearby Potter Places

The Death Eaters' **Bridge (Site #1):** A 15 minute walk.

Hogwarts Staircase (Site #6): A 15 minute walk.

Going to Gringotts Bank

No matter how you get here, when you arrive at the Australia House you'll want to check whether the curtains of the Exhibition Hall's windows are open. The windows are located on Melbourne Place, which runs along the west side of Australia House between Aldwych and the Strand. If the curtains aren't open, take some Pouty-Face pix there. If the curtains *are* open, take a bunch of Happy-Face pix!

When finished on Melbourne Place, walk south and turn left to walk east along the Strand—*or* walk north and turn right to walk southeast along Aldwych. Either way, you'll soon reach the Australia House's front (east) entrance. There, you can cross the island to the plaza in front of Saint Clement Danes Church and snap your Australia House front entrance pix.

From Original Tour Bus Aldwych Red/Yellow Stop *or* Big Bus Stop 44/17

A 2 minute walk.

After disembarking, the northwest corner of Australia House can be seen across the street to the south and east (left). But you can't cross to it directly. Walk west (*away from* Australia House) along the north side of **Aldwych** to **Kingsway**. ♦ Use the triangular crosswalk island to reach the south side of Aldwych. ♦ Turn left and walk east along Aldwych as it curves around to the south. ♦ At **Melbourne Place** you've reached the northwest corner of Australia House

From Temple Tube Station

A 5 minute walk.

You'll emerge from Temple Tube Station in a courtyard below street level. Head left to go up the steps to **Temple Place** and cross over to **Arundel Street**. ♦ Walk north on the east side of Arundel Street to its end at the **Strand**. The Australia House will be in front of you, to the left.

From the Death Eaters' Bridge (Site #1)

A 15 minute walk.

Walk to the north-bank end of the **Millennium Footbridge** and make a U-turn to your left. ♦ Go down the steps to the Thames River and turn right on **Paul's Walk**. ♦ Walk west along the Thames as Paul's Walk passes under **Blackfriars Bridge** and becomes **Victoria Embankment**. ♦ Cross to the north side of Victoria Embankment as soon as convenient, and continue walking west, watching for **Temple Place** (just west of **Middle Temple Lane**) on your right. ♦ Turn right at Temple Place and walk north, continuing as it curves west until you reach **Arundel Street** (on your right). ♦ Turn right and walk north on the east side of Arundel Street to its end at the **Strand**. The Australia House will be in front of you, to the left.

From Hogwarts Staircase (Site #6)

A 15 minute walk.

If you leave from the **South Churchyard** entrance, walk west on **Saint Paul's Churchyard Street**, continuing west as it becomes **Ludgate Hill**. If you leave from **Saint Paul's Great West Door** entrance, head west on **Ludgate Hill**. ♦ Continue west on Ludgate Hill as it becomes **Fleet Street**. ♦ Continue west as Fleet Street becomes the **Strand**. You'll soon see the east entrance of the Australia House.

From the Diagon Alley Wizard Entrance: Charing Cross Road (Site #3)

A 15 minute walk.

🚶 Walk east from **Charing Cross Road** along the north side of **Great Newport Street** to **Saint Martin's Lane**. This is a confusing intersection. Be sure you're on the north side of Great Newport Street when you reach it. ♦ Cross Saint Martin's Lane and continue forward to walk *northeast* on **Long Acre**. You'll soon reach another confusing intersection with **Endell Street** jogging north on the left, followed a few feet later by **Bow Street** jogging south on the right. ♦ Continue forward to stay on Long Acre, and keep walking northeast until you see **The Prince of Wales Pub** on the southeast corner of Long Acre and **Drury Lane**. ♦ Cross to the pub-side of Drury Lane, turn right and walk southeast on Drury Lane until you reach **Aldwych**. ♦ Cross to the south side of Aldwych and turn left. Follow Aldwych until you reach **Melbourne Place** (at the northwest corner of Australia House).

From Number 12 Grimmauld Place: Claremont Square (Site #15)

A 5 to 7 minute walk, an 18 minute tube journey, a 5 minute walk.

🚶 When finished on the southern **Claremont Square** (street), walk to whichever end is closest. ♦ Turn north and walk to **Pentonville Road**. ♦ Turn right and walk east to the intersection where Pentonville Road becomes **City Road**. ♦ Turn left and walk north to **Angel Underground Station**.

🚇 Take the **Northern Line** towards **Morden**, to reach **Bank Tube Station**.

🚶 Follow station signs to **Monument Underground Station** (a 4 minute walk).

🚇 Take the **District Line** towards **Ealing Broadway**, **Richmond**, or **Wimbledon**—*OR* take the **Circle Line** towards **Embankment**—to reach **Temple Underground Station**.

🚶 You'll emerge from Temple Tube Station in a courtyard below street level. Head left to go up the steps to **Temple Place** and cross over to **Arundel Street**. ♦ Walk north on the east side of Arundel Street to its end at the **Strand**. The Australia House will be in front of you, on the left.

Hogwarts Staircase

Saint Paul's Cathedral Geometric Staircase
http://www.stpauls.co.uk
http://en.wikipedia.org/wiki/St_Paul%27s_Cathedral

Google Maps UK: St Paul's Church Yard, City of London, EC4M 8
Bensons Mini: K-4 / **Bensons Street:** M-4
Collins Mini: pg 39, E-3 / **Collins Atlas:** pg 16, C,D-2

Tube Station: St Paul's

Original Tour Bus Red/Yellow Stop or **Big Bus Stop 45/18.**

Operation Hours and Entry Fees: Visit the cathedral's website for the most up-to-date schedules and ticket fees.

Operation Hours: On Sundays, the cathedral is open only to those who wish to worship, no sightseeing is allowed. Mondays to Saturdays, the cathedral is usually open for general sightseeing (*not* including **Hogwarts Staircase**) from 8:30 am to 4:00 pm. Special services or events may occasionally close all, or part, of the cathedral. Check the cathedral calendar before you visit.

Entry Fees: Adult cathedral sightseeing admission is £14.50 ($23); Children 6-16 y/o £5.50 ($9); Students and Seniors £13.50 ($21). For Potterites with a **London Pass**, entry is free. Group discounts for 10 or more are available.

Guided Tours: See the information below.

Visit Time: Allow at least 30 minutes to visit only the cathedral shop. For general cathedral sightseeing and shopping, 1.5 hours ought to do. Schedule at least 2 hours for a Guided Tour and shopping.

Saint Paul's Cathedral is one of the most famous and recognizable sights of London, its distinctive dome having dominated the city's skyline for over 300 years. The present structure is the fifth cathedral to occupy this site since

604 AD, and was built between 1675 and 1710, after Old Saint Paul's was destroyed in the Great Fire of London.

Because it has always been an inspirational British icon, the cathedral was targeted during the Blitz of the Second World War. Although hit by 28 bombs, Saint Paul's miraculously survived. Visit the websites above to learn more about this magnificent church.

Saint Paul's is home to a gorgeous staircase that served as a film site for several Harry Potter movies.

[*Prisoner of Azkaban* screenshot (enhanced)]

Spiraling upward within the **South West Bell Tower** of Saint Paul's Cathedral, the **Geometric Staircase** most often served as the staircase leading to Professor Trelawney's Divination classroom or the Astronomy Tower. Like any other Hogwarts stairway, however, you never know where it might be found.

[*Sherlock Holmes* screenshot segment (enhanced), ©2009 Warner Bros.]

Saint Paul's Geometric Staircase also was a film site for the 2009 Sherlock Holmes movie, starring Robert Downey Jr. and Jude Law, a second Potter/ Holmes film association [see **Number 12 Grimmauld Place (Site #15)**].

Site Rating

👓 Saint Paul's Cathedral earns a **Skip It** rating because:
- The Geometric Staircase is the only Harry Potter site in the cathedral.
- Access to the Hogwarts Staircase is only allowed during Guided Tours, which cannot be pre-booked.
- At least 90 minutes are required to obtain a brief peek at the staircase.
- **No photography** is allowed *anywhere* within the cathedral!

http://www.stpauls.co.uk/FAQS#photography

We suggest that Potterites pop into **Saint Paul's Shop** while traveling between nearby Potter Places, and purchase one of their Geometric Staircase postcards. The Saint Paul's Guidebook includes Geometric Staircase photos and info, and is available for only £4 ($6).

Happily, Saint Paul's Shop is open seven days a week: on Sundays from 10am to 4:30pm, from 8:30am to 5pm all other days.

The shop is reached via the **Crypt Entrance** at the west end of the cathedral's northern side, off of Paternoster Square.

http://www.stpauls.co.uk/Visits-Events/Shop

That said, Potterites with tons of time and additional interest in Saint Paul's Cathedral, or cathedrals in general, will certainly enjoy visiting this marvelous church.

The general sightseeing entrance fee allows you to freely wander through the public areas of Saint Paul's Cathedral, including its Crypt (the largest in Europe). You'll walk down the processional nave where Lady Diana Spencer passed, the 25-foot-long train of her dress cascading behind her, on the day she married Prince Charles in 1981. You can climb into the famous dome to visit the three circular galleries of Saint Paul's Cathedral.

The **Whispering Gallery** is 259 steps above ground level and runs around the interior of the dome. A *whisper* uttered at any point against the wall of this gallery can be clearly heard by a listener with an ear held to the wall at any other point in the gallery. Oddly enough, it only works for whispers. Normally-voiced speech is not transmitted this way.

The **Stone Gallery** is 119 steps above the Whispering Gallery, and the **Golden Gallery** is 172 steps higher still. Your climb to either of these two external galleries will be rewarded with spectacular, panoramic views of London. And, since you'll be outside, photography *is* allowed from these vantage points.

Guided Tours of Saint Paul's Cathedral are included in the price of general cathedral admission, and are offered 4 times each day — apart from Sundays. Lasting 90 minutes, the tours include the Hogwarts Staircase! However, the number of participants is limited and you cannot book a tour in advance. Reserve your tour place at the Guiding Desk when you arrive at the cathedral.

Tour Times: 10:45am, 11:15am, 1:30pm, and 2pm.
http://www.stpauls.co.uk/Visits-Events/Multimedia-Guides-Tours/Guided-Tours

For Potterites who visit, here are a few more screenshots showing what you'll be able to see, but not snap.

[*Goblet of Fire* screenshot (enhanced)]

[*Prisoner of Azkaban* screenshot (enhanced)]

The beautiful tiled floor at the bottom of Saint Paul's Geometric Staircase was altered each time Hogwarts scenes were filmed here. However, because filmmakers weren't attempting to disguise the cathedral as some other place for the *Sherlock Holmes* movie, the true tiles are seen in those shots.

[*Sherlock Holmes* screenshot segment (enhanced), ©2009 Warner Bros.]

One last note of interest, the Hogwarts Staircase **set** built for filming *Deathly Hallows Part Two* was clearly designed based on Saint Paul's Geometric Staircase. But, for some unknown reason, the distinctive railing was *not* reproduced. Perhaps your Tour Guide will be able to explain. If so, please blog about it on the *Harry Potter Places* website.

[*Deathly Hallows Part Two* screenshot (enhanced)]

Nearby Potter Places

Death Eaters' Bridge (Site #1): A 5 minute walk.

Gringotts Bank (Site #5): A 15 minute walk, or a 10-15 minute bus ride.

Leaky Cauldron: *Sorcerer's Stone* (Site #8): A 17 minute walk.

Going to Hogwarts Staircase / Saint Paul's Cathedral

Access to Saint Paul's Shop is via the **Crypt Entrance** at the west end of the cathedral's northern side, off of Paternoster Square.

From Original Tour Bus Red/Yellow Stop and Big Bus Stop 45/18

A 1 to 2 minute walk.

The open-top tour bus stop is just a block west of the **Great West Door** entrance to Saint Paul's Cathedral. You'll see the cathedral and its western entrance as you approach this stop. Walk east to reach it.

From Saint Paul's Tube Station

A 4 minute walk.

Follow station signs to **Newgate Street Exit #2.** ♦ After you exit the station, turn left and look for the tall sign with directions to nearby sites. Just past the sign, you'll see the north side of Saint Paul's Cathedral to your left. ♦ Walk toward the cathedral keeping right to reach the **Crypt Entrance**, continuing west to reach the **Great West Door** entrance.

From the Death Eaters' Bridge (Site #1)

A 4 minute walk.

The **South Churchyard** entrance to Saint Paul's Cathedral can be seen from any spot on the Millennium Footbridge. Walk north to reach it.

From Gringotts Bank (Site #5)

A 10 to 15 minute tour bus ride from the Australia House **Original Tour Bus Red/Yellow Stops** *or* **Big Bus Stops 44/17,** or a 15 minute walk from the Australia House main entrance.

Ride a Tour Bus to Hogwarts' Staircase: Walk east from the main entrance of Australia House and cross the island to the east side of **Aldwych** in front of Saint Clement Danes Church. ♦ Turn left to walk north and then west as Aldwych curves around to the Tour Bus stop. ♦ Board the next tour bus and ride to the next stop, just a block west of the **Great West Door** entrance to Saint Paul's Cathedral. You'll see the cathedral as you approach the stop. ♦ Walk east to reach the cathedral's western entrance.

Walk to Hogwarts' Staircase: Head east from the main entrance of Australia House and cross the island to the plaza in front of Saint Clement Danes Church. ♦ Walk straight ahead, keeping right of the church, to walk east on the north side of **The Strand.** ♦ Continue east as The Strand becomes **Fleet**

Street, then **Ludgate Hill**. You'll see the cathedral and its western entrance as you approach the end of Ludgate Hill. ♦ Walk east to reach the cathedral.

From the Leaky Cauldron; *Sorcerer's Stone* (Site #8)

A 17 minute walk.

♈ Head west from any point in Leadenhall Market to **Gracechurch Street**. ♦ Turn left and walk south, crossing to the west side when convenient. ♦ Keep right at the southern end of Gracechurch Street, following the curve to walk west along the north side of **Cannon Street** until you reach the **South Churchyard** entrance to the Cathedral on your right.

7

LEAKY CAULDRON
PRISONER OF AZKABAN

Borough Market
http://www.boroughmarket.org.uk/
http://en.wikipedia.org/wiki/Borough_Market

Google Maps UK: 7A Stoney Street, Southwark, London SE1 9AA
Bensons Mini: L-6 / **Bensons Street:** N-6
Collins Mini: pg 52, A-2,3 / **Collins Atlas:** pg 17, F-5,6

⊖ **Tube Station:** London Bridge

🚌 **Original Tour Bus London Dungeon Red/Yellow Stop** *or* **Big Bus Stop 46/19**

Retail Market Hours: Thurs 11am to 5pm; Fri 12pm to 6pm; Sat 8am to 5pm

Wholesale Market Hours: Every weekday morning, from 4am to 8am.

TIP: Borough Market doesn't have to be **open** to visit the *exterior* HP film sites.

Visit Time: Schedule at least an hour here, perhaps two.

Parseltongue Pointers:
- Borough = "BUR-oh"
- Chez Michele = "SHAY mee-SHELL"
- Southwark = "SUTH-uck"

J.K. Rowling's **Leaky Cauldron** is located on **Charing Cross Road**, where it serves as a gateway between the Muggle World and a hidden courtyard containing the magical **Diagon Alley Wizard Entrance (Site #3)**. Harry Potter movie scenes featuring the Leaky Cauldron's Muggle entrance were filmed in **Leadenhall Market (Site #8)** for *Sorcerer's Stone*, and in **Borough Market** for *Prisoner of Azkaban*.

Borough Market is London's oldest food market. It began operation on **London Bridge** soon after the Romans built it around 40 to 50 AD. Sometime in 1276, congestion caused the market to move off of London Bridge and into the first of two areas where it operated for the next several hundred years. In 1756, Borough Market relocated again to its present—permanent—location, where it has remained for over 250 years.

[©2009 Tara Bellers]

The exterior *Prisoner of Azkaban* Borough Market film sites consist of two buildings immediately adjacent to each other, **#7A Stoney Street** and **#8 Stoney Street**.

[©2009 Tara Bellers] [*POA* screenshot segment (enhanced)]

The **Chez Michele** flower shop at **#7A Stoney Street** is situated in an ancient brick building located directly beneath a railway bridge.
http://www.chezmichele.org.uk/

This store front was modified with a scary-looking façade before being filmed as the Muggle entrance to the Leaky Cauldron for *POA*. Additionally, Chez Michele's doorstep is commonly festooned with flowers when the shop is open. Even so, here is where you should snap the first of your Leaky Cauldron *POA* screenshot recreation pix.

Leaky Cauldron *POA* Screenshot #1

[*Prisoner of Azkaban* screenshot (enhanced)]

Above, Harry is seen standing in front of the Leaky Cauldron (Chez Michele) entrance, just after the Knight Bus vanished. He's immediately under the railway bridge, with the north end of Stoney Street in the background. Unfortunately, there's no **Walker & Hughes** fruit and vegetable vendor sign there anymore.

#8 Stoney Street is Immediately North of Chez Michele

[©2009 Tara Bellers] [Internet *POA* film set photo; ©Unknown]

As demonstrated by the photos above, little more than paint was required to transform this store front's roll-up door and overhead façade into the **Third Hand Book Emporium**. Unfortunately, this wonderful paint treatment is only fleetingly seen on screen, and no longer exists in real-life.

111

Leaky Cauldron *POA* Screenshots #2 & #3

[*Prisoner of Azkaban* screenshot (enhanced)]

[*Prisoner of Azkaban* screenshot (enhanced)]

Inside #8 **Stoney Street**, at the southeast corner of its fourth (top) floor, is a room with a window from which some special *POA* film footage was shot.

[©2009 Tara Bellers]

Although **Harry's Leaky Cauldron bedroom** was a Leavesden Studio **set**, film footage of the real-life view from this #8 Stoney Street window was shot here and digitally inserted into the movie as the view from his Leaky Cauldron bedroom window.

Leaky Cauldron *POA* Screenshot #4

[*Prisoner of Azkaban* screenshot (enhanced)]

Harry's Leaky Cauldron bedroom window view featured the Southwark Cathedral tower rising up beyond the rooftops of Borough Market, as a train passed by on the railway bridge right next to the window. In the screenshot above, the tower's four spires appear to be rising out of Harry's head—like a crown.

[©2009 Tara Bellers]

The photo above left was taken *from* the window seen above right. The real-life architecture of #8's fourth floor room interior and its window is completely different from the Leaky Cauldron bedroom set. But, the view from this window is exactly the same as the view seen in the movie. When this room and its window become publicly accessible—*we're thinking positively!*—Potterites will enjoy a unique opportunity to have their photo taken with Harry's Leaky Cauldron bedroom window view behind them.

#8 Stoney Street Now Owned by The Market Porter

[©2009 Tara Bellers]

According to our research, Market Porter owners intend to eventually renovate all four floors of #8's building so that some kind of business can be conducted on each. Thus, Harry's Leaky Cauldron bedroom window may someday become publicly accessible. We'll be sure to post updates for this entry as soon as it is.

Unfortunately, it could take over a year to obtain the proper permits for renovation. Thus, construction may not begin until mid-to-late 2012—perhaps not even until 2013—completion may take up to 2 years.

[©2011 Tara Bellers]

In the mean time, Market Porter is operating the UK version of a fast-food shop in #8 Stoney Street's ground floor space, **The Posh Banger Boys**. A variety of quickly cooked items are offered: beef burgers, chicken wraps, and *cones of chips* (paper cartons of French-fried potatoes). But, the shop's specialty is **Posh Bangers in a BAP**. *Posh* means high quality. *Bangers* are sausages. And, a *BAP* is a soft bread roll.

Oddly enough, the fast-food served by The Posh Banger Boys is of *gourmet* quality. Although there sometimes are complaints about the price (£5 a pop), Posh Bangers' fare is universally praised as being extraordinarily delicious.

> "The food was so incredibly fresh. They serve 'fast food' but everything is made to order. The chicken was just fried (so juicy) …This made all the difference in taste. There was also this strange hot sauce with mixed greens that I couldn't quite identify … [It] literally blew me away!"

http://www.qype.co.uk/place/1638691-The-Posh-Banger-Boys-London
http://www.facebook.com/pages/The-Posh-Banger-Boys/151962661491527

The Posh Banger Boys shop commonly opens at noon every day of the week. On Monday, Tuesday, and Wednesday, they close at 9 or 10 pm. On Thursday and Friday they stay open "even later, if it's busy and we haven't run out of sausages." On Saturday and Sunday they close at 6 or 7 pm.

[©2009 Tara Bellers]

Although no filming took place *within* the **Market Porter**, actors and crew members spent much of their between-film-shots time here, making it a great place for Potter fans to enjoy a sip or a sup. If business is *slow* during your visit, politely ask to speak with someone about the Harry Potter window on the fourth floor of #8 Stoney Street. Market Porter personnel have been marvelously helpful to visiting Potterites.

To view Market Porter's peculiar operating hours, visit these websites:
http://www.markettaverns.co.uk/the_market_porter.html
http://www.facebook.com/pages/The-Market-Porter/127281513991013

Please Note: For some unknown reason, neither the Market Porter, nor the Posh Banger Boys, have an official website. Both have registered pages on Facebook. But, there ain't much info found on either of those Facebook pages. Apparently, both of these businesses have no need of social network advertisement. Happy for them!

The Non-Potter Parts of Borough Market Are *Marvelous*

[©2009 Tara Bellers]

You can easily spend more than a hurried Harry Potter hour here. In addition to scads of English fare purveyors, Borough Market boasts many International food vendors.

[©2009 Tara Bellers]

Offering everything from *Soup to Nuts*, Borough Market abounds with unusual and exotic—sometimes hilarious—sights, sounds, and smells.

[©2009 Tara Bellers] [©2008 C.D. Miller]

Best of all, because it isn't considered a popular London "sightseeing" attraction, few non-Potterite tourists visit Borough Market. Thus, even when the market is busy, you'll mostly be rubbing elbows with savvy indigenous London Muggles. Chat up the vendors or other shoppers while you wander. Folk who frequent Borough Market are friendly.

The Borough Market Potterite Suggested Plans of Attack

• When following the *Harry Potter Places* **Quick-Quill Trip** or **Kwikspell Crusade** itineraries on a Thursday or Saturday, you'll arrive at Borough Market very near the Market Stalls' closing time. Meander through the market *before* snapping your Potter Pix.

• When following any of the other *Harry Potter Places* **Suggested Itineraries** on a Thursday, Friday, or Saturday, you'll have plenty of time to snap exterior Potter Pix before or after visiting the market stalls.

• Once finished with exterior *POA* Potter Pix on any day, go to the Market Porter pub for a *SIP* of something. While there, politely ask to speak with someone about the #8 Stoney Street property, and its top-floor Harry Potter window. If you can gently persuade someone into helping you gain entrance to that room, do so!

• Finally, enjoy a *SUP* at the Posh Banger Boys stall. If chatting-up the Market Porter folks didn't gain you entrance to the #8 Stoney Street Harry Potter window, see if you can charm one of the Posh Banger employees into taking you up to the top floor of their building.

[In 2009, Potterite Tara Bellers discovered that the stairway entrance giving access to the floors above #8 Stoney Street's Posh Bangers space was blocked by a refrigerator. Her Unnamed Guide had to have the refrigerator moved aside so that he could take her up to Harry's window.]

Nearby Non-Potter Places

There is an amazing variety of interesting non-Potter attractions nearby.

Between Borough Market and Original Tour Bus/Big Bus Stops

The Old Operating Theatre Museum and Herb Garret
http://www.thegarret.org.uk/

Southwark Cathedral
http://cathedral.southwark.anglican.org/

The London Bridge (and Tombs) Experience (more info below.)
http://www.thelondonbridgeexperience.com/

The London Dungeon (See extra info below.)
http://www.the-dungeons.co.uk/london/en/index.htm

The HMS Belfast (See the Fly-By Bridges & Buildings, Site #4, entry for more info.)
http://www.iwm.org.uk/visits/hms-belfast

Between Borough Market & the Millennium Footbridge (Site #1)

The Golden Hind

(A recreation of Sir Francis Drake's English galleon, best known for circumnavigating the earth between 1577 and 1580.)
http://www.goldenhind.co.uk/

The Clink Prison Museum (See extra info below.)
http://www.clink.co.uk/

Shakespeare's Globe Theater (See Death Eater's Bridge, Site #1, entry for more info.)
http://www.shakespeares-globe.org/

The Tate Modern Art Museum (See Death Eater's Bridge, Site #1, entry for more info.)
http://www.tate.org.uk/modern/

A Prison, a Dungeon, or a Bridge with Tombs—*Oh, My!*

If you're interested in visiting such spooky non-Potter Places as these, here are a few tips for choosing between them.

Clink Prison offers the cheapest, fastest, and lowest-tech experience; a good choice if you have very young children with you.

The London Dungeon and **the London Bridge with Tombs** attractions offer loads of high-tech gore, live actors and rides—but, at more than twice the cost, even with discounted advance tickets purchased via the Internet.

Trip Advisor Traveler Reviews for *all three* of these attractions seem evenly split between "well worth a visit" and "a complete rip-off."

[©2008 C.D. Miller]

The Clink Prison Museum
http://www.clink.co.uk/

This museum occupies the original site of Clink Prison, a notorious London lockup that operated from 1144 to 1780, when it was burned to the ground by rioting Protestants. The prison's name was derived from the *clinking* noise made by the various manacles, fetters, and chains worn by its prisoners. In fact, Clink Prison is the origin of the phrase, *"in the clink."* Plan to spend at least 30 to 45 minutes here.

Opening Hours: 7 days a week at 10am. Check the website for closing times.

Admission: Adults £7 ($11); Children under 16, Seniors over 60, and Students with an ID, £5.50 ($9).

The London Bridge Experience and the London Tombs
http://www.thelondonbridgeexperience.com/

According to the official website, you will;

> "See, hear, feel, taste, even smell what London Bridge was like over the ages. ... Experience London of old with Romans, Vikings and the odd pick-pocket or two. ... The Tombs are not for the faint hearted! It's an adrenalin pumping experience ... When you venture down from the vaults, you will enter the real tombs of the bridge."

Allow about 45 minutes for the London Bridge Experience, and an additional 25 minutes if you continue to the London Tombs tour.

Opening Hours: Mon to Fri, 10am-5pm; Sat & Sun, 10am-6pm; Dec 24 to Jan 1, 11am-4pm; Closed Christmas Day & Boxing Day.

Tickets are cheaper when pre-booked online.

The London Dungeon
http://www.the-dungeons.co.uk/london/en/index.htm

From the official website:

> "In the dark and dingy underbelly of the capital the London Dungeon dwells, waiting to scare the life out of you and any willing visitors brave enough to cross the threshold. Confront your fears, face your worst nightmares and uncover the gory truth behind some of history's most horrific events!"

The London Dungeon tour lasts approximately 60 to 90 minutes.

Opening Hours: Mon to Fri, 10:30am-5pm; Sat & Sun, 10am-5pm; Dec 26, 11am-4pm; Closed Christmas Day.

Tickets are cheaper when pre-booked online.

Nearby Potter Places

Death Eaters' Bridge (Site #1): A 10 minute walk.

Leaky Cauldron; *Sorcerer's Stone* (Site #8): A 15 minute walk.

Going to the Leaky Cauldron, *Prisoner of Azkaban* Site

From London Bridge Tube Station
A 7 to 10 minute walk from your train, but only a 2 minute walk from the street exit.

🚶 Follow station signs to the **Borough High Street West exit**. Upon reaching the street, walk straight ahead (southwest) to **Stoney Street**. ♦ Turn right and walk northwest to Chez Michele—the Leaky Cauldron *POA* entrance.

If you accidentally leave the London Bridge tube station from its exit on **Duke Street Hill**, head west and follow the directions from the Original Tour Bus and Big Bus stops.

🚌 **From Original Tour Bus London Dungeon Red/Yellow Stop *or* Big Bus Stop 46/19**
A 9 minute walk.

🚶 Head northwest on **Tooley Street**, continuing as it curves west and becomes **Duke Street Hill**. At the end of Duke Street Hill, cross to the west side of **King William Street**. ♦ Turn left and walk southwest as King William Street becomes **Borough High Street**. Continue until you reach **Bedale Street**. ♦ Turn right and walk northwest. The Borough Market entrance will be on your left. ♦ Shop your way south through the market. When you reach **Stoney Street**, look left for the railway bridge above Chez Michele—the Leaky Cauldron *POA* entrance.

From the Death Eaters' Bridge (Site #1): *ALL HPP* Suggested Itineraries
A 10 minute walk.

🚶 From the south bank of the Millennium Footbridge (or the north entrance of the Tate Modern Art Museum), head east on the walkway along the south bank of the **Thames River**. ♦ As you near the Globe Theater, head slightly away from the river and walk east on **Bankside Jetty**, continuing east when Bankside Jetty becomes **Bankside**. ♦ At **Southwark Bridge**, follow Bankside to the right as it goes south and then east again, to cross under the bridge. ♦ On the other side of the bridge, turn left and go back toward the river, then turn right to walk east on **Thames Path**, continuing as it turns right and heads southeast, becoming Bankside again. ♦ Follow Bankside until it ends at **Bank End**. ♦ Turn right and go south to **Clink Street**. ♦ Turn left and walk east, passing under the railway bridge. (You'll see the Clink Prison Museum ahead of you.) Continue east to **Stoney Street**. ♦ Turn right and walk south until you see the Market Porter and the railway bridge over Chez Michele, the Leaky Cauldron *POA* entrance.

From the Leaky Cauldron; *Sorcerer's Stone* (Site #8)
A 15 minute walk.

♀ Go west from any place in Leadenhall Market to **Gracechurch Street**. ♦ Turn left and walk southwest down the east side of Gracechurch Street to its end at **Eastcheap**, and cross to the south side. ♦ Turn right and walk west to follow the sidewalk as it curves south and becomes the east side of **King William Street**. Continue southwest, over the new **London Bridge**. [**TIP:** From the bridge's east side you can take pix of **Tower Bridge** without traffic in the way.] After you reach the south bank of the Thames River, cross to the far west side of King William Street. ♦ Turn left and walk southwest, until King William Street becomes **Borough High Street**, continuing southwest until you reach **Bedale Street**. ♦ Turn right and walk northwest on Bedale Street. The northern Borough Market entrance will be on your left. ♦ Shop your way south through the market. When you reach **Stoney Street**, look left to see the railway bridge above Chez Michele—the Leaky Cauldron *POA* entrance.

8

LEAKY CAULDRON
SORCERER'S STONE

Leadenhall Market
http://www.leadenhallmarket.co.uk/
http://en.wikipedia.org/wiki/Leadenhall_Market

Google Maps UK: 41 Leadenhall Market, London EC3V 1LT, or 51.512395,-0.083815

Bensons Mini: M-5 / **Bensons Street:** P-5

Collins Mini: pg 40, C-3 / **Collins Atlas:** pg 17, H-2

⊖**Tube Station:** Monument *or* Bank (These two stations are actually *one* vast underground station.)

🚌 **Original Tour Bus London Dungeon Red/Yellow Stop** *or* **Big Bus Stop 46/19**

🚌 **Original Tour Bus Saint Paul's Cathedral Red/Yellow Stop** *or* **Big Bus Stop 45/18**

Operation Hours: Market stalls are open from 11am to 4pm *only* on Monday through Friday, as are most shops and restaurants. Potterite visits to Leadenhall Market on Saturday or Sunday are *not* recommended.

Entry Fee: None

Visit Time: Schedule at least 45 minutes here to snap your Potter pix at the film sites. To enjoy the food or shops, plan to spend 1.5 to 2 hours here.

Parseltongue Pointer:
- Leadenhall = "LED-in-hall"

J.K. Rowling's **Leaky Cauldron** is located on **Charing Cross Road**, where it serves as a gateway between the Muggle World and a hidden courtyard containing the magical **Diagon Alley Wizard Entrance (Site #3)**. Harry Potter movie scenes featuring the Leaky Cauldron's Muggle entrance were filmed in **Borough Market (Site #7)** for *Prisoner of Azkaban*, and in **Leadenhall Market** for *Sorcerer's Stone*.

[©2009 Tara Bellers]

Since the first century AD, there has been a *forum* (the Roman term for *market place*) where Leadenhall Market stands today. Named for a lead-roofed mansion that stood nearby in the 14th Century, the main area of Leadenhall Market first became a covered structure when it was rebuilt after the Great Fire of 1666. In 1881, Sir Horace Jones, a well-known Victorian architect, redesigned the market's main building, replacing the simple stone walls with wrought iron, glass, and a marvelously ornate roof.

In addition to a wide variety of traditional and ethnic cafés, pubs, and restaurants in all price ranges, modern day Leadenhall Market is loaded with specialty shops and stalls that sell flowers, pens, cheeses, leather goods, chocolates, craftwork, greeting cards, jewelry, wines and spirits. You'll also find professional services such as a tailor, a drycleaner, and a fantastic shop that offers rapid watch and shoe repair at reasonable prices.

Modern day Leadenhall Market stalls are more upscale than the traditional produce sellers of old. You'll find gourmet foods, fancy breads and pastries. Ready-to-eat food vendors offer a wide variety of luncheon fare such as piping hot pastas, duck or goose liver foie gras, garden fresh salads, and sumptuous sandwiches. Leadenhall Market also has outdoor seating areas where you can sit and enjoy your food.

Potter Places in Leadenhall Market

The store front where the Leaky Cauldron's entrance was filmed for *Sorcerer's Stone* can be found in **Bulls Head Passage**, a pedestrian alley that leads east from Gracechurch Street, into the heart of Leadenhall Market.

[©2008 CD Miller] [©2009 Tara Bellers]

The easy-to-spot royal blue building was home to The I Glass House (an optician) when *SS* filming took place. A **Capital Aesthetics** clinic (cosmetic and aesthetic medicine) was its occupant in 2009.

[©2009 Tara Bellers]

The unique architecture and leaded glass are what probably caught the eye of Harry Potter location scouts. Unfortunately, set designers blackened all the gorgeous glass with soot-colored paint (perhaps to make the Leaky Cauldron less inviting to Muggles).

Leaky Cauldron *SS* Screenshot #1

[*Sorcerer's Stone* screenshot (enhanced)]

Happily, in spite of the color differences between the *SS* screenshot and its real-life film site, recognizable Harry Potter pix can be taken here.

After taking your Leaky Cauldron entrance pix, resume walking east on Bull's Head Passage to Lime Street Passage and you'll arrive at the corner seen in the next screenshot.

Leaky Cauldron *SS* Screenshot #2

[*Sorcerer's Stone* screenshot (enhanced)]

In real-life, this Leadenhall Market area still looks almost exactly the same as it did when filming took place in 2000. The John Kent Greengrocer on the corner closed in 2003 and was replaced by a Ben's Cookies store, but **The Market Café** next door—where the tables and a scooter are seen in the screenshot—hasn't changed at all. Their Potterite-friendly staff shared the following story with us in October of 2008.

> "The scooter in that screenshot belonged to the Indian man who runs the cigarette store across from us. It was stolen from his house a few weeks after filming."

The Market Café offers delicious, inexpensive food from 6am to 4pm on Mondays through Fridays; 6am to 11am on Saturdays. Buy a cuppa or snack here and chat up the staff. (Please report any new Harry Potter filming stories they share on the *Harry Potter Places* blog.) Then, have your pic taken while sitting at the tables outside, with the magnificent arched enclosure of Leadenhall Market's main building in the background.

The Market is *Deserted* on Weekends & After 4pm Weekdays

[©2009 Tara Bellers] [©2008 CD Miller]

Above left, a weekend shot of Leadenhall Market. Above right, Leadenhall Market on a weekday. All Leaky Cauldron *SS* screenshots can be accomplished when the market is closed. But, it's much more fun to visit while the stalls are open and the area is bustling with people.

After you've finished at The Market Café, walk north to the arched enclosure (seen above) and enjoy the Leadenhall Market Stalls. The stalls extend west from this point, so you'll be shopping your way back toward Gracechurch Street.

Nearby Potter Places

 Leaky Cauldron: *Prisoner of Azkaban* (Site #7): A 15 minute walk.

 Hogwarts Staircase (Site #6): A 17 minute walk.

Going to the Leaky Cauldron: *Sorcerer's Stone* Film Site

[©2008 C.D. Miller]

Please Note: If you somehow miss **Bull's Head Passage** while following any of the directions below, you'll soon arrive at the huge Gracechurch Street entrance to Leadenhall Market—something you cannot possibly miss, even if it's still surrounded by renovation scaffolding. Turn around and go back the way you came, watching on your left for *Bull's Head Passage*. ♦ Turn left and walk east until the alley suddenly widens. There, on your left, is the Leaky Cauldron's *SS* Muggle front entrance.

⊖ From Monument Tube Station
A 9 minute walk.

🚶 Follow the signs to reach the **Gracechurch, near House of Fraser Exit**, or the **King William Street, near House of Fraser Exit**. Both of these exits emerge at the intersection of Cannon Street, Eastcheap, King William Street, and Gracechurch Street. Cross to the east side of **Gracechurch Street** and walk northeast. After crossing **Fenchurch Street**, watch on your right for **Ship Tavern Passage**, a pedestrian alley. Continue to the *next* pedestrian alley, **Bull's Head Passage**, also on your right. ♦ Turn right and walk east until the alley suddenly widens.

From Bank Tube Station
An 11 minute walk.

𝕏 Follow station signs to reach **Exit #6**, the **Lombard Street and King William Street Exit**. You'll emerge from this exit at the northeast corner of King William and Lombard Streets. Turn left and walk east on **Lombard Street** until you reach **Gracechurch Street**. ♦ Cross to the east side, turn left and walk northeast on Gracechurch Street. ♦ Watch on your right for **Ship Tavern Passage**, a pedestrian alley. Continue to the *next* pedestrian alley, **Bull's Head Passage**, also on your right. ♦ Turn right and walk east until the alley suddenly widens.

From Original Tour Bus London Dungeon Red/Yellow Stop/ Big Bus Stop 46/19
A 15 minute walk.

[**TIP:** If you'll also be visiting the **Leaky Cauldron:** *Prisoner of Azkaban* **(Site #7)** in Borough Market today, go *there* first.]

𝕏 Head northwest on **Tooley Street**, continuing as it curves west and becomes **Duke Street Hill**. ♦ At the end of Duke Street Hill, turn right and walk north along the east side of **King William Street**, crossing over the new London Bridge. [**TIP:** From the bridge's east side you can take pix of **Tower Bridge** without traffic in the way.] ♦ When you reach the intersection of Cannon Street, Eastcheap, King William Street, and Gracechurch Street, cross to the east side of **Gracechurch Street** and walk northeast. ♦ After crossing **Fenchurch Street**, watch on your right for **Ship Tavern Passage**, a pedestrian alley. Continue to the *next* pedestrian alley, **Bull's Head Passage**, also on your right. ♦ Turn right and walk east until the alley suddenly widens.

From the Leaky Cauldron: *Prisoner of Azkaban* (Site #7)
A 15 minute walk.

𝕏 Whether leaving from **Stoney Street** or **Bedale Street**, walk southeast until the street ends. ♦ Turn left and walk northeast to the crosswalk just a few steps north of Bedale Street. ♦ Cross to the east side of **Borough High Street**, turn left and walk northeast. ♦ After passing under the railway bridge, Borough High Street becomes **King William Street**. Continue north, crossing over the new London Bridge. [**TIP:** From the bridge's east side you can take pix of **Tower Bridge** without traffic in the way.] ♦ When you reach the intersection of Cannon Street, Eastcheap, King William Street, and Gracechurch Street, cross to the east side of **Gracechurch Street** and walk northeast. ♦ After crossing **Fenchurch Street**, watch on your right for **Ship**

Tavern Passage, a pedestrian alley. Continue to the *next* pedestrian alley, **Bull's Head Passage**, also on your right. ♦ Turn right and walk east until the alley suddenly widens.

From the Hogwarts Staircase (Site #6) *OR From*

Original Tour Bus Saint Paul's Cathedral Red/Yellow Stop/ Big Bus Stop 45/18
A 17 minute walk.

🕴 Walk east on **Cannon Street** to the intersection of Cannon Street, Eastcheap, King William Street, and Gracechurch Street. ♦ Cross to the east side of **Gracechurch Street** and walk northeast. ♦ After crossing **Fenchurch Street**, watch on your right for **Ship Tavern Passage**, a pedestrian alley. Continue to the *next* pedestrian alley, **Bull's Head Passage**, also on your right. ♦ Turn right and walk east until the alley suddenly widens.

⊖ From Camden Town Tube Station: Kwikspell Crusade and Huffandpuff Expedition *SS* Day itineraries
A 14 minute underground journey and an 11 minute walk.

Take the **Northern Line** towards Morden to reach **Bank Underground Station**. ♦ Follow walking directions from Bank Tube Station above.

9

LITTLE WHINGING ZOO

The London Zoo
http://www.zsl.org/zsl-london-zoo

Google Maps UK: 51.535556, -0.155833 (The Zoo's *street address* doesn't bring up a map that accurately identifies the entrance.)

Zoo Address: ZSL London Zoo, Regent's Park, London NW1 4RY
   Warning! Do not trust any directions that route you *through* the park, or *through* the Zoo. You cannot enter the Zoo from any place other than its main entrance, at the northern section of Regent's Park Outer Circle.

Bensons Mini: C-1 / **Bensons Street:** E-1
(The Zoo's main entrance is *beyond* the north edge of both Bensons maps.)
Collins Mini: pg 10, A-2 / **Collins Atlas:** pg 41, F,G-1, pg 42, A-1

🚇 **Tube Station:** Camden Town

🚌 **Original Tour Bus Madame Tussauds Red/Yellow/Black/Gray Stop** *or* **Big Bus Stop 32/5**

Operation Hours: Open at 10am every day of the year except Christmas Day. The Zoo closes at 4pm in the Winter, 5:30pm in the Summer.

Entry Fee: Consult the Zoo's website for ticket prices and special offers available during the dates of your visit. Tickets can be purchased online up to six months in advance, however Internet-purchased tickets are dedicated to a specific date and are non-refundable. Discount family tickets are available online. Individuals tickets cost the same online as they do at the Zoo's entrance, but you can avoid the queues by booking online and enter via the fast track gate. (The London Pass includes free, fast track entry to the Zoo.)

Visit Time: Our directions are designed to facilitate a **Rapid 1 Hour Harry Potter Pic & Shop Visit**. A 90 minute Zoo visit is optimal, as it allows extra time to enjoy the Potter sites and the gift shop. Schedule 2 to 6 hours if you have time to enjoy *more* of the London Zoo—it's a world-class Zoo, after all!

General Zoo Visit Tips:

(1) To be safe, schedule at least 45 minutes total travel time before *and* after your Zoo visit. The journey to the Zoo is longer and more complicated than jaunts to other Central London Potter places. Whether traveling via the Tube or an open-top Tour Bus, you'll be walking or City-Bussing it between your arrival point and the Zoo's entrance.

(2) Maps of the Zoo layout are available on the Visitor Information webpage. http://www.zsl.org/zsl-london-zoo/visit/

These maps are available for free *at* the Zoo, so you don't need to print one from the website to pack and bring with you.

Parseltongue Pointers:

- Whinging = "WIN-jeeng" (*not* "WINE-jeeng") [To "whinge" is to complain or protest in an annoyingly persistent manner. Although similar to "whining," the pronunciation is different.]
- Madame Tussauds = "mah-DAM too-SODS" ... *French*: "mah-DAM chew-SO"
- Marylebone = "MERRILY-bone"

CRAC

J.K. Rowling's **Little Whinging** is a fictional town just south of London, in Surrey, England, where Harry lived with the Dursleys at #4 Privet Drive. In *Sorcerer's Stone*, Harry was grudgingly allowed to accompany his cousin to the **Little Whinging Zoo** on Dudley's birthday. It was while visiting the Zoo's **Reptile House** that Harry discovered he could speak **Parseltongue**— communicate with a snake.

All of the *Sorcerer's Stone* Little Whinging Zoo scenes were filmed in and around the London Zoo's Reptile House.

Potter Zoo Pic #1

[*Sorcerer's Stone* screenshot (enhanced)]

After entering the Zoo via its main entrance, look ahead and to your right (south and slightly west) for the path that leads to the Reptile House. Have your photo taken outside the entrance.

Just inside the Reptile House is the snake display tank used to film *Sorcerer's Stone* scenes. You can't miss it! A Harry Potter information sign featuring a promotional photo is posted next to the tank.

Potter Zoo Pix #2, 3, and 4

[*SS* promotional photo (enhanced)] [©2009 Tara Bellers]

[*Sorcerer's Stone* screenshot (enhanced)]

In real life, the snake tank used to film *Sorcerer's Stone* scenes contains a **Black Mamba**. The London Zoo's Reptile House doesn't have a **Brazilian Boa Constrictor** (the *book's* snake), nor a **Burmese Python** (the *movie's* snake). However, there *is* a **Basilisk** on display here! After taking pix at the Black Mamba tank, find a Zoo employee to direct you to the **Plumed Basilisk** display tank.

[*Chamber of Secrets* screenshot (enhanced)]

The Basilisk Harry battled in *Chamber of Secrets* was based on a Greek mythological creature composed of rooster, snake, and lion aspects, that could turn a person to stone with its gaze.

[©2008 C.D. Miller]

The London Zoo's Plumed Basilisk cannot turn you into stone with its gaze, nor is it the same size or shape as the movie's Basilisk. In fact, *Basiliscus plumifrons*' average length is 2 feet from tail-tip to nose, with 3 feet long being its maximum size. The Basilisk seen in the Zoo pic above was barely a foot long at the time. Still, it *is* a Basilisk—and no one can deny that it's kind of adorable.

If you are following the **Rapid 1-Hour Visit Schedule**, exit the Reptile House immediately after visiting the Black Mamba and Plumed Basilisk display tanks.

Sad News: *HP* Screenshot Recreation Photo-Op Lost Forever

In *Sorcerer's Stone*, **Guy the Gorilla** could be seen outside the Reptile House as the Burmese Python made his escape. Unfortunately, after *SS* filming, Zoo officials became concerned about the safety risk of children climbing on Guy and falling off. Alas and alack, Guy was relocated to an inaccessible grassy area at the center of **Barclay Court**—the next stop on your Zoo tour.

To console yourself for this loss, quickly visit one of the sweets vendors outside the Reptile House. In 2008, vendors didn't offer a **cheap lemon ice pop**—the treat bought for Harry after large chocolate ice creams were purchased for Dudley and his pal, Piers. But, a *raspberry* ice pop was available for only 50 pence (80 cents). It was delicious!

Enjoy your cheap ice pop while making your way to Barclay Court.

Head southeast from the Reptile House and turn left at the next lane.

Potter Zoo Pic #5

[*Sorcerer's Stone* screenshot (enhanced)]

When you arrive at Barclay Court you'll see Guy the Gorilla in the center of his unfortunately inaccessible enclosure. Using your camera's zoom feature, you can snap Guy pix that look similar to his appearance outside the Reptile House door.

[©2008 C.D. Miller]

But, you might as well have fun with him.

[©2009 Conny Rhode] [©2009 Tara Bellers]

After taking pix of Guy, visit the **Barclay Court Gift Shop**—the Zoo's largest.

The **Rapid 1 Hour Harry Potter Pic & Shop Visit** ends when you're done shopping. But, before you leave, dash into Barclay Court's **Oasis Café** to use the restroom. It isn't always easy to find an accessible public restroom once you're back on the streets of London.

When ready to leave, you'll find the Zoo exit to the northwest of Barclay Court, on the east side of the Zoo entrance.

Nearby Non-Potter Places

Regent's Park Open Air Theatre
http://openairtheatre.org/

Google Maps UK: Open Air Theatre, Inner Circle, Regent's Park, London NW1 4NU

London has loads of live performance theaters, but the outdoor theater experience is uniquely enjoyable. Operating between May and September, Regent's Park Open Air Theatre productions are always of the highest quality. Its roofless auditorium boasts 1240 individual seats.

Per the Regents' Park Open Air Theatre website:

> "It's best to come prepared for all types of weather: bringing your own shade in the afternoon is particularly important as is a jumper for the end of evening performances. So sun hats, sun cream, sunglasses, raincoats and rain hats should all be considered."

If you forget to bring something, the shop sells most of those items at reasonable prices. In the event of a weather cancellation (very rare), there is no time limit for the exchange of your tickets.

> "We've had people exchanging years later."

A wide variety of food as well as a full-service bar is available before, during, and after each production. Or, you can pre-purchase a pretty-darn-tasty Box Picnic that includes a complimentary program. Although eating during a performance is discouraged, you can enjoy drinks at any time.

Show Times: Most shows run Monday through Saturday at 8pm, with 2:30pm matinees also offered on Thursday and Saturday. Occasionally, individual shows offer Sunday performances.

Ticket Prices: These vary, depending on the type of production and whether or not seating is assigned. When seating is assigned, ticket prices are based on the view-related location of the seat. 2012 assigned seating ticket prices range between £17.50 ($28) and £49.50 ($78). Tickets for Open-Seating productions and Preview performances are commonly far less than the cheapest assigned-seating tickets.

If you cannot time your London Zoo visit to immediately precede or follow a Regents' Park Open Air Theatre production, it's well worth your effort to make a special trip back to this area to enjoy a show.

The following Nearby Non-Potter Places are located on the route between the Zoo and Madame Tussauds.

The Sherlock Holmes Museum
http://www.sherlock-holmes.co.uk/

Google Maps UK: 221b Baker Street, London NW1 6XE

Built in 1815, the Georgian townhouse that lies between numbers 237 and 241 Baker Street closely resembles Sir Arthur Conan Doyle's structural description of Mrs. Hudson's boarding house. Additionally, this building operated as a real-life boarding house from 1860 to 1936, a time frame that accurately corresponds to the years when the fictional Sherlock Holmes and Doctor Watson were tenants of 221b Baker Street (1881 to 1904).

However, the address Sir Arthur attributed to Holmes' boarding house—number **221b**—had never been assigned to any structure on Baker Street until after the Sherlock Holmes Museum opened in March of 1990. At that time, the Westminster City Council gave permission for the museum to use that address, and bestowed upon them a historical blue plaque identifying it.

[©2002 C.D. Miller]

Run by the non-profit **Sherlock Holmes International Society**, the museum's highlight is the famous first floor study overlooking Baker Street. Faithfully maintained as it would have appeared in Victorian times, this study is stuffed full of Sherlock Holmes memorabilia. Holmes fans can easily spend an entire hour in this one room, as most of the study's artifacts are associated with various individual cases.

The museum's other rooms contain wax figures arranged in tableaus representing famous scenes from Holmes' many adventures. Although they aren't of the same quality found at Madame Tussauds, these wax figures succeed in stimulating the imagination — occasionally giving one a start!

Open every day (except Christmas Day), from 9:30am to 6pm.
Admission: Adult, £6 ($10); Children under 16, £4 ($7).

The London Beatles Store
http://www.beatlesstorelondon.co.uk/

Google Maps UK: 231 Baker Street, London NW1 6XE

Just two shops south of the Sherlock Holmes Museum, this store sells everything *Beatles*: music, photos, high quality collectibles, as well as low cost souvenirs and trinkets.

Open every day from 10am to 6:30pm. No Admission fee.

It's Only Rock 'n' Roll
http://www.itsonlyrocknrolllondon.co.uk/

Google Maps UK: 230 Baker Street, London NW1 5RT

Directly across the street from the London Beatles Store, this store is dedicated to all *other* rock 'n' roll stars and bands' memorabilia. The wares found here are not limited to English rock-n-rollers. Elvis fans will thoroughly enjoy this store. **Open every day** from 10am to 6:30pm. No Admission fee.

Nearby Potter Places

👓 Muggle Wax Museum: Madame Tussauds (Site #14): A 35 minute walk or walk/bus journey.

Going to Little Whinging Zoo
⊖ From Camden Town Underground Station

From Camden Town Tube Station, you can either walk all the way to the Zoo, or do a walk-ride-walk journey via a City Bus. Both of these options take approximately 30 minutes.

TAXI If you'd rather just take a taxi to the Zoo, ignore Camden Town Tube Station's **To The Zoo** signs. Instead, head in the opposite direction, following signs to the **Camden High Street** exit. ♦ Walk about 1 ½ blocks south on Camden High Street to **Greenland Street** for the nearest 24-hour Taxi Queue. Taxi fare to the Zoo may range from £7 to £12 ($11 to $19), depending on the day, the time, and the traffic.

Take a City Bus to the Zoo from Camden Town Tube Station

🚶🚌🚶 A 7 minute walk to the bus stop, a 13-15 minute bus ride, then a 7 minute walk to the Zoo.

🚶 Follow the Camden Town Tube Station's **To The Zoo** signs. They'll lead you to the **Kentish Town Road** exit, which is on the station's east side—the side *opposite* to the Zoo, but closest to where you can catch a City Bus to the Zoo. ♦ When you emerge, turn right and walk to the intersection of Kentish Town Road, Camden Road and Greenland Road. Look for the **World's End Pub**. ♦ Cross **Camden Road** and turn right to walk west toward the pub's entrance. As you pass the pub's front door, keep left to walk east on the north side of **Greenland Road**. ♦ At the next intersection, Greenland Road and **Bayham Street**, cross to the southeast corner and turn right. Bayham Street's **Bus Stop T** is but a few steps away.

🚌 **Board Bus 274 towards Lancaster Gate.** Get off at the nearest Zoo stop, **Bus Stop A** on **Regent's Park Road.**

🚶 From Bus Stop A, walk a few steps east to the street named **Saint Mark's Square**. ♦ Turn right and walk a block south to **Prince Albert Road**. ♦ Cross over and continue south on the footpath to the **Regent's Canal Footbridge**. ♦ Cross over the footbridge and continue south until you reach **Regent's Park Outer Circle Road**. ♦ Turn right and walk southwest along Outer Circle Road to the Zoo's main entrance.

Walk to the Zoo from Camden Town Underground Station
A 30 minute walk.

🚶 Ignore Camden Town Tube Station's **To The Zoo** signs. Instead, head in the opposite direction, following signs to the **Camden High Street** exit. ♦ Cross to the west side and turn left, heading southeast to **Parkway**. ♦ Turn right and walk west along the north side of Parkway until you reach the **Prince Albert Road** intersection, where you'll see tree-lined parkland across the street to the right. ♦ Cross to the park side (west side) of Prince Albert Road, turn right and walk north, continuing as the road curves west. ♦ When you reach the first crosswalk stoplight, walk just past it and turn left on the footpath to the **Regent's Canal Footbridge**. ♦ Walk south on that footpath, crossing over Regent's Canal Footbridge, continuing until you reach **Regent's Park Outer Circle Road**. ♦ Turn right and walk southwest along Outer Circle Road to the Zoo's main entrance.

From Madame Tussauds (Site #14), *OR*
🚌 From the Madame Tussauds Open-top Tour Bus Stops
You can either walk all the way to the Zoo, or do a walk-ride-walk journey via a City Bus. Both of these options take approximately 30 to 35 minutes.

TAXI If you'd rather just take a taxi to the Zoo, ask for directions to the Marylebone/Baker Street 24-hour Taxi Queue. Taxi fare to the Zoo may range from £7 to £12 ($11 to $19), depending on the day, the time, and traffic.

Take a City Bus from Madame Tussauds, or the Tour Bus Stop
🚶🚌🚶 A 7 minute walk to the city bus, a 16 to 20 minute bus ride, then a 7 minute walk to the Zoo.

🚶 Walk southwest on the north side of **Marylebone Road**, past **Baker Street**, to **Gloucester Place**. ♦ Cross over and turn right to walk northwest along the west side of Gloucester Place. ♦ **Bus Stop T** is just past **Dorset Square Park**.

🚌 Board Bus 274 toward Islington/Angel. Get off at the nearest Zoo stop, **Bus Stop H** on **Prince Albert Road** near **Ormonde Terrace**.

🚶 Walk a few yards southwest on the north side of Prince Albert Road to the cross walk just *before* Ormonde Terrace. ♦ Turn left and cross to the south side of Prince Albert Road. ♦ Turn right and follow the south-curving sidewalk, crossing over the **Regent's Canal Footbridge**. ♦ Continue southeast to **Regent's Park Outer Circle Road**. ♦ Turn left and walk northeast along Outer Circle Road to the Zoo's main entrance.

Walk from Madame Tussauds or the Open-top Tour Bus Stop

A 35 minute walk.

🚶 Walk southwest on **Marylebone Road** to Baker Street. ♦ Turn right and walk northwest on the east side of Baker Street until you reach the intersection of Baker Street, Allsop Place, and Ivor Place. ♦ Cross the mouth of **Allsop Place** and continue northwest on Baker Street until it merges into **Regent's Park Outer Circle Road**. ♦ Cross to the east side and follow Outer Circle Road as it curves north, and then northeast, until you reach the Zoo's main entrance.

Leaving from Little Whinging Zoo

🚶 If you **walked *to* the Zoo** from Camden Town Tube Station, or Madame Tussauds, *or* from the open-top Tour Bus Stops nearby Madame Tussauds, simply reverse those directions for **walking *back*** to the same point.

If you **walked *to* the Zoo** but would rather ride a **City Bus** to Camden Town Tube Station, or Madame Tussauds, *or* the open-top Tour Bus Stops nearby Madame Tussauds, follow the bus directions below.

🚌 If you traveled to the Zoo via a **City Bus** from Camden Town Tube Station, or Madame Tussauds, or from Madame Tussauds' **Original Tour Bus**/Big Bus stops, you must go to a *different* bus stop to catch the City Bus that will return you to your starting point.

🚕 Alternatively, there are usually several **Taxis** waiting outside the Zoo.

Take a City Bus from the Zoo to Camden Town Tube Station

🚶🚌🚶 A 30 minute walk-bus-walk journey.

🚶 Exit the Zoo, turn right, and walk northeast along **Regent's Park Outer Circle Road**. ♦ Watch for a sign indicating a path to the **Regent's Canal Footbridge**. ♦ At the path, turn left and walk north, crossing over the footbridge. ♦ Continue north to **Prince Albert Road**. ♦ Use the crosswalk on your right to cross Prince Albert Road and walk north on the street named **Saint Mark's Square** for one block, to **Regent's Park Road**. ♦ Cross to the north side of Regent's Park Road and turn right. **Bus Stop K** is just a few steps east.

🚌 **Board the 274 bus and request to get off at Bus Stop CX near the Camden Town Tube Station.** Riding in the *top* of the bus will allow you to better enjoy the scenery on your way back to Camden Town Tube Station. As soon as you can see the **World's End Pub** straight ahead of the bus, get off at the next stop.

[©2009 Tara Bellers]

🚶 After stepping off the bus, turn right and head northeast to **Camden High Street**. Look to your left, and you'll see the entrance to **Camden Town Tube Station**.

Take a City Bus from the Zoo to Madame Tussauds, *or* to the Open-top Tour Bus Stops Near Madame Tussauds

🚶🚌🚶 A 30 to 35 minute walk-bus-walk journey.

🚶 Exit the Zoo and cross to the north side of **Regent's Park Outer Circle Road**. ◆ Turn left, and walk southwest. Watch on your right for a break in the iron railing where a footpath leads northwest. ◆ Turn right and walk northwest on the footpath, crossing over the **Regent's Canal Footbridge** and continuing until you reach **Prince Albert Road**. ◆ Turn left and walk southwest to **Bus Stop C**.

🚌 **Board Bus 274 toward Lancaster Gate**. Get off at the **Baker Street Bus Stop** closest to **Madame Tussauds**.

🚶 From there, walk southeast on Baker Street to Marylebone Road. ◆ Turn left and walk northeast to Madame Tussauds or the Tour Bus Stops.

10

THE MINISTRY OF MAGIC AREA

Old Scotland Yard, Whitehall, Westminster

http://en.wikipedia.org/wiki/Ministry_of_Magic

Google Maps UK: Scotland Pl, City of Westminster, SW1A
Bensons Mini: G-6 / **Bensons Street:** J-6
Collins Mini: pg 48, C-2,3 / **Collins Atlas:** pg 15, E-5,6

Tube Stations: Embankment *or* Westminster

Original Tour Bus Whitehall Red/Yellow/Green Stops *or* Big Bus Stops 38/11 and 48/21

Operation Hours and Entry Fee: None

Visit Time: Schedule at least 45 minutes to quickly snap Potter Pix at the two film sites in this area. Consider allowing an hour here so that you don't have to rush.

᥊᥊

Ministry of Magic film footage for *Order of the Phoenix* and *Deathly Hallows Part One* was shot in the **Whitehall** area of the **City of Westminster**, a section of Central London that once housed the original **Scotland Yard**. There are two Ministry of Magic (**MoM**) film sites in this area, and 10 Potter Pix possibilities.

For Potterites who want to print a detailed map of this area, we used a **Google Maps UK** image segment to create our **Potter Whitehall Map Supplementum**.

A = Red Phone Box corner B = Gentleman's Toilet

[© 2011 Google]
http://HarryPotterPlaces.com/b1/WhitehallMapSupplementum.pdf

Scotland Yard
http://en.wikipedia.org/wiki/Scotland_Yard
http://knowledgeoflondon.com/bobby.html

In 1829, the first Metropolitan Police Headquarters in London was established at **#4 Whitehall Place**. You can see the building's Blue Historical Plaque just east of Whitehall (street), on the north side of Whitehall Place. The entrance most often used by the detectives, however, was at the *back* of the building, on **Great Scotland Yard,** which is why London's Police Headquarters (HQ) became commonly known as **Scotland Yard.**

By 1887 Scotland Yard had grown to include a number of buildings on Whitehall Place, Great Scotland Yard, and Palace Place—also including various nearby stables and outbuildings. When there was no more room for expansion in this area, a new building was constructed on the Victoria Embankment, overlooking the River Thames. The Metropolitan Police (**Met**) HQ moved there in 1890. This new location was called **New Scotland Yard** and the vacated area became known as **Old Scotland Yard.**

In 1967, having outgrown its Victoria Embankment building, the Met HQ moved to its present location at #10 Broadway, retaining the name of New Scotland Yard.

The only surviving (still functioning) element of the original Scotland Yard is the **Great Scotland Yard Metropolitan Police Stable,** located at **7-11 Great Scotland Yard**. It is one of eight **Met Mounted Branch** stables in London. This stable is not open to the public. However, if they're not trotting off to an appearance or task, mounted officers will happily stop and speak with tourists. If politely asked, they'll even pose for photos.

Order of the Phoenix Whitehall Area MoM Potter Pix

In *OOTP*, Harry James Potter is accused of violating the Decree for the Reasonable Restriction of Underage Sorcery, as well as the International Statute of Secrecy, and is ordered to attend a hearing at the **Ministry of Magic**. Mr. Weasley takes Harry to his hearing by traveling the Muggle underground via **Westminster Station (Site #13)**, then walking to the **Ministry of Magic Visitor's Entrance (Site #11)**, an old-fashioned, British red telephone box.

The first Whitehall area Harry Potter film site is located at the southwest corner of **Scotland Place** and **Great Scotland Yard**. Although several *DHp1* scenes were also shot in the area of this corner, we are calling this the **Red Phone Box corner**, because all *OOTP* Ministry of Magic Visitor's Entrance Red Phone Box footage was filmed here.

[©2009 Tara Bellers] [©2011 Tara Bellers]

Much of what is seen on screen in *OOTP* can still be found at this real-life location, such as the stone arch structure that spans Scotland Place. Unfortunately, there's no Red Phone Box, and black traffic posts were installed along streets soon after *DHp1* filming finished.

Two Set Pieces Were Installed for *OOTP* Scenes

An iconic British **Red Phone Box** was placed between the first window west of the Red Phone Box corner and the first wooden door (seen above left). An **arch structure** exactly like the one spanning Scotland Place was built to span Great Scotland Yard, with its southern end covering the first wooden door.

MoM Potter Pic #1: *OOTP*

[*Order of the Phoenix* screenshot (enhanced)]

Recreate this screenshot by having your photo taken after walking across the northern mouth of Scotland Place and reaching the Red Phone Box corner.

[©2009 Tara Bellers]

The wooden door that was covered by the Great Scotland Yard Arch set piece can be seen at the left in the pic above. To recreate the next screenshot, have your photo taken while standing on the sidewalk between the window and that door, with the **Old Admiralty Building** on Whitehall (street)—the one with the columns—visible in the background.

MoM Potter Pic #2: *OOTP*

[*Order of the Phoenix* screenshot (enhanced)]

Deathly Hallows Part One Whitehall Area MoM Potter Pix

In *Deathly Hallows*, Harry, Ron, and Hermione learn that Dolores Umbridge has one of Voldemort's Horcruxes. To obtain it, they must sneak into the Ministry of Magic.

In all three of these next screenshots, Ron is watching for Mafalda Hopkirk at the *southeast* corner of Great Scotland Yard and Scotland Place, directly across from the Red Phone Box corner.

MoM Potter Pic #3: *DHp1*

[*Deathly Hallows Part 1* screenshot (enhanced)]

MoM Potter Pic #4: *DHp1*

[*Deathly Hallows Part 1* screenshot (enhanced)]

Screenshot #5 shows Harry looking out from the doorway of the only *DHp1* **set piece** that was constructed for April of 2009 filming, a wooden façade that covers the gray, metal garage door found here in real-life.

MoM Potter Pic #5: *DHp1*

[*Deathly Hallows Part 1* screenshot (enhanced)]

To recreate the next two screenshots, have your photographer walk south on the west side of Scotland Place to the arch, turn around and take pix with the entrance to the **Great Scotland Yard Metropolitan Police Stable** building in the background.

MoM Potter Pic #6: *DHp1*

[*Deathly Hallows Part 1* screenshot (enhanced)]

Even if you've only three persons in your Potter party, screenshot #7 is doable. Have your Mafalda stand-in simply hide her/his body by pressing it against the garage door, and raise **one** leg (the right leg) to be grasped by your Ron stand-in.

MoM Potter Pic #7: *DHp1*

[*Deathly Hallows Part 1* screenshot (enhanced)]

The last two screenshots for this area should be snapped by someone standing on the Red Phone Box corner, with the building across from the southern mouth of Scotland Place seen in the background.

MoM Potter Pix #8 and9: *DHp1*

[Deathly Hallows Part 1 screenshots (enhanced) above and below.]

Whitehall Area *Deathly Hallows Part One* MoM Film Site #2

Another area where *DHp1* filming took place is only a few blocks south of the Red Phone Box corner area—a 3 minute walk. If you approach the Ministry of Magic Whitehall area from Westminster Tube Station, stop at this film site first.

Head south on Scotland Place to Whitehall Place (the street in the distance of both pix above). ♦ Turn right and walk to Whitehall (street). ♦ Turn left and walk to the next street, **Horse Guards Avenue**. At the mouth of that avenue is a large stone pedestal topped by a bronze statue of **Spencer Compton, Eighth Duke of Devonshire** (below left).

[©2011 Tara Bellers]

Directly behind the statue is a safe area to stand while taking pix of the white-diagonal-striped lane that runs down the middle of Horse Guards Avenue. The **Gentlemen's Toilet** set piece for *Deathly Hallows Part One* filming was erected *in* the striped lane. With your back to the Duke's statue, look east and slightly left for the **Gurkha Soldier Monument** (above right) on the northwest corner of Whitehall Court and Horse Guards Avenue. Line up your last MoM Potter Pix with the Gurkha Soldier seen in the upper left corner of your camera frame.

MoM Potter Pic #10: *DHp1*

[*Deathly Hallows Part 1* screenshot (enhanced)]

BOLO!

While Pottering around the Whitehall area—or any other place in London—
Be On the Look Out for a public Gentlemen's Toilet (or Ladies' Toilet!) that
has architectural features similar to those seen when polyjuice-disguised
Ron and Harry had to **flush** themselves into the Ministry of Magic. If you
find one, please blog about its location on the *Harry Potter Places* website.

[*Deathly Hallows Part 1* screenshots (enhanced) above and below]

Nearby Non-Potter Places
The Horse Guards Building and the Horse Guards Parade
http://www.frommers.com/destinations/london/A24150.html
http://en.wikipedia.org/wiki/Horse_Guards_%28building%29

Google Maps UK: Horse Guards Av, Whitehall, London, SW1A 2HB

Original Tour Bus Whitehall Red/Yellow/Green Stops or Big Bus Stop
39/12

On the west side of Whitehall (street), approximately 3 blocks south of Great Scotland Yard and just north of Downing Street, is the **Horse Guards building**. Thirty minutes before the Queen's **Household Cavalry** (her mounted guards) parade to **Buckingham Palace** to participate in the famous **Changing of the Guard** ceremony *there*, a similar ceremony takes place at **Horse Guards Arch**. Knowledgeable London visitors may prefer to attend the far less crowded Horse Guards Arch ceremony, which occurs on Monday through Saturday at 11am, and at 10am on Sundays. (Extremely wet conditions sometimes result in cancellation of *both* Changing of the Guard ceremonies.)

Additionally, two mounted sentries stand on duty at the Horse Guards Arch each day. To benefit the horses, mounted sentries are relieved every hour. Thus, a small Changing of the Guard ceremony takes place here every hour between 10 am and 4pm. Finally, the Chief Guard performs an Inspection of the Troops here, at 4pm each day. (Foot sentries take over between 4pm and 10am.)

If you walk west through the Horse Guards Arch, you'll arrive at the **Horse Guards Parade,** a large parade ground which opens onto Saint James's Park. Formerly the Palace of Whitehall's tiltyard where King Henry the 8th held jousting tournaments, Horse Guards Parade is where the Queen's *official* birthday is celebrated. Queen Elisabeth II was born on April 21st. However, since 1748 it has been an English tradition to publicly celebrate the Sovereign's birthday on a Saturday in June, when good weather is more likely. This nationally televised, annual event is called **Trooping the Colour.** On the preceding two Saturdays, **Reviews** take place on the parade ground, effectively functioning as rehearsals for the big event. The first review is free to the public. The second review—as well as Trooping the Colour—requires tickets that must be *applied for* prior to the end of February each year.
http://www.trooping-the-colour.co.uk/

During the **2012 Summer Olympics**, Horse Guards Parade will be the site of beach volleyball competition.

Trafalgar Square
http://en.wikipedia.org/wiki/Trafalgar_Square
http://www.london.gov.uk/trafalgarsquare/

Google Maps UK: Trafalgar Square, Westminster, London WC2N 5, UK

⊖**Tube Station:** Charing Cross

🚌 **Original Tour Bus Trafalgar Square Red/Yellow Stops *or* Big Bus Stops 37/10/77**

[*Half-Blood Prince* screenshot (enhanced)]

Briefly seen at the beginning of *Half-Blood Prince*, Trafalgar Square is one of the most famous places in the United Kingdom. Located in the heart of London, the square's name commemorates the **Battle of Trafalgar**, an 1805 British naval victory during the Napoleonic Wars. Honoring Admiral Horatio Nelson, who was killed in action during that battle, **Nelson's Column** stands at the center of the square, guarded by four bronze lion statues. The granite column is 151 feet high, and is topped by an 18 foot tall sandstone statue of the Admiral. Trafalgar Square is located halfway between the **Diagon Alley Wizard Entrance (Site #3)** and the **Ministry of Magic Film Sites**.

The National Gallery

http://www.nationalgallery.org.uk/
http://en.wikipedia.org/wiki/National_Gallery_%28London%29

Spanning the entire northern border of **Trafalgar Square**, England's National Gallery is world-renown for its extensive collection of Western European paintings dating from the 13th to 19th centuries. Although special exhibitions usually require entry fees, the National Gallery belongs to the public of the United Kingdom, and entry to its main collection is FREE of charge. (The London Pass includes a free audio guide.)

Open: Saturday to Thursday, 10am-6pm; Fridays 10am-9pm.

Nearby Potter Places

DHp1 **Café-Related Film Sites (Site #2):** A 15 minute walk

Diagon Alley Wizard Entrance (Site #3): A 15 minute walk.

Muggle Portrait Gallery (Site #12): A 10 minute walk.

Muggle Underground Station (Site #13): A 12 minute walk.

The following two Nearby Potter Places do *not* have **Harry Potter Places Site Entries** of their own.

Number 10 Downing Street
http://en.wikipedia.org/wiki/10_Downing_Street
http://www.number10.gov.uk/

Google Maps UK: 10 Downing Street, London, SW1A 2AA

Original Tour Bus Whitehall Red/Yellow/Green Route Stops *or* Big Bus Stop 40/13

Chapter One of *Half-Blood Prince* begins with a very disgruntled **Muggle Prime Minister** sitting in his office before receiving a surprise visit from the Wizarding World's **Minister of Magic**, Cornelius Fudge, who pops out of a dirty oil painting stuck on a corner wall.

Although it doesn't appear on film, number 10 Downing Street is the internationally-renown address of **Great Britain's Prime Minister**—the location of his office, as well as his family residence (a private flat on the second floor). Prior to a 1991 bombing attempt here, Downing Street was publicly accessible. Since then, iron gates and armed guards have been installed at both ends of the street, and visitors can only view the famous residence from a distance.

To visit the gates and guards that bar entrance to the Muggle Prime Minister's Downing Street office from the Ministry of Magic Film Sites (about a 4 minute walk), head west on Great Scotland Yard, Whitehall Place, or Horse Guards Avenue to Whitehall (street). ♦ Turn left and walk south. Just after Whitehall becomes Parliament Street, you'll see Downing Street on your right.

Trafalgar Studios & Potted Potter
http://www.trafalgar-studios.co.uk/

Google Maps UK: Trafalgar Studios, 14 Whitehall, London SW1A 2DY

Original Tour Bus Whitehall Red Stop or Big Bus Stops 38/11

On the west side of Whitehall (street), approximately one block north of Great Scotland Yard and a block south of Trafalgar Square, is **Trafalgar Studios theater**, the original home of **Christmas Season *Potted Potter*** performances.

Potted Potter is a Harry Potter parody written and performed by British comedians Daniel Clarkson and Jefferson Turner; aka the Dan and Jeff Duo. Since it first premiered in August of 2006 at the **Edinburgh Fringe Festival**, the duo's "Unauthorized Harry Experience" has consistently garnered rave reviews, both nationally and internationally. Because it is such a perfectly penned and executed parody, *Potted Potter* is enormously enjoyed by both Potterites and Potter-Poopers.

Since 2011, *Potted Potter* has been performed at other London theatres. When planning your trip to London, be sure to check the *Potted Potter* website to learn whether any performances are scheduled during your holiday.
http://www.pottedpotter.com/

Going to the Ministry of Magic Film Sites
Via an Open-Top Tour Bus

To design your own London Harry Potter itinerary utilizing a tour bus, download both companies' Tour Maps from their websites.
http://www.theoriginaltour.com/tour-information/tour-info.htm
http://www.bigbustours.com/eng/london/custompage.aspx?id=maps

The closest tour bus stop to the Ministry of Magic Film Sites (a minute's walk away) is the northern of three **Whitehall** (street) Original Tour Bus Red Route stops *or* Big Bus Stop 38/11—the first bus stop south of **Trafalgar Square**. However, that stop can only be accessed when traveling *southbound* from Trafalgar Square. Northbound Original Tour Bus Yellow/Green stops are slightly farther away, but may be helpful to your personal itinerary planning.

Depending on the order of your travel plans for reaching the Ministry of Magic Film Sites, you may want to get off the tour bus at the southbound Original Tour Bus Embankment Pier Red/Yellow Stop or Big Bus Stop 48/21 on **Victoria Embankment**—also known as the **Embankment Tube Station** tour bus stops. From there, it is only a 5 minute walk to the Ministry of Magic Film Sites.

From Original Tour Bus Whitehall Red Stop *or* Big Bus Stop 38/11
A 1 minute walk.

After disembarking the bus on the east side of **Whitehall** (street), turn right and walk south to the next intersection (which should be **Great Scotland Yard**, but may be **Whitehall Place**). ♦ Turn left and walk to **Scotland Place**.

From Original Tour Bus Embankment Pier Red/Yellow Stop or Big Bus Stop 48/21
A 5 minute walk.

After disembarking the bus on the east side of **Victoria Embankment**, turn right and head south, walking under the railway bridge. ♦ Beyond the bridge, cross to the south side of westbound **Northumberland Avenue.** ◆ Walk west on Northumberland Avenue to **Whitehall Place** (a short block) and turn left. ◆ Walk south on Whitehall Place, following it as it curves west, watching for **Scotland Place** on your right.

⊖ Embankment Tube Station *vs* Westminster Tube Station

If you wish to visit the Ministry of Magic Film Sites *before* visiting the Muggle Underground Station, head for Embankment Tube Station. However, if you wish to follow in Harry's footsteps and visit the **Muggle Underground Station (Site #13)** *first*, head for Westminster Tube Station and follow those directions before walking to the Ministry of Magic Sites.

⊖ From Embankment Tube Station

A 5 minute walk.

🚶 Follow station signs to the **Victoria Embankment Exit**. When you emerge, turn right and head south, walking under the railway bridge. ◆ Beyond the bridge, cross to the south side of westbound **Northumberland Avenue.** ◆ Walk west on Northumberland Avenue to **Whitehall Place** (a short block) and turn left. ◆ Walk south on Whitehall Place, following it as it curves west, watching for **Scotland Place** on your right.

⊖ From Westminster Tube Station: The Muggle Underground Station (Site #13)

A 12 minute walk.

🚶 After accomplishing your Muggle Underground Station visit, follow station signs to the **Bridge Street** exit. ◆ Turn right and walk west (away from **Big Ben**) to the next street corner, **Parliament Street**. ◆ Turn right and walk north, continuing as Parliament Street becomes **Whitehall** (street). [You can stop at the iron gates barring **#10 Downing Street**, or at the **Horse Guards Building** on your way.] ◆ Turn right at **Whitehall Place** and walk east to **Scotland Place.**

From the Muggle Portrait Gallery (Site #12)

A 10 minute walk.

🚶 Exit via the National Portrait Gallery's main entrance on **Saint Martin's Place.** ◆ Turn right and head south until you are walking along the eastern perimeter of **Trafalgar Square.** ◆ When you reach the southeast corner of Trafalgar Square, you'll see a large, circular island, containing a bronze statue of King Charles I on a horse. Several streets intersect here, making this a very confusing area. Your goal is to reach **Whitehall** (street), which begins south of the island. ♦ Cross to **King Charles I Island**, then cross to the east side of **Whitehall**. ♦ Turn right and walk south along the east side of Whitehall to **Great Scotland Yard**. ♦ Turn left and walk east to **Scotland Place**.

From the Diagon Alley Wizard Entrance (Site #3)
A 15 minute walk.

⋀ Walk west on **Great Newport Street** to **Charing Cross Road**. ♦ Turn left and walk south on the east side of Charing Cross Road to the next crosswalk. ♦ Turn right and cross to the west side of Charing Cross Road. ♦ Turn left and continue south. ♦ After crossing the mouth of Irving Street, keep right to walk south on **Saint Martin's Place**. You'll pass the **Muggle Portrait Gallery (Site #12)** on your right. [Consider popping into the Gallery's Shop to buy Radcliffe, Watson, and Grint portrait postcards before continuing your trek to the Ministry of Magic.] ♦ Continue following Saint Martin's Place south until you end up walking along the eastern perimeter of **Trafalgar Square**. ♦ When you reach the southeast corner of Trafalgar Square, you'll see a large, circular island, containing a bronze statue of King Charles I on a horse. Several streets intersect here, making this a very confusing area. Your goal is to reach **Whitehall** (street), which begins at the south side of the island. ♦ Cross to **King Charles I Island**, then cross to the east side of **Whitehall**. ♦ Turn right and walk south along the east side of Whitehall to **Great Scotland Yard**. ♦ Turn left and walk east to **Scotland Place**.

From the *DHp1* Café-Related Film Sites (Site #2)
A 15 minute walk.

⋀ Head south on **Shaftesbury Avenue** to **Coventry Street**. ♦ Turn left and walk east to **Great Windmill Street**, *OR*, head south through the outdoor walkway tucked under the second floor of the Trocadero building that runs along the east side of **Great Windmill Street** to **Coventry Street**.

Directly across the intersection of Coventry Street and Great Windmill Street is the four **Horses of Helios** fountain, on the southwest corner of Coventry Street and Haymarket. Cross to the fountain-side of Coventry Street. ♦ Turn left and walk around the fountain to head south on the west side of **Haymarket** to its end at **Pall Mall**. ♦ Cross the street toward the Bank of Scotland building and turn left to walk east on **Cockspur Street**. ♦ When you pass Warwick House Street, you'll see Nelson's Column on **Trafalgar Square** ahead of you. Continue east on Cockspur Street until you reach **King Charles I Island** (a large, circular island, containing a bronze statue of King Charles I on a horse). ♦ Keep right and follow the street as it curves south around the island. ♦ Cross the mouth of The Mall (street) and continue as the street curves east again, until you've crossed to the east side of **White-**

hall (street). ♦ Turn right and walk south on Whitehall to **Great Scotland Yard**. ♦ Turn left and walk east to **Scotland Place**.

From the Leaky Cauldron, *POA* (Site #7) in Borough Market: Huffandpuff Expedition *POA* Day

🚶☉🚶 A 10 minute walk, a 12 minute tube trip, a 5 minute walk.

🚶 If leaving from the southern Borough Market entrance, walk southeast on **Stoney Street** to the intersection of **Southwark Street** and **Borough High Street**.

If leaving from the northern Borough Market entrance, walk southeast on **Bedale Street** to **Borough High Street**.

A stairway leading down to the **London Bridge Underground Station** lies on Borough High Street, between Stoney Street and Bedale Street.

☉ Take the **Northern Line** towards Morden to reach **Elephant & Castle** Tube Station. ♦ Take the **Bakerloo Line** towards Queen's Park, or Harrow & Wealdstone, or Stonebridge Park, to reach **Embankment Tube Station**.

🚶 Follow the directions above for walking to the Ministry of Magic Area from Embankment Tube Station.

11

MINISTRY OF MAGIC VISITOR'S ENTRANCE

Red Phone Box Guide
http://en.wikipedia.org/wiki/Red_telephone_box

Operation Hours or **Entry Fee:** None

Visit Time: Snap your Red Phone Box Potter Pix wherever you encounter one while touring London.

CXEXO

In *Order of the Phoenix*, Mr. Weasley takes Harry to his Ministry of Magic hearing by traveling the Muggle underground to Westminster Station, then walking to the Ministry's **Visitor Entrance**: a distinctively-British red phone box.

OOTP film footage of the Ministry's Visitor Entrance was shot at the southwest corner of **Scotland Place** and **Great Scotland Yard**, in the **Whitehall** section of London. [See **Ministry of Magic Area (Site #10)**.] The Red Phone Box seen on screen was a **set piece**. No phone box, of any kind, exists where filming took place.

Up to eight different designs of the iconic, British phone box exist today.
http://heritage.elettra.co.uk/phonebox/

The first Red Telephone Box design was introduced in 1924. The Potter-like Red Phone Boxes, Kiosk style number 6, were designed by Giles Gilbert-Scott in 1935 to commemorate the Silver Jubilee of King George V. Happily, they're located all over London, so you can recreate the Potter Phone Box screenshots almost anywhere.

We suggest that you perform screenshot recreation pic sessions at *several* Red Phone Boxes, as you travel around London. When using a digital camera, you cannot take too many pix. Be especially vigilant for a Red Phone Box located in front of a **white stone building**.

Red Phone Box Screenshot #1

[*Order of the Phoenix* screenshot (enhanced)]

If your party consists of three or more people, take turns snapping Screenshot #1 pix from a distance, while two of you are standing inside the phone box. If your party consists of only two people, or you're alone, have a **disposable** camera handy to give to a helpful bystander willing to take a few pix for you.

Red Phone Box Screenshot #2

[*OOTP* screenshot segment (enhanced)]

This is an enlarged *segment* of Screenshot #1. As long as someone's snapping, take closer full-box pix, as well. Then, round out your collection with the very close-up shots below.

Red Phone Box Screenshots #3 and 4

[*Order of the Phoenix* screenshots (enhanced), above and below.]

*And, that's **IT** for this entry!*

12

MUGGLE PORTRAIT GALLERY

The National Portrait Gallery
http://www.npg.org.uk/
http://en.wikipedia.org/wiki/National_Portrait_Gallery_%28London%29

Google Maps UK: National Portrait Gallery, St Martin's Place, London WC2H 0HE
Bensons Mini: G-5 / **Bensons Street:** J-5
Collins Mini: pg 48, B,C-1 / **Collins Atlas:** pg 14, E-4

Tube Station: Leicester Square *or* Charing Cross

Original Tour Bus (OTB) Loop Line Start/End point at Leicester Square Tube Station.

OTB Trafalgar Square Red/Yellow Stops *or* **Big Bus Stops 37/10/77**

Operation Hours: Saturdays to Wednesdays 10am-6pm, Thursday and Friday 10am-9pm. Closed 24-26 December.

Entry Fee: The National Portrait Gallery is **free.** However, donating at least £1 per person will help support its operation. If you can afford £5 per person, so much the better. [The London Pass includes your choice of **free entry** to Gallery Exhibits that charge a fee, *or* a free copy of the National Portrait Gallery's fully illustrated Visitor's Guide.]

Visit Time: To visit *only* the National Portrait Gallery Gift Shop, schedule about 30 minutes. To dash to the Potter-related portraits and visit the gift shop, you'll need at least 2 hours.

Parseltongue Pointers:
- Charing = "CHAR-ing" (like CHARcoal, not "CHAIR-ing")
- Leicester = "LES-ter"

CXEXO

In September of 2005, **Joanne Kathleen Rowling** was present at the National Portrait Gallery unveiling of a *3-D* portrait painted of her by artist Stuart Pearson Wright. Rowling is also represented in the National Portrait Gallery by two pencil and charcoal Wright portraits, and well as two photos in the gallery's Photographs Collection.

National Portrait Gallery Images of J.K. Rowling are Online at:
http://www.npg.org.uk/collections/search/person.php?search=ss&firstRun=true&sText=Rowling&LinkID=mp14871

Fourteen year old **Daniel Radcliffe** posed for Stuart Pearson Wright, in 2004. Wright's pencil drawing portrait of Radcliffe premiered at a Royal National Theatre exhibition in April of 2006, and was purchased by the National Portrait Gallery. At the age of sixteen, Radcliffe became the youngest non-royal ever to have an individual portrait displayed in England's National Portrait Gallery.

In June of 2006, the gallery purchased and displayed Emma Hardy's color photograph landscape portrait of Radcliffe standing in a wheat field. The most recent gallery addition was in March of 2009, when Matt Holyoak's color photograph portrait of the Primary Potter Trio of actors—**Daniel Radcliffe, Emma Watson, and Rupert Grint**—was purchased by the National Portrait Gallery and placed on display.

National Portrait Gallery Images of Daniel Radcliffe are Online at:
http://www.npg.org.uk/collections/search/person.php?LinkID=mp83293

[*Order of the Phoenix* screenshot (enhanced)]

The many portraits mounted on Hogwarts walls contain characters who are magically able to interact with those who view them. Unfortunately, the

National Portrait Gallery is a Muggle World gallery. As such, the characters trapped within this gallery's portraits are lifeless and entirely unaware of the people who pass by.

Site Rating

The National Portrait Gallery earns a **Skip It** rating because:
- **No photography** is allowed inside the gallery, and mobile phones are prohibited, so sneaking pix is pretty much right out!

- You can see ALL the Potter-related portraits *online.* You can even order Prints of some portraits online. (**Please Note:** a set of Harry Potter actors postcards once was offered online. It contained ten copies of *the same postcard,* the trio's photo. Just a head's up in case they offer it again.)

- The National Portrait Gallery's Shop offers only *two* Potter-related **postcards:** the Stuart Pearson Wright 3-D portrait of J.K. Rowling, and Matt Holyoak's color photograph of Radcliffe, Watson, and Grint. No Harry Potter souvenirs are available here.

If you want to buy the two Potter-related postcards, schedule about 30 minutes to pop into the National Portrait Gallery Shop when **walking between:**
- The **Diagon Alley Wizard Entrance (Site #3)** and the **Ministry of Magic Area (Site #10)**

- The **Trafalgar Square Tour Bus Stops** and the **Diagon Alley Wizard Entrance**

- The *DHp1* **Café-Related Film Sites (Site #2)** and the **Diagon Alley Wizard Entrance**

That said, here are some tips for Potterites divinely inspired to view the National Portrait Gallery's Potter-related portraits

Whether you enter the gallery via the main entrance on Saint Martin's Place or the secondary entrance on Orange Street, go to the **Main Hall** and find the **Information Desk** to ask for directions to the current locations of the various Potter-related portraits.

After you've enjoyed the portraits, head toward the main entrance on Saint Martin's Place and visit the National Portrait Gallery Shop. There you'll find the gallery's **Portrait Printer.**

The Portrait Printer is a touchscreen kiosk located inside the Gallery Shop. Not only does this print-on-demand device keep the gallery's stock overhead to a minimum, it saves visitors a ton of time. You won't have to spend time rifling through multiple bins loaded with pre-printed stock to find posters of the portraits you wish to purchase.

Using the Portrait Printer, search for *Daniel Radcliffe* or *Joanne Kathleen Rowling*. Select the one(s) you want to buy, the size and paper type you want, and place your order. Your order will be printed in minutes by the helpful Shop Assistants.

Print prices vary according to paper size and quality, ranging between £12.50 ($20) and £40 ($63).

The Holyoak photo of the Potter Trio is *not* available for purchase as a **print**, either online or at the Shop. The gallery doesn't own the digital reproduction rights for that image. However, several of the Rowling and Radcliffe portraits are available.

Please Note: Prints purchased online—at the same price as in the shop—will be safely packed and sent to you for a modest postage fee, saving you the trouble of carrying prints with you as you travel and risking their damage. Postage within the UK is £2.99. Postage for prints sent to nearby European countries is £7.99 (€10). Postage for prints sent to the USA and other non-European countries (Japan, Australia, and the like) is £9.99 ($16).

Nearby Potter Places

Diagon Alley Wizard Entrance (Site #3): An 8 minute walk.

Ministry of Magic Area (Site #10): A 10 minute walk.

DHp1 **Café-Related Film Sites (Site #2):**A 10 minute walk.

Going to the National Portrait Gallery

From Leicester Square Tube Station, *OR*
Original Tour Bus Loop Line Start/End Point
A 5 minute walk.

Please Note: Follow directions for visiting the **Diagon Alley Wizard Entrance (Site #3)** *before* walking to the National Portrait Gallery from this tube station or tour bus stop. Use these directions only if you've already visited that site and are returning to this area at a different time.

Follow station signs to the **Charing Cross Road (West Side) Exit #2.** You'll emerge at almost the same spot as the **Original Tour Bus Loop Line Start/ End point.** ♦ Turn right and walk south on the west side of **Charing Cross Road.** ♦ After the street begins to curve east (left), pass Irving Street and keep right to walk south on **Saint Martin's Place.** ♦ Look to your right for the Saint Martin's Place National Portrait Gallery entrance.

From Charing Cross Tube Station
A 5 minute walk.

Follow station signs to the **Strand North Side Exit #9**. When you emerge at street level on **The Strand**, turn right and walk southwest to the next corner. ♦ Keep right to cross to the north side of **Duncannon Street**. ♦ Turn left and walk west to **Saint Martin's Place**. ♦ Turn right to walk north to the crosswalk just *before* Saint Martin's Place meets the southeastern curve of **Charing Cross Road**. ♦ Turn left and cross to the National Portrait Gallery's Café entrance. The Saint Martin's Place entrance is but a few steps to the north.

From Original Tour Bus Trafalgar Square Red/Yellow Stops *or* Big Bus Stops 37/10/77
A 5 minute walk.

Disembark the tour bus near the northwestern corner of **Trafalgar Square**. ♦ Walk east across Trafalgar Square to the northeastern corner, passing by the National Gallery. ♦ Turn left and walk north along **Saint Martin's Place** to the National Portrait Gallery's entrance.

From the Diagon Alley Wizard Entrance (Site #3)
An 8 minute walk.

Walk west on **Great Newport Street** to **Charing Cross Road**. ♦ Turn left and walk south, crossing to the opposite (west) side of Charing Cross Road. ♦ Continue south until the street begins to curve east (left). ♦ After passing Irving Street, keep right to walk south on **Saint Martin's Place**. Look to your right for the National Portrait Gallery entrance.

From the *DHp1* Café-Related Film Sites (Site #2)
A 10 minute walk.

Walk east on **Coventry Street** from Piccadilly Circus as it turns northeast and becomes **Swiss Court**. ♦ At the northwest corner of **Leicester Square**, cross to the park side and head right to walk southeast on the diagonal path that leads through the park to the southeast corner. ♦ Cross to **Irving Street** and walk southeast to **Charing Cross Road**. ♦ Turn right to walk south on the west side of Charing Cross Road as it curves east. ♦ Keep right to walk south on **Saint Martin's Place**. Look to your right for the National Portrait Gallery entrance.

From the Ministry of Magic Area (Site #10)
A 10 minute walk.

🚶 Walk southwest on **Great Scotland Yard** or **Whitehall Place** to **Whitehall** (street). ♦ Turn right and walk north on Whitehall to its end at **King Charles I Island** (a large, circular island directly south of **Trafalgar Square**, containing a bronze statue of King Charles I on a horse). Several streets intersect here, making this a very confusing area. Your goal is to cross to King Charles I Island, and then cross to the southeast corner of **Trafalgar Square**. ♦ Once there, walk north along the eastern border of Trafalgar Square, continuing north as you begin walking along the west side of **Saint Martin's Place**. Look to your right for the National Portrait Gallery entrance.

13

THE MUGGLE UNDERGROUND STATION

☻Westminster Tube Station
http://en.wikipedia.org/wiki/Westminster_tube_station

Google Maps UK: Bridge Street, London SW1A 2JR
Bensons Mini: G-7 / **Bensons Street:** J-7
Collins Mini: pg 60, C-1 / **Collins Atlas:** pg 21, E-2

🚌 Original Tour Bus Red/Yellow/Green Stops. Big Bus Stops 40/13 or 49/22.

Operation Hours: Most London Underground Stations operate between 5:30am and 12:30am on Monday through Saturday, 7:30am to midnight on Sunday.

Entry Fee: If you arrive at, or leave from, Westminster station via the Tube system, you won't have to pay anything extra to take Muggle Underground Potter pix. Visiting Westminster station via surface transportation will cost you an underground fare.

Visit Time: Schedule at least 45 minutes to snap your Potter pix. Consider allowing 60 to 75 minutes here so that you don't have to rush—especially if visiting during the afternoon.

!!!Flash OFF!!! Photography is forbidden in underground and surface train stations for security reasons.

Parseltongue Pointers:
- Westminster = "WEST-min-stah"
- Parliament / Parliamentary = "PAR-lah-ment" / "PAR-lah-MEN-tree"

೮ৼৡ

In *Order of the Phoenix*, Harry Potter is accused of violating the Decree for the Reasonable Restriction of Underage Sorcery, as well as the International Statute of Secrecy, and is ordered to attend a hearing at the **Ministry of Magic**. Harry is escorted to his hearing by Mr. Weasley, via the Muggle underground train system. Although he's a **Misuse of Muggle Artifacts Office** official, Mr. Weasley isn't particularly familiar with the procedures of navigating the Muggle Underground.

"Trains. *Underground!* Ingenious things, these Muggles."

The **Westminster London Underground station** is located in the **City of Westminster**, a section of Central London. The station is served by the Circle, District and Jubilee Lines. For an entire day in October of 2006, all of Westminster Tube station was closed while *OOTP* Muggle Underground Station scenes were filmed here. The scenes that appeared on screen were shot at the ticket gates and escalators associated with Westminster station's **Jubilee Line**.

Westminster/Muggle Underground Station Potter Pix Tips

[©2009 Tara Bellers (taken late on a Saturday afternoon)]

Avoid Westminster Station During Weekday Rush Hours

For the best possible Potter pix, you want at least *some* people around you while riding the Jubilee Line escalator and going through the ticket gates. But, taking pix in the midst of weekday rush hours, morning or evening, is not a good idea. You'll only be a face in the mob, and even the most minor pic-taking delays might irritate Muggles dashing to meet a train. Weekday rush hours are commonly 8am to 9:30am and 4pm to 6:30pm.

Morning Hours Are the Best Time to Visit

Muggle Underground Station screenshots show Mr. Weasley and Harry traveling **down** on the **middle** of a triple Jubilee Line escalator. Only in the mornings are **two** of the triple escalators dedicated to sending commuters down toward the trains. Thus, the hour just before or after the weekday morning rush is the best time to take your Muggle Underground Station Potter Escalator pix.

If your London itinerary requires you to visit Westminster Station during hours before or after evening rush, all is not lost! You can step on the *up*-**going** middle escalator and carefully turn around to **face downward** for your pic. (Something Samantha is seen demonstrating in the pic below.)

[©2009 Tara Bellers]

Caution: Traveling *backwards* on an *up* escalator is not as easy as it sounds. Be careful! Another drawback to this technique: if there are any Muggles on the escalator above or below you, they'll be facing the other way—making it rather obvious that you're standing backwards on an up escalator.

!!!Flash OFF!!!

Be sure your camera flash is **off** before you start snapping, and be discreet. Even with your flash off, station personnel who observe you taking pictures may ask you to stop taking them. Be Potterly Polite, and they won't confiscate your camera.

If Arriving at Westminster Station via the Underground System

Save your Ticket Gate Potter Pix for LAST. You'll be exiting through the ticket gates, and can only pass through them once.

If you arrive at Westminster Tube station *via* the **Jubilee Line**, you'll encounter the *OOTP* triple escalator before reaching the ticket gates, anyway. If you arrive via the **Circle** or **District Lines**, follow station signs to the Jubilee Line. You'll see where the ticket gates are before you ride down the escalators to the Jubilee platforms.

If Departing via the Underground System

Snap your Ticket Gate Potter Pix FIRST. You'll be entering the station through the ticket gates, and can only pass through them once.

After taking ticket gate pix, follow station signs to the **Jubilee Line** escalators. Once you reach the bottom of a triple escalator set, take your Potter Escalator pix.

When finished, head to your **Jubilee Line** train departure platform. If you're departing via the **Circle** or **District Lines**, return to the station's main area (ground level) and follow station signs to your departure train's platform.

If Only *Visiting* Westminster Station from the Surface

Take your Ticket Gate Potter Pix FIRST. You'll have to pay an underground fare to go through the ticket gates and gain entry to the Jubilee Line escalators. But, even though you'll be leaving the station through the same ticket gates, you can snap pix of passing through them only when you **enter**. Why? Because you're going to need help to get out.

After snapping ticket gate pix, head for the **Jubilee Line** escalators and take your *OOTP* escalator pix. Then, return to the ticket gate area and find a station employee to help you exit.

When leaving a London Tube Station without traveling to another station, the ticket gate will **reject your ticket** as you attempt to pass back through it. To get out, you'll have to ask station personnel for assistance. They'll be happy to help you leave the station. But, since they'll be right there *with you*, you won't be able to take pix as you exit the gates.

Muggle Underground Station Escalator Potter Pix

Although you may be taking ticket gate pix before escalator pix, we've presented the Muggle Underground Station Potter Pix in order of their appearance in OOTP.

Please Note: Potterites with time to accomplish a full set of escalator screenshot reproductions will enjoy **Potter Pix #1, 2, and 3**. Potterites in a *hurry* should skip to **Potter Pic #4**.

Muggle Underground Pic #1: Bracing for Escalator Dismount

[*Order of the Phoenix* screenshot segment (enhanced)]

Muggle Underground Pic #2: Assume Dismount Position

[*Order of the Phoenix* screenshot segment (enhanced)]

Muggle Underground Pic #3: Standing Tall for Dismount

[*Order of the Phoenix* screenshot (enhanced)]

Muggle Underground Potter Pic #4: Successful Dismount

[*Order of the Phoenix* screenshot (enhanced)]

Muggle Underground Station Ticket Gate Potter Pix

Please Note: If you accidentally take any of the ticket gate pix from a side opposite that seen in the screenshot, you can use your photo-editing program to flip a pic horizontally. Below left is Tara's original photo. Below right is her screenshot reproduction pic.

[©2009 Tara Bellers]

Muggle Underground Potter Pic #5: Entering the Ticket Gate

[*Order of the Phoenix* screenshot (enhanced)]

This pic doesn't require the photographer to go through the ticket gate. The next two pix are out of order in relationship to the footage seen on screen, because they should be taken before anyone passes through the ticket gates.

Muggle Underground Potter Pic #6: Explaining the Pass Card

[*Order of the Phoenix* screenshot (enhanced)]

Muggle Underground Pic #7: Demonstrating the Pass Card

[*Order of the Phoenix* screenshot (enhanced)]

Muggle Underground Pic #8: The Ineffective Button Whack

[*Order of the Phoenix* screenshot (enhanced)]

Although this scene appears on screen before Harry's Muggle Pass Card demonstrations, someone must go ahead of you, *through* the ticket gate, to take this pic. Since your photographer won't get a similar pic of her-/himself, be sure to reward that person with extra escalator pix.

Muggle Underground Potter Pic #9: Leaving the Ticket Gate

[*Order of the Phoenix* screenshot (enhanced)]

Nearby Non-Potter Places

Big Ben

http://www.parliament.uk/about/living-heritage/building/palace/big-ben/
http://en.wikipedia.org/wiki/Big_Ben

Located just south of Westminster Underground station's Bridge Street exit, Big Ben is the nickname for a **13-ton bell** mounted within **Saint Stephen's Clock Tower**, a structure at the northern end of **Westminster Palace**. Over the years, however, both the clock and its tower have become commonly known as Big Ben.

The largest four-faced chiming clock and the third-tallest free-standing clock tower in the world, Big Ben celebrated its 150th anniversary in May of 2009. Only UK residents are eligible to tour inside Big Ben's tower, and *they* have to apply to their Parliamentary representative months in advance to obtain a tour appointment.

Happily, foreign visitors can snap as many pix of Big Ben's exterior as they wish. But, because it is difficult for the common camera to capture its entirety, you may be better off buying Big Ben postcards.

The Houses of Parliament, aka Westminster Palace

http://www.parliament.uk/about/living-heritage/building/
http://en.wikipedia.org/wiki/Palace_of_Westminster

The Houses of Parliament building is also known as Westminster Palace and contains the United Kingdom's two legislative Parliamentary houses: the **House of Lords** and the **House of Commons**. Located in the heart of London, on the north bank of the River Thames, the Houses of Parliament are south of Westminster Station's Bridge Street exit.

Westminster Abbey

http://www.westminster-abbey.org/
http://en.wikipedia.org/wiki/Westminster_Abbey

Approximately two blocks southwest of Westminster Station's Bridge Street exit, Westminster Abbey is a huge, internationally famous, Gothic church. The traditional coronation ceremony site for British monarchs since 1066 AD, the Abbey also houses the burial tombs of many royals and aristocrats— as well as many historically famous poets, artists, and scientists. (*Da Vinci Code* fans flock here to visit the tomb of **Sir Isaac Newton**.) The *Royal Wedding* Ceremony of Prince William and Catherine Middleton took place in Westminster Abbey on April 29, 2011.

Opening Times: Westminster Abbey is usually open to the public from Monday to Saturday at 9:30am. Closing times vary throughout the week. On Sundays and religious holidays such as Easter and Christmas, the Abbey is open only for those attending worship services. All visitors are welcome to attend worship services, free of charge.

Entry Fees: Adults, £16 ($25), Students with a valid ID card or Seniors 60+ (Concessions), £13 ($20), Children 11 to 18 years old, £6 ($9); Children under 11 years old, free with adult.

The Horse Guards Building and the Horse Guards Parade

http://www.frommers.com/destinations/london/A24150.html
http://en.wikipedia.org/wiki/Horse_Guards_%28building%29

Google Maps UK: Horse Guards Av, Whitehall, London, SW1A 2HB

Original Tour Bus Whitehall Red/Yellow/Green Stops or Big Bus Stop 39/12

On the west side of Whitehall (street), approximately 1 block north of Downing Street, is the **Horse Guards building**. Thirty minutes before the Queen's **Household Cavalry** (her mounted guards) parade to **Buckingham Palace** to participate in the famous **Changing of the Guard** ceremony *there*, a similar ceremony takes place at **Horse Guards Arch**. Knowledgeable London visitors may prefer to attend the far less crowded Horse Guards Arch ceremony, which occurs on Monday through Saturday at 11am, and at 10am on Sundays. (Extremely wet conditions sometimes result in cancellation of *both* Changing of the Guard ceremonies.)

Additionally, two mounted sentries stand on duty at the Horse Guards Arch each day. To benefit the horses, mounted sentries are relieved every hour. Thus, a small Changing of the Guard ceremony takes place here every hour between 10 am and 4pm. Finally, the Chief Guard performs an Inspection of the Troops here, at 4pm each day. (Foot sentries take over between 4pm and 10am.)

If you walk west through the Horse Guards Arch, you'll arrive at the **Horse Guards Parade,** a large parade ground which opens onto Saint James's Park. Formerly the Palace of Whitehall's tiltyard where King Henry the 8th held jousting tournaments, Horse Guards Parade is where the Queen's *official* birthday is celebrated. Queen Elisabeth II was born on April 21st. However, since 1748 it has been an English tradition to publicly celebrate the Sovereign's birthday on a Saturday in June, when good weather is more likely. This nationally televised, annual event is called **Trooping the Colour.** On the preceding two Saturdays, **Reviews** take place on the parade ground, effectively functioning as rehearsals for the big event. The first review is free to the public. The second review — as well as Trooping the Colour — requires tickets that must be *applied for* prior to the end of February each year.
http://www.trooping-the-colour.co.uk/

During the **2012 Summer Olympics**, Horse Guards Parade will be the site of beach volleyball competition.

Follow directions below to Number 10 Downing Street from Westminster Station, and then continue north for another block to reach the Horse Guards Building.

Nearby Potter Places

👀 **Fly-By Bridges & Buildings (Site #4):** A 5 minute walk.

👀 **Ministry of Magic Area (Site #10):** A 12 minute walk.

The following two Nearby Potter Places do *not* have **Harry Potter Places Site Entries** of their own.

The London Film Museum
http://www.londonfilmmuseum.com/

Google Maps UK: 51.502505,-0.118747

The London Film Museum contains a few static displays of Harry Potter movie costumes and props. It isn't all that interesting — except for a particularly fun Potter Pic op.

[©2011 Tara Bellers]

In honor of this Potter Pic op, there's a **London Film Museum Supplementum**.
http://HarryPotterPlaces.com/b1/LondonFilmMuseumSupplementum.pdf

Interested Potterites can read that free PDF file and consider including a visit to the London Film Museum during your London holiday.

Number 10 Downing Street
http://en.wikipedia.org/wiki/10_Downing_Street
http://www.number10.gov.uk/

Chapter One of *Half-Blood Prince* begins with a very disgruntled **Muggle Prime Minister** sitting in his office before receiving a surprise visit from the Wizarding World's **Minister of Magic**, Cornelius Fudge, who pops out of a dirty oil painting stuck on a corner wall.

Although it doesn't appear on film, Number 10 Downing Street is the internationally-renown address of **Great Britain's Prime Minister**—the location of his office, as well as his family residence (a private flat on the second floor). Prior to a 1991 bombing attempt here, Downing Street was publicly accessible. Since then, iron gates and armed guards have been installed at both ends of the street, and visitors can only view the famous residence from a distance.

To visit the gates and guards that bar entrance to the Muggle Prime Minister's Downing Street office from the Muggle Underground Station (a 4 minute walk), follow station signs to the **Bridge Street** exit. ♦ Turn right and walk west (away from Big Ben) to **Parliament Street**. ♦ Turn right and walk north, watching for **Downing Street** on your left.

Going to the Muggle Underground Station
⊖ Westminster Tube Station
Arrive via Circle, District, or Jubilee Lines.

🚌 From the *Southbound* Whitehall/Parliament Street Original Tour Bus Red Stop *or* Big Bus Stop 40/13
OR
🚌 From the *Northbound* Parliament Street Original Tour Bus Yellow/Green Stop
A 5 minute walk.

🚶 Get off the bus at the **Big Ben** stop on **Parliament Street**. ♦ Walk south to **Bridge Street**. ♦ Turn left and walk east to the Westminster Underground Station entrance.

🚌 From the *Southbound* Victoria Embankment/Westminster Pier Original Tour Bus Red/Green Stop *or* Big Bus Stop 49/22
OR
🚢 From the Westminster Millennium Pier: Huffandpuff Expedition *POA* Day
A 5 minute walk.

Please Note: To snap ticket gate pix first, do not use the Victoria Embankment Underground entrance.

🚶 Walk south on **Victoria Embankment** to **Bridge Street** ♦ Turn right and walk west to the Westminster Underground Station entrance.

From the Muggle Wax Museum (Site #14): Padfoot Prowl and Potter Promenade POA Day
A 1 minute walk and a 7 minute Underground journey.

🚶 Walk one block southwest on **Marylebone Road** to the **Baker Street Tube Station**.

⊖ Take the **Jubilee Line** towards Stratford to reach Westminster Underground Station.

From the Ministry of Magic Area (Site #10)

A 12 minute walk.

🚶 Walk west on **Great Scotland Yard** or **Whitehall Place** to **Whitehall** (street). ♦ Turn left and walk south on Whitehall (you'll pass by the Horse Guards Building). ♦ Continue south as Whitehall becomes **Parliament Street** (you'll pass by #10 Downing Street). ♦ Continue south on Parliament Street to **Bridge Street**. ♦ Turn left and walk east to the Westminster Underground Station entrance.

From the Golden Tours Coach Departure Point: Warner Bros. Studio Tour (Site #27) 10am or 1pm Ticket Package
http://HarryPotterPlaces.com/b1/08aHPSTitineraryPlan.pdf

A 3 minute walk and 10 minute tube journey.

🚶 Walk a block northeast on **Buckingham Palace Road** to the **Victoria Underground Station.**

⊖ Take the **District Line** towards Tower Hill, Dagenham East, Upminster, or Barking, to reach Westminster Underground Station.

From Number 12 Grimmauld Place (Site #15): Quick-Quill Trip and Kwikspell Crusade *POA* Day Itineraries

A 7 minute walk and a 30 minute Underground journey.

🚶 Walk to either end of the southern **Claremont Square** (street). ♦ Turn north and walk to **Pentonville Road**. ♦ Turn right and walk east to the intersection where Pentonville Road becomes **City Road**. ♦ Turn left and walk north to **Angel Underground Station.**

⊖ Take the **Northern Line** toward Edgware or High Barnet to reach **Euston Tube Station.** ♦ Take the **Victoria Line** toward Brixton to reach **Green Park Tube Station.** ♦ Take the **Jubilee Line** toward Stratford to reach Westminster Underground Station.

14

Muggle Wax Museum

Madame Tussauds
http://www.madametussauds.com/London/
http://en.wikipedia.org/wiki/Madame_Tussauds

Google Maps UK: 51.522778, -0.155278

[Madame Tussauds' *address* doesn't bring up a map that accurately identifies its entrance.]

Address: Marylebone Road, London, NW1 5LR
Bensons Mini: C,D-3 / **Bensons Street:** E,F-3
Collins Mini: pg 22, A-3 / **Collins Atlas:** pg 7, F-4

⊖**Tube Station:** Baker Street

🚌 **Original Tour Bus Madame Tussauds Red/Yellow/Black/Gray Stop** *or* **Big Bus Stop 32/5**

Operation Hours: Madame Tussauds is open at 9 or 9:30am almost every day of the year. Visit their website to determine the closing times during your visit.

Entry Fee: Madame Tussauds' website offers a wide variety of ticket options and prices, some that include entry to other venues. Museum-only tickets purchased online 24 hours or more in advance are assigned to a specific day and a half-hour entry timeslot, but offer a 10% discount. London Original Tour Bus and Big Bus websites offer similarly discounted prepaid tickets. Madame Tussauds tickets purchased at the museum on the day of your visit cost £28.80 ($45) for Adults, £24.60 ($39) for Children.

Visit Time: Schedule 30 to 45 minutes to merely get in, find Daniel, snap a Potter Pic, and get back out again. Schedule at least 2 hours to enjoy *all* Madame Tussauds has to offer.

Parseltongue Pointers:
- Madame Tussauds = "mah-DAM too-SODS" ... *French*: "mah-DAM chew-SO"
- Marylebone = "MERRILY-bone"

⊂ℜℬↄ

On July 2nd, 2007 — the day before *Harry Potter and the Order of the Phoenix* premiered in London — Madame Tussauds unveiled a wax figure of (then) seventeen year-old Daniel Radcliffe, making him the youngest actor to be immortalized in wax. Although not featured on the Madame Tussauds London website, Daniel's wax sculpture is on permanent display in their **A-List Party room**.

[©2007 Wolfgang Mletzko]

New as of March, 2010

A wax figure of **Robert Pattinson** has joined Daniel Radcliffe in the A-List Party room. Although known to Harry Potter fans as **Cedric Diggory** (the boy killed by Voldemort in the *Goblet of Fire* graveyard), Robert's entry to Madame Tussauds was brought about by the popularity of his role as vampire **Edward Cullen** in the *Twilight* movie series.

Site Rating

Madame Tussauds Earns a Might-Be-Fun Rating Because:
Some Potterites may consider the expense required to simply have a photo taken with Radcliffe and Pattinson's wax figures to be *prohibitive*.

Madame Tussauds London is the birthplace of this remarkable, world-wide wax museum franchise. There are hundreds of celebrities, royals, world leaders, and historical figures.

[©2002 C.D. Miller]

Your wax museum admission ticket also includes entry to Madame Tussauds' *SCREAM* Chamber of Horrors exhibit, and the *Spirit of London* Black Cab ride.

Please Note: Both of these exhibits are rather short, each lasting only *five minutes*.

The SCREAM Chamber of Horrors

This is the horror section of Madame Tussauds, showcasing serial killers and murders. The Scream experience is an actor-led trek through a maze of live-action and wax figure tableaus. This attraction may not be suitable for children under 12 years of age.

The Spirit of London Ride

Visitors sit in open cars resembling iconic London black taxicabs, connected into a train. The cars revolve to offer the best view as they are pulled on a journey through tableaus depicting the history of London. The ride starts in Tudor times and ends in the 1980s. Shakespeare, the Great Fire of London, the Industrial Revolution and the Swinging Sixties are featured along the way. Audio commentary is available in several languages. Near the end of the ride, your photo is taken and can be purchased when you disembark.

Nearby Non-Potter Places

See Little Whinging Zoo (Site #9) for Information About These Non-Potter Places
The Sherlock Holmes Museum
The London Beatles Store
It's Only Rock 'n' Roll Store

Nearby Potter Places

👓 **The Little Whinging Zoo (Site #9):** A 35 minute walk or walk/bus/walk journey.

Going to Madame Tussauds

Please Note: Madame Tussauds has five entrances. Doors 1, 2, 3, and 4 are on Marylebone Road, just east of the Green Dome at the northeast corner of Alsop Place and Marylebone Road. If you don't have a ticket, go to Door 1. Potterites with prepaid tickets can use Doors 2, 3 or 4. Groups enter via Door 5 on Alsop Place.

🚌 **From Original Tour Bus Madame Tussauds Red/Yellow/Black/Gray Stop *or* Big Bus Stop 32/5**
A 1 minute walk.

🚶 Disembark the bus and look to your right for Madame Tussauds' iconic Green Dome, less than a block northeast of the bus stop.

🚇 **From Baker Street Tube Station**
A 1 minute walk.

🚶 Follow station signs to the **Marylebone Road Exit**. Walk one block northeast to Madame Tussauds' Green Dome.

From the Leaky Cauldron, *POA* (Site #7) in Borough Market: Padfoot Prowl or Potter Promenade *POA* Day
🚶🚇🚶 A 10 minute walk, a 12 minute tube trip, a 1 minute walk.

🚶 If leaving from the southern Borough Market entrance, walk southeast on **Stoney Street** to the intersection of **Southwark Street** and **Borough High Street**.

If leaving from the northern Borough Market entrance, walk southeast on **Bedale Street** to **Borough High Street**.

A stairway leading down to the **London Bridge Underground Station** lies on Borough High Street, between Stoney Street and Bedale Street.

⊖ Take the **Jubilee Line** towards Wembley Park or Stanmore to reach **Baker Street Tube Station**.

🕴 Follow the directions above for walking to the Muggle Wax Museum from the tube station.

From Little Whinging Zoo (Site #9)

🕴🚌🕴 A 35 minute walk *or* a 35 minute walk/ride/walk journey.

TAXI Alternatively, there usually are several Taxis waiting outside the Zoo. The fare to Madame Tussauds from the Zoo may range from £7 to £12 ($11 to $19), depending on the day, the time, and traffic.

Take a City Bus from the Zoo to Madame Tussauds
A 35 minute walk-bus-walk journey.

🕴 Exit the Zoo and cross to the north side of **Regent's Park Outer Circle Road**. ♦ Turn left, and walk southwest. Watch on your right for a break in the iron railing where a footpath leads northwest. ♦ Turn right and walk northwest on the footpath, crossing over the **Regent's Canal Footbridge** and continuing until you reach **Prince Albert Road**. ♦ Turn left and walk southwest to **Bus Stop C**.

🚌 Board **Bus 274 toward Lancaster Gate**. Get off at the **Baker Street Bus Stop** closest to **Madame Tussauds**.

🕴 From there, walk southeast on Baker Street to **Marylebone Road**. ♦ Turn left and walk northeast to Madame Tussauds.

Walk from the Zoo to Madame Tussauds
A 35 minute walk.

🕴 Exit the Zoo, turn left, and walk southwest along the park-side of **Regent's Park Outer Circle Road**. Follow Outer Circle Road as it curves further south, and then southeast. ♦ Just before Outer Circle Road splits into two streets like a "V," cross to the west side of the road and follow **Baker Street** to continue southeast. ♦ At the intersection of Baker Street, **Allsop Place**, and **Ivor Place**, keep left to cross the island at and continue southeast on Baker Street to **Marylebone Road**. ♦ Turn left and walk northeast to the entrance to Madame Tussauds, about one block away.

NUMBER 12
GRIMMAULD PLACE

Number 25 Claremont Square
http://harrypotter.wikia.com/wiki/12_Grimmauld_Place

Google Maps UK: 25 Claremont Square, Islington, London N1
Bensons Mini: J-1 / **Bensons Street:** L-1
Collins Mini: pg 14, A-3 / **Collins Atlas:** pg 43, G-1

Tube Stations: Angel *or* King's Cross/Saint Pancras

Original Tour Bus Station Connector (Black route), King's Cross/Saint Pancras stop

Operation Hours or **Entry Fee:** None. This is a private neighborhood in Islington, London.

Please Note: Due to a high crime reputation associated with the King's Cross/Saint Pancras Station area, it is safer to visit Islington during the daytime. Although *OOTP* Grimmauld Place screenshots were filmed at night, daytime pix will **not** disappoint.

Visit Time: Schedule at least 45 minutes here to rapidly snap your Grimmauld Place Potter Pix. Schedule an hour or more to enjoy Grimmauld Place at a more leisurely pace.

ભ૩৪

Number 12 Grimmauld Place is a Georgian townhouse **located in a London Muggle neighborhood near King's Cross Railway Station, and is** the ancestral home of **Sirius Black**'s family. After escaping from Azkaban, Sirius volunteered his home as **Headquarters** for the *Order of the Phoenix*. When Sirius was killed, Harry inherited the townhouse. In *Deathly Hallows*, #12 Grimmauld Place became a sanctuary where Harry, Ron, and Hermione hid from Voldemort's Death Eaters while beginning their search for the remaining Horcruxes.

In fiction, the location of Grimmauld Place was protected by an Unplottability Spell. In real-life, its location has long been protected by a Confundus Charm!

Erroneous information perpetuated by **multiple movie databases and HP Fan websites has long caused** Potterites to believe that exterior **Grimmauld Place** *Order of the Phoenix* scenes were filmed at **Lincoln's Inn Fields**. Yet, absolutely nothing observed at that real-life London location supports this claim. None of the four streets bordering Lincoln's Inn Fields contain structures that look anything like Grimmauld Place buildings. And, none of the fences or gates surrounding Lincoln's Inn Fields' park look anything like the park-side of Grimmauld Place. Finally, not a single **Fan Report** of filming having occurred at Lincoln's Inn Fields has ever surfaced.

Lincoln's Inn Fields is Not a Film Site, Don't Waste Your Time

Another cause of confusion regarding the real-life Grimmauld Place location is the erroneous information published in many Harry Potter location guidebooks. Below are examples from two authors who came *close* to finding Grimmauld Place—*but DIDN'T.*

From Steve Vander Ark's *In Search of Harry Potter* (© 2008)

"And then we walked into Lonsdale Square. I knew immediately that I had finally found Grimmauld Place. ... We found number 12 opposite a gate into the small grassy square."

From J.P. Sperati's *Harry Potter On Location* (©2010)

"For Georgian terrace houses you must look to Bloomsbury and Islington and indeed people have variously cited Regent Square, Argyle Square, Tavistock Square, Bedford Square and Gordon Square as the true location [of Grimmauld Place] with the favorite actually being New Square in Lincoln's Inn where there are even reports of a friendly gatehouse keeper telling interested tourists all about the filming that took place here. ... [This] 'location detective' firmly believes that Grimmauld Place is based on Canonbury Square in Islington, which coincidently would perfectly fit with the locations indicated in the book."

The moment *Harry Potter Places* is published, the fictional Unplottability Spell will be broken, and the real-life Confundus Charm shattered—because Grimmauld Place *does* exist in real-life, and **we found it!**

Claremont Square is Grimmauld Place

Claremont Square is located in the **Borough of Islington**—a community in the northern area of what is considered Central or Greater London. Pentonville Road runs along Claremont Square's north side. The streets bordering its eastern, southern, and western sides are *each* called Claremont Square.

Thanks to Sarah Moore and Conny Rhode, we found the following personal Internet Blog posted by a former Claremont Square resident, who describes *OOTP* **Grimmauld Place location scouts visiting this site.**
http://jostamon.blogspot.com/2007/10/richer-or-poorer-in-pentonville.html

> "Believe it or not, but the location agents for the film Harry Potter and the Order of the Phoenix came to Claremont Square around the end of 2005, asking the local residents for permission to film the Grimmauld Square scene in the area. Nina was very excited about this, especially when we were told that our flat might be used for props. Even the fact that J.K. Rowling describes Grimmauld Square as grimy and run down didn't dampen her spirits. In the event, the filming was done after we moved out, and Nina (barely able to contain her excitement) was only able to see the results when we went to the cinema in July to watch the film."

Thanks to Tara Bellers' devoted attention to detail while watching behind-the-scenes **Focus Points** footage found on the **Blu-Ray *HbP* DVD**, we confirmed the rumors that a **Leavesden Studios SET** was built for Grimmauld Place street filming.

[*Half-Blood Prince* DVD Focus Point screenshots (enhanced)]

When we compared set photos with **Claremont Square** photos, it became quite clear that the Grimmauld Place street set was designed as an *exact* **reproduction** of the real-life street and buildings that exist on the **south side of Claremont Square.**

Each of the buildings found there have the same number of floors and the same façade as those built for the set—the same first floor wrought-iron balconies, the same number of steps leading up to each door, and the same design for the railings flanking steps. Even the set's street lamps are the exactly the same as those seen on the southern Claremont Square street.

After comparing real-life Claremont Square photos with OOTP screenshots, we found the address: #25 Claremont Square is #12 Grimmauld Place.

Grimmauld Place Set Trivia

For *Half-Blood Prince*, the Grimmauld Place street set was used to film the brief Pensieve flashback scene of Dumbledore's approach to the orphanage where he first met Tom Riddle.

[*Half-Blood Prince* screenshot (enhanced)]

Digital blurring of the Grimmauld Place buildings prevents recognition of the set while watching the movie. Additionally, the set's western end-cap was reconstructed, becoming Wool's Orphanage, and its park-side was digitally replaced with a street-long façade of other buildings.

[*Half-Blood Prince* DVD Focus Point screenshot (enhanced)]

As nothing of Wool's Orphanage can be seen in **Claremont Square's** real-life location, you won't be able to snap pix resembling Dumbledore's *HbP* orphanage approach. Sorry.

Potterites who watch the 2009 *Sherlock Holmes* movie (starring Robert Downey Jr. and Jude Law) will easily recognize that the Grimmauld Place street set was used to film **Baker Street** exterior shots.

[2009 *Sherlock Holmes* screenshots (enhanced) above and below, ©2009 Warner Bros.]

The door that corresponds to Holmes' **221b Baker Street** abode is real-life **#20 Claremont Square**—four doors west of #12 Grimmauld Place.

Please Note: The Grimmauld Place/Baker Street set is one of *two* Potter/Holmes film associations. See **Hogwarts Staircase (Site #6)**.

Grimmauld Place Potter Pix

Claremont Square is a Real-Life Muggle Neighborhood

Please remember the Potterite Prime Directive.

To **POLITELY** Go Where Potterites Need to Go
— without **PERTURBING** anybody —
So That Other Potterites Can *Continue* to
ENJOY GOING THERE!

Your behavior while visiting Claremont Square will significantly affect how Potterites are greeted here long after you're gone. Please be as quiet and unobtrusive as Potterly possible while visiting this private Muggle neighborhood.

Prime Directive Pointers:
- Visit on a weekday, during hours when indigenous Muggles are likely to be at work.
- Invoke the Quietus Spell, or activate a Silencio Charm, while visiting.
- Stay OFF Muggle property. Keep to the street while taking your Potter Pix.
- Do not approach, nor take any photos of, indigenous Muggles who might be out and about.
- Get IN … Get your Potter Pix … Get OUT!

Grimmauld Place Potter Pic #1

[*Order of the Phoenix* screenshot (enhanced)]

The moment you arrive here, you'll no longer have any doubts that the street bordering the south side of Claremont Square's park *IS* **Grimmauld Place.**

[©2009 Tara Bellers]

Tara came very close to recreating the first screenshot. But, you can do even better. Take your Grimmauld Place Potter Pic #1 while approaching from the **east** end of the street along Claremont Square's south side, before reaching the street's midpoint and while standing closer to the *park-side* sidewalk. (Tara stood smack-dab in the middle of the street when snapping the pic above.) Angle your shot so that the open space at the end of the **western** Claremont Square buildings isn't seen.

Grimmauld Place Potter Pic #2

Use the door of **#25 Claremont Square** to center your reproduction of the following screenshot(s). That address is the second door west of a street lamp, flanked by a drain pipe after fully emerging in the film, *exactly* as #12 Grimmauld Place is.

[*Order of the Phoenix* screenshot (enhanced)]

Only one #12 Grimmauld Place exterior scene appeared in *DHp1*, and it's exactly like the *OOTP* screenshot above.

[*Deathly Hallows Part One* screenshot (enhanced)]

[©2009 Conny Rhode]

The angle of your reproduction pic will be closer to that of the screenshot if you *stand in the street* and your photographer *sits down* on the curb behind you to snap the photo. Happily, there isn't much traffic on the south side of Claremont Square.

Grimmauld Place Potter Pic #3

Next, take close-up pix of the shallow, wrought-iron-railed balcony above #25 Claremont Square, with the drain pipe seen in the far right of your camera frame. That drain pipe is the point from which #12 Grimmauld Place emerges into the Muggle World when a **Secret Keeper** deactivates the **Fidelius Charm** protecting it.

[*Order of the Phoenix* screenshot (enhanced)]

[©2009 Conny Rhode]

Grimmauld Place Potter Pic #4

[*Order of the Phoenix* screenshot (enhanced)]

Even though you cannot gain the height required to accurately recreate screenshot #4 (film crews had the luxury of using a crane), your pic will best resemble that scene if you visit when snow is on the ground.

[©2009 Tara Bellers]

No snow? No problemmo. Just stand on the sidewalk and take a pic of the buildings along the length of Claremont Square's southern street.

Grimmauld Place Potter Pic #5

[*Order of the Phoenix* screenshot (enhanced)]

Similarly, snow isn't absolutely necessary for recreating Grimmauld Place Potter Pic #5's screenshot, either. All you really need to capture is a close-up of #25 Claremont Square's door and front steps from its eastern side.

[©2009 Tara Bellers]

Grimmauld Place Potter Pic #6

Among the several charms and spells Sirius and other *Order of the Phoenix* members invoked to protect their headquarters was an **anti-Apparation Charm** which prevented apparation into, or out of, the *interior* of #12 Grimmauld Place. Due to that charm, there was only one way for Harry, Ron, and Hermione to come and go clandestinely from their *Deathly Hallows* hideaway: by precisely apparating to or from the **landing** in front of #12 Grimmauld Place's door, while crouched beneath Harry's invisibility cloak.

[©2009 Tara Bellers]

Well, *Blast-Ended Skrewt!* No Grimmauld Place landing apparation scenes were filmed for *Deathly Hallows Part One*. Still, many Potterites may want to have their pic taken **on the landing of #25 Claremont Square**, while they pose crouched-over as if covered by an invisibility cloak. (A clear plastic rain poncho might be nice to have for this pic.)

Again, *Please* Remember the Potterite Prime Directive

● Do not ring the doorbell of #25 Claremont Square, or in any other way attempt to contact those who live there.

● If no one is around, quickly and quietly dash up on #25's doorstep landing and have your crouched-over pic snapped. Quickly and quietly trade places with your photographer and snap a reciprocal pic. Then quickly and quietly *run away*.

● If one or more residents of #25 Claremont Square happen to be outside during your visit, **politely ask permission** to take pix while posing on their doorstep's landing. If they refuse, thank them anyway and profusely apologize for bothering them. Then walk away.

Don't forget that you can always do as Tara did, and simply take a pic of the #25 Claremont Square landing while standing on the sidewalk.

Park-Side Grimmauld Place Potter Pix

Claremont Square's park is surrounded by a 19th-century wrought-iron fence that also was reproduced for the Grimmauld Place set. At the southwestern corner of the real-life fence (directly across from #20 Claremont Square) is a gate and curb that look exactly like what is seen in *OOTP* footage. The only difference between Claremont Square's southwestern corner and the Grimmauld Place set's park-side is that the real-life park perimeter is rather bare, and the ground is steeply mounded up behind the fence.

Even so, at Claremont Square's southwestern fence gate you *can* snap reasonably similar pix of the screenshot showing Mad Eye Moody leading Harry and other Order members out of the park found across the street from #12 Grimmauld Place.

Grimmauld Place Potter Pic #7

[*Order of the Phoenix* screenshot (enhanced)]

One last point of consideration: Claremont Square's park isn't truly a *park*. It's an old open-pond reservoir that was covered over with dirt and turf in 1852. As such, it has been *privately owned* by the **Thames Water** utility company since 1989, and is **not accessible to the public.** Even those who live on Claremont Square aren't allowed access.

If you **climb over** the southwestern gate of Claremont Square reservoir's fence and go inside the reservoir park, you will be **trespassing on private property.** Then, again, it is entirely unlikely that anyone who observed you climbing over the gate would rush to report you to the Thames Water utility company.

Please Note: We are *not* advising you to *trespass* on Thames Water reservoir property, and we hereby disclaim responsibility for any liability or penalty, resulting directly or indirectly from any person or persons who independently elect to do so after reading this travel guidebook.

We are merely mentioning the fact that, if someone *did* climb over the southwestern Claremont Square gate, that person or persons could take pix recreating the last *OOTP* Grimmauld Place screenshot from *inside* the reservoir park … while they were trespassing.

Grimmauld Place Potter Pic #8

[*Order of the Phoenix* screenshot (enhanced)]

If a person or persons independently elected to trespass on the reservoir's property, there is no need to worry about which Claremont Square door is seen on the other side of the fence. Apart from the drain pipe on the west side of #25 Claremont Square, all the south-side Claremont Square doors look the same.

Nearby Non-Potter Place

Filthy McNasty's Pub

68 Amwell Street, Clerkenwell, London, EC1R 1UU

Hours: Mon-Thurs Noon to 11pm, Fri-Sat Noon to 2am, Sun Noon to 10:30pm.

View London Review:
http://www.viewlondon.co.uk/pubsandbars/filthy-mcnastys-review-11461.html

> "Inside, the pub is all stripped wooden furniture with mismatched pieces from old church chairs to high stools and low armchairs. The tables are covered in punters' scrawl—most of it pretty hard to decipher but that's half the fun. ... Pie fans are in for a treat here—they serve **Pieminster's pies** with mash and veggie gravy for £6.50. Pieminster's pies are something of an institution ... They come with a range of fillings including sweet potato and feta or chicken with tarragon. They are delicious and offer a golden flaky pastry that just cries out comfort food as you break open the crust with your fork. ... There is also a **Thai menu** for those after a red, green, yellow or matsuman curry. These are also priced around £6.50."

Time Out Review:
http://www.timeout.com/london/bars/reviews/13015.html

> "You can tell a lot about a bar by its toilet graffiti. To judge from the misspelt poetry and smut scrawled on these walls, Filthy McNasty's is still Islington's most rock 'n' roll boozer ... the tiny back room hosts acoustic sessions, sweaty bebop and Latin DJ nights. By day the pub is a surprisingly quiet, bookish refuge from the traffic-choked streets."

To find Filthy McNasty's Pub:

🚶 Walk to the west end of the southern Claremont Square (street). ◆ Turn left and walk south to the next corner.

Nearby Potter Place

👀 **Platform Nine & Three Quarters (Site #16):** A 15 minute walk.

Going to #12 Grimmauld Place

⊖ From Angel Tube Station
A 7 minute walk.

🚶 Turn left after exiting the station and head south on **Upper Street** to the intersection of **City Road** and **Pentonville Road**. ♦ Turn right and walk west to the *first* **Claremont Square** (street) that you encounter, the one bordering the park's eastern edge. Several black traffic posts prevent automobiles from entering this street. ♦ Turn left and walk south until you reach the southeastern corner of Claremont Square's park. ♦ Turn right and you'll be looking down the street that was the design model for Leavesden Studios' Grimmauld Place street set.

⊖ From King's Cross/Saint Pancras Tube Station, aka Platform Nine & Three Quarters (Site #16)

OR

🚌 From the Original Tour Bus Station Connector (Black route) King's Cross/Saint Pancras Stop:
A 15 minute walk.
Please Note: If arriving via King's Cross/Saint Pancras tube station or the OTB Black route stop, accomplish your **Platform Nine & Three Quarters** visit *before* going to Grimmauld Place. When finished at Grimmauld Place, you can leave by reversing the directions above and going **to Angel Tube Station.**

🚶 Go to the King's Cross/Saint Pancras station exit on **Euston Road** and stand with your back to the station. Turn left and walk northeast along Euston Road. ♦ Continue east along the northern side of Euston Road as it becomes **Pentonville Road**. ♦ Go past the *first* Claremont Square (street) — the one open to automobiles — to the *second* Claremont Square (street), which borders the park's eastern edge and is blocked by black traffic posts. ♦ Turn left and walk south until you reach the southeastern corner of Claremont Square's park. ♦ Turn right and you'll be looking down the street that was the design model for Leavesden Studios' Grimmauld Place street set.

16

PLATFORM NINE
& THREE QUARTERS

King's Cross/Saint Pancras Railway & Tube Stations
http://www.networkrail.co.uk/aspx/867.aspx
http://www.stpancras.com/
http://en.wikipedia.org/wiki/London_King%27s_Cross_railway_station
http://en.wikipedia.org/wiki/St_Pancras_railway_station

Google Maps UK: 51.530397,-0.123858
Bensons Mini: G-1 / **Bensons Street:** J-1
Collins Mini: pgs 12 and 13 / **Collins Atlas:** pg 43, D,E-1,2

Original Tour Bus: Station Connector (Black Route), King's Cross/ Saint Pancras Stop

Original Tour Bus Woburn Place Blue Stop *or* **Big Bus Stops 74 and 75**

Operation Hours: King's Cross Station is open 24 hours a day, 7 days a week. Due to the area's high crime reputation, it's best to visit between morning and evening rush hours (between 9:30am and 4pm), when other folks are around, but it's not too crowded.

Entry Fee: None. Even if you arrive and leave via surface transportation, you can visit interior King's Cross Railway Station interior film sites without paying for an underground or railway fare.

Visit Time: If you're willing to *race* to accomplish Potter Pix at both these locations, schedule only one hour here. For a more leisurely visit (allowing time to explore and more thoroughly enjoy yourself.), plan to spend at least 90 minutes at this site.

!!!Flash OFF!!! For security reasons, photography is forbidden inside underground and surface train stations.

Parseltongue Pointers:
- Euston = "YOU-stun"
- Saint Pancras = "sent PAN-crus"

[*Sorcerer's Stone* screenshot segment]

After being abruptly abandoned at **King's Cross Railway Station** in *Sorcerer's Stone*, 11-year-old Harry Potter had no idea how to find **Platform Nine and Three Quarters** and board the train that would take him to **Hogwarts School of Witchcraft and Wizardry**. Thankfully, the Weasley family arrived to help in the nick of time.

In real-life, no common platform exists between Tracks 9 and 10 of **King's Cross Railway Station**. To overcome this dilemma, filmmakers used the platform between Tracks 4 and 5 to shoot **Platform 9¾** scenes for *Sorcerer's Stone*, and all other HP movies requiring Hogwarts Express London boarding footage.

Exterior King's Cross station scenes needed for *Chamber of Secrets* were shot outside **Saint Pancras Railway Station**. Filmmakers found its gorgeous Victorian Gothic architecture far more cinematically attractive than King's Cross station's rather drab real-life exterior. Who can blame them?

[©2009 Tara Bellers]

The two London locations associated with Platform 9¾ are immediately adjacent to each other, and are connected by underground passageways. Thus, they often are referred to as though they're a single station, **King's Cross/Saint Pancras Station.**

Our discussion and directions begin with the **interior** Potter pix available at King's Cross Railway Station. Should you arrive here via surface transportation, however, follow our **exterior** Potter pix directions for Saint Pancras Station (and the King's Cross Potter Trolley) before entering King's Cross Railway Station.

King's Cross Railway Station

Soon after the 2001 release of *Sorcerer's Stone*, **Network Rail** recognized the Potter franchise's incredible popularity and wisely erected a cast-iron **Platform 9¾** sign on a brick wall just outside the suburban rail service building at King's Cross station (the building containing real-life Platforms 9 and 10) to attract tourists.

A year or so later, they brilliantly improved this Potterite destination by installing *part* of a luggage trolley below the Platform 9¾ sign. With only the push-handle half visible, the trolley's body seems to have disappeared into the magical realm of Platform 9¾, thus affording a fabulous King's Cross Potter pic opportunity.

[©2008 C.D. Miller] [©2009 Tara Bellers]

Unfortunately, things rapidly went downhill from there!

The Potterite King's Cross Conundrum

Beginning in 1997, the King's Cross Railway Station's **modernization, renovation, and reconstruction** project was launched, with an estimated completion date of 2013. One of its goals is to renovate and restore portions of the station's original **Victorian** architecture. Unfortunately, the sites where iconic Harry Potter scenes were filmed are not included in the renovation and restoration plan. In fact, they've been demolished.

The first casualty was the **Victorian Overhead Pedestrian Footbridge** that once spanned the main section of King's Cross Railway Station between Platforms 1 and 8.

[*Sorcerer's Stone* screenshot (enhanced)]

Even before *Sorcerer's Stone* was filmed here in 2000, the footbridge railing had been lined with unsightly plywood—presumably to prevent debris from falling onto the tracks below. The plywood was removed for filming, then immediately replaced.

[*Order of the Phoenix* screenshot (enhanced)]

The last film footage shot on the overhead footbridge was for *OOTP*, in 2006.

[©2008 C.D. Miller] [©2009 Tara Bellers]

In October of 2008, the King's Cross Railway Station plywood-lined footbridge was still intact. Eight months later, the footbridge was *gone!* Only a few skeletal remnants remained above its elderly support pillars in July of 2009.

The next casualty was the stairway lined with beautiful Victorian railings, that connected the overhead footbridge with Platform 1—stairs traversed by Sirius in his Padfoot form in *OOTP*.

[*Order of the Phoenix* screenshot (enhanced)]

Though barricaded since 2008, this beautiful example of Victorian iron work could still be seen behind a fenced enclosure in July of 2009. Perhaps Padfoot's staircase may be restored and reopened to the public in some capacity by 2013. We can only hope.

[©2009 Tara Bellers: a pic snapped through the fence]

The **Waiting Room** once found at the bottom of Padfoot's Platform 1 staircase still exists, but will *not* be restored to a state that can be recognized as an *OOTP* film set.

[*COS* Ultimate Edition *OOTP* extras screenshot (enhanced)]

After all, only Potterites would wish this waiting room to remain so drab in appearance.

[*Order of the Phoenix* screenshot (enhanced)]

According to the current King's Cross Station facility map, this room is now called the **First Class Lounge**. We seriously doubt that the new lounge is populated by tacky plastic chairs. If the fire place mantel is still there when you visit, please blog about it on the *Harry Potter Places* website.

Interior King's Cross Railway Station Potter Pix

[©2009 Tara Bellers] [©2008 C.D. Miller]

Various phases of the King's Cross construction project have caused the **Platform 9¾ Trolley Potter Pic Photo Op** to be moved from time to time. At this writing (December of 2011), it can be found *outside* of the station! Although the Platform 9¾ trolley may one day be returned to an interior King's Cross Station location, we currently provide directions for taking these pix in our **exterior** Potter pix directions.

Please Note: If you arrive *within* King's Cross Railway Station, find the nearest station employee and ask for the current location of the Harry Potter Platform 9¾ Trolley. Perhaps it's been moved back inside. If it has, please blog about it on the *Harry Potter Places* website.

!!!Flash OFF!!! Just a quick reminder. When inside King's Cross Railway Station, be sure your camera flash is **off** before you start snapping. Even with your flash off, station personnel who observe you taking pictures may ask you to stop taking them. Be Potterly Polite, and they won't confiscate your camera.

To begin interior pic-taking, go to the main King's Cross Railway Station section containing Platforms 1 to 8. Rent a luggage trolley (£1). Head left to **Platform 8.**

King's Cross Railway Station Potter Pic #1

[*Chamber of Secrets* screenshot (enhanced)]

When on Platform 8, look overhead for this clock. If it's still there, snap it. When finished go back the way you came and turn left at the head of Platform 8 to reach the platform between Tracks 4 and 5.

King's Cross Railway Station Potter Pix #2 and 3

Scenes involving Platform 9¾ were filmed on the platform between Tracks 4 and 5 at the low-arch section just beyond the overhead footbridge. Unfortunately, overhead footbridge demolition has made directing Potterites to the base of the *actual* film site arch somewhat problematic.

Go to the platform between **Tracks 4 and 5** and look for the low-arch *before* the **last overhead iron support truss,** the truss closest to the station's open train exit. Pile everything you can strip off without indecently exposing yourself into your trolley. Then, do what you can to reproduce these last two interior King's Cross Railway Station Platform 9¾ screenshots.

[*Sorcerer's Stone* screenshots (enhanced), above and below.]

Happily, the bases of all arches found on the real-life platform between Tracks 4 and 5 are barely wider than a luggage trolley. Thus, filmmakers had to install a **set piece** that made one arch base **wider** for shooting the **Muggle Platform 9¾** entrance scenes. This means that you can use any of the real-life arches found between Tracks 4 and 5 to recreate your screenshots.

[©2009 Tara Bellers]

215

Kings Cross Trivia

King's Cross Railway Station reappears on screen twice in *Deathly Hallows Part Two*.

Chapter 35 of the seventh and final Harry Potter book is titled, **King's Cross**, and describes the dream-like scenes that Harry experienced after meeting Voldemort in the Forbidden Forrest. These King's Cross scenes were filmed on a Leavesden Studios set.

Scenes filmed of the *Deathly Hallows* **Epilogue** ("Nineteen Years Later"), were originally shot inside King's Cross Railway Station in May of 2010. But, because director David Yates was dissatisfied by several aspects of that footage, the epilogue cast was recalled to shoot additional scenes inside King's Cross Railway Station in December of 2010.

Exterior King's Cross Railway Station Potter Pix

Outside the **Euston Road exit** of King's Cross Railway Station, head northeast toward **York Way**—the direction *away from* Saint Pancras Station.

[©2011 Sarah Greene]

Just before reaching the corner of York Way, turn left and look for the December 2011 location of the **Platform 9¾ Trolley Potter Pic Photo Op**.

[©2011 Sarah Greene]

This tiny enclosure severely limits the range of Potter pix that can be snapped. But, hopefully, this is a temporary location.

[©2011 Sarah Greene]

Basically, there's only room enough to accomplish a cramped pic like the one seen below.

[©2011 Sarah Greene]

But, make the best of it! Stuff your packs and purses, jackets and jumpers, into the tiny bit of trolley that remains in the Muggle world. Then, shoot as many poses as you can manage.

Someday, if the **Platform 9¾ Trolley Potter Pic Photo Op** is moved back inside the station, there will be plenty of room to shoot a variety of pix—as there once was.

[©2009 Tara Bellers]

Exterior Saint Pancras Railway Station Potter Pix

Saint Pancras Railway Station is a major railway terminus in central London. In 2007, after a security-sealed terminal area was completed for **Eurostar** services to Continental Europe via High Speed 1 and the Channel Tunnel, the station became known as **Saint Pancras International**.

Often called the "Cathedral of the Railways," Saint Pancras' gorgeous Victorian architecture has made it a popular shooting location for loads of TV and film productions, such as *Harry Potter*, *Bridget Jones's Diary*, and *Batman Begins*.

Filming for *Chamber of Secrets* took place in front of the station, outside the area once known as **Saint Pancras Chambers**—which used to house the **Midland Grand Hotel**.

After years of renovation and reconstruction that has periodically interfered with Potter Pic opportunities, the station is now free of scaffolding and the upscale **Marriott Renaissance Saint Pancras Hotel London** has opened. Potterites with plenty o' pounds (*beaucoup bucks) will enjoy staying here.*
http://www.marriott.co.uk/hotels/travel/lonpr-st-pancras

Happily, you don't have to go into the hotel or station to snap Potter pix. All Saint Pancras Potter pix are exterior photos.

To snap exterior King's Cross Station Potter screenshot recreation shots, head east on **Euston Road** to Saint Pancras Station. You may find it best to snap pix from the side of Euston Road across from the station. If you have time, shoot photos from both sides.

Saint Pancras Potter Pic #1

[*Chamber of Secrets* screenshot (enhanced)]

The Saint Pancras Potter Pic #1 examples we snapped in the past were all marred by construction blights.

219

[©2008 C.D. Miller] [©2009 Tara Bellers]

In December of 2011, Sarah (a non-Potterite friend) shot the pic below, confirming that the Saint Pancras Potter Pic #1 area is now free of obstruction.

[©2011 Sarah Greene]

Saint Pancras Potter Pic #2

[*Chamber of Secrets* screenshot (enhanced)]

Reconstruction of the Saint Pancras Chambers **Clock Tower** was completed prior to July of 2009. Thus, perfectly wonderful Saint Pancras Potter Pic #2 shots have long been available.

[©2009 Tara Bellers]

Nearby Non-Potter Places

Potterites interested in such should search the Internet. We're too focused on the Nearby Potter Place to care!

Nearby Potter Place

👓 **Number 12 Grimmauld Place (Site#15):** A 15 minute walk.

Going to Platform 9 & Three Quarters

≋ From King's Cross Railway Station

🚶 You're there! Wherever you arrive, find a station employee and ask for directions to the *current location* of Platform 9¾'s trolley. Follow interior King's Cross Railway Station Potter Pix directions above. ♦ When finished, head to the main exit on Euston Road and follow the exterior Potter pic directions above.

⊖ From King's Cross/Saint Pancras Underground Station

Walk time varies depending on your arrival platform, but shouldn't be more than 3 minutes.

🚶 Follow station signs to the **Euston Road/King's Cross Railway Station** exit. ✦ After emerging from the underground, look to your left for the main entrance to King's Cross Railway Station. ✦ Go inside and follow King's Cross Railway Station interior Potter Pix directions. ✦ When finished, return to the main exit on Euston Road and follow Potter pic directions above.

🚌 From the Original Tour Bus Station Connector (Black Route) King's Cross/Saint Pancras Stops
A 2 to 5 minute walk.

🚶 There appears to be **two** King's Cross/Saint Pancras Black Route Original Tour Bus stops, but the OTB maps don't clearly identify where each is actually located. Wherever you disembark, ask for directions to King's Cross *Railway Station* so that you can take interior Potter Pix first. ✦ If you find yourself walking past Saint Pancras Chambers and Clock Tower, take your exterior Potter Pix first.

🚌 From Original Tour Bus Woburn Place Blue Stop *or* Big Bus Stops 74 and 75
A 15 minute walk.

🚶 Head northwest on **Woburn Place**, continuing as it becomes **Tavistock Square** (*aka* **Upper Woburn Place**), until you reach **Euston Road**. ✦ Turn right and walk east on the south side of Euston Road until you see Saint Pancras Chambers and Clock Tower to your left, across the street. Take your exterior Potter Pix first. ✦ When finished, continue east on Euston Road to reach King's Cross Railway Station's entrance. ✦ Go past that and complete your exterior Potter Pix at the current location of Platform 9¾'s trolley. ✦ Return to the Euston Road King's Cross Railway Station's entrance and follow interior Potter Pix directions.

From Number 12 Grimmauld Place (Site #15)
A 15 minute walk.

🚶 Head west on the south side of **Claremont Square** (street) to **Amwell Street**. ✦ Turn right and walk north to **Pentonville Road**. ✦ Head left to cross to the opposite (north) side of the road. Then turn left and walk west on the north side of Pentonville Road for several blocks, until Pentonville has become **Euston Road** and you cross **York Way**. ✦ Take Potter Pix at the current exterior location of Platform 9¾'s trolley. ✦ Return to Euston Road and turn right to reach King's Cross Railway Station's entrance. Go inside and follow interior King's Cross Potter Pix directions above. ✦ When finished, leave via the main exit on Euston Road. ✦ Turn left and walk to the Saint Pancras Station Clock Tower. Follow the Potter pic directions above.

17

Saint Mungo's Hospital for Magical Maladies and Injuries

Saint Mungo's Charity
http://www.mungos.org/

~ ⋘⋙ ~

In the Potterverse, **Saint Mungo's Hospital for Magical Maladies and Injuries** is located somewhere in London. It is disguised as a condemned, red-bricked, Muggle department store (perpetually under renovation) called, **Purge and Dowse, Ltd**.

In real-life, **Saint Mungo's** is London's largest charitable organization, dedicated to providing housing and rehabilitation programs for people who are homeless or disabled. In July of 2009, their charity benefited from the auction of two tickets donated by Warner Bros, allowing entry to the UK premiere of *Harry Potter and the Half-Blood Prince*. Thus, Saint Mungo's is well aware of its unintended relationship with the wizarding world of Harry Potter.

Site Rating

Saint Mungo's Charity Earns a Skip It Rating Because:
- Saint Mungo's Hostels are a refuge for homeless and disabled individuals, victims of domestic abuse, and the like. Their privacy is important.

- Even perfectly polite Potterites may frighten or upset Saint Mungo's residents, causing them concern or offence.

• None of the Saint Mungo's hostels look *anything* like a condemned, red-bricked, Muggle department store.

• Saint Mungo's hostels have no exterior sign to pose in front of. The few that do bear identification have only a tiny, nondescript plaque.

Internet Clues to Saint Mungo's Locations are Misleading

The **Harry Potter Lexicon** website identifies the **Holborn** area of London as the most likely location of Saint Mungo's Hospital for Magical Maladies and Injuries.
http://www.hplex.info/atlas/britain/atlas-b-london.html

Potterites who perform further research will discover the real-life Saint Mungo's **Endell Street Hostel** located near the Holborn Tube Station. Endell Street Hostel's beautiful, *beige*-brick building has no exterior sign or plaque.

Potterites who find the **Flickr** photo of a Saint Mungo's Hostel door with a plaque, will learn that it is located between **#12 Grimmauld Place (Site #15)** and **King's Cross/Saint Pancras Station (Site #16)**.

[©2006 Stephen Spencer]

The **Argyle Walk Hostel** is discretely hidden away at the mouth of an alley that leads west from a pedestrian street. Many individuals who live here suffer with severe physical and mental health needs. Some have alcohol- and drug-related disabilities.

Potterites Should Avoid Saint Mungo's Hostels

We do not provide directions for finding them. Instead, consider going to their website and contributing to **Saint Mungo's Charity for Muggle Maladies and Injuries**.

WIZARD CHESSMEN

The British Museum
http://www.britishmuseum.org
http://en.wikipedia.org/wiki/British_Museum

Google Maps UK: 51.519444, -0.126944

[The museum's street address doesn't bring up a map that accurately indicates the front or rear entrances.]
Street Address: Great Russell Street, London, WC1B 3DG
Bensons Mini: G-4 / **Bensons Street:** J-4
Collins Mini: pg 36, B,C-1 / **Collins Atlas:** pg 14, D-1

Tube Station: Tottenham Court Road

Original Tour Bus Blue Museum Link Stop *or* **Big Bus Stops 74 & 75**

Operation Hours: Open daily from 10am to 5:30pm. Closed on December 24-26, January 1, and Good Friday.

Entry Fee: The British Museum is free. However, the enormous cost of its operation is almost entirely dependant upon visitor donations. Please contribute at least £1 per person. If you can afford £5 or more per person, so much the better.

Visit Time: Schedule at least one hour here to snap Lewis Chessmen pix before dashing to one of the gift shops for a 20 minute visit.

The Museum's Potterly Exhibit: the Lewis Chessmen

[©2008 C.D. Miller]

[*Sorcerer's Stone* screenshot (enhanced)]

👓 The British Museum merits a **Great Site** rating because it houses a world-renown collection of incredibly interesting non-Potter exhibits. If your London Harry Potter itinerary includes a Wizard Chessmen visit, please consider scheduling three to four (or more) hours here so you can enjoy more of the amazing exhibits found at the British Museum.

From the British Museum Website

"The British Museum was founded in 1753, the first national public museum in the world. From the beginning it granted free admission to all 'studious and curious persons.' Visitor numbers have grown from around 5,000 a year in the eighteenth century to nearly 6 million [per year] today. The British Museum's collection of seven million objects representing the rich history of human cultures mirrors the city of London's global variety. In no other museum can the visitor see so clearly the history of what it is to be human."

[*Sorcerer's Stone* screenshot (enhanced)]

The **Wizard Chess Set** that Harry and Ron used in *Sorcerer's Stone* was modeled after the Lewis Chessmen, an ancient Nordic chess set consisting of:

"elaborately worked walrus ivory and whales' teeth in the forms of seated kings and queens, mitered bishops, knights on their mounts, standing warders [rooks], and pawns in the shape of obelisks."

http://en.wikipedia.org/wiki/The_Lewis_Chessmen

Lewis Chessmen Are Shrouded in Mystery and Controversy

[Wikipedia image (segments) © Finlay McWalter]

Below is an irreverent but surprisingly accurate summary of what little is known about the Lewis Chessmen history, obtained from an article by Geoff Chandler, "*Not Even From Lewis, Mate.*"
http://textualities.net/tag/lewis-chessmen/

227

"At an unknown date, an unknown ship is sheltering from a storm in a bay on the Isle of Lewis [in Scotland]. Onboard, an unknown cabin boy seizes his chance to escape from the ship, sneaks into the Captain's cabin, steals a sack containing 128 carved walrus pieces (four chess sets) and swims ashore. The boy is spotted by an unknown person, who, unaccountably, murders him. The murderer disposes of the body in an unknown grave, buries the bag of pieces in an unknown location and leaves. He goes to Stornoway [a village on the Isle of Lewis] and whilst awaiting execution for an unknown crime confesses to killing the cabin boy. One day a herdsman's cow sticks its [horn] into a sandbank and pulls out 93 of the chess pieces. The herdsman sells the find to a Captain Pyrie, who takes it to Edinburgh and sells it to a Mr. Forrest. Forrest sells 82 of the pieces to the British Museum; the remaining eleven pieces, he sells to a Mr. Sharpe, who later sells them to the Society of Antiquaries of Scotland."

No matter how they came to be buried in a sandbank on the Isle of Lewis, the Lewis Chessmen were discovered in 1831, and experts agree that they were probably carved in **Norway**, sometime between 1150 and 1200 AD.

Of the 93 Lewis Chessmen in existence, 82 are currently in the custody of London's British Museum. The remaining 11 pieces belong to the **National Museum of Scotland (Site #52)**, in Edinburgh. Because they are indisputably *Scottish* artifacts, the fact that so many of them are "owned" by an English museum is an ongoing source of contention.

Tips for Visiting the Wizard Chessmen

Because they occasionally get moved, go to the British Museum Information Desk in the Great Court when you arrive, and ask for directions to the Lewis Chessmen exhibit while picking up a copy of the museum floor plan. Dash to that location and snap your Lewis Chessmen pix. If you have time to visit more of the museum's exhibits after that, do so.

The British Museum Has Three Cafés and a Restaurant
http://www.britishmuseum.org/visiting/eat.aspx

Visit the British Museum website before your holiday to determine which one best suits your itinerary and pocketbook.

Whether or not you'll only be visiting the Lewis Chessmen while at the British Museum, be sure to schedule time to peruse at least one of the *four* British Museum gift shops—something you'll want to research beforehand.
http://www.britishmuseum.org/visiting/shop.aspx

The Book Shop is located just within the museum's main entrance, to the west (left), before you enter the Great Court. Here, you'll find a few Lewis Chessmen books and postcards.

The Culture Shop is located just within the museum's main entrance, to the east (right), before you enter the Great Court. This shop sells luxury items, such as high-quality British Museum artifact reproductions, at a premium price.

Two different versions of a hand-finished resin **Lewis Chessmen Set**, each including a wooden board, are sold in the Culture Shop. In 2011, the Medium-quality set cost £199 ($326). The Premium-quality set cost £495, approximately $811.

The Collections Shop, found on the west side of the Great Court, sells souvenirs, replicas, postcards, jewelry, stationery and inexpensive gifts.

The Family Shop, found on the north side of the Great Court, sells games, books, DVDs, souvenirs and educational items for children of all ages.

Both shops in the Great Court sell a *miniature*, Lewis Chessmen set. The miniature set's King is 4.2cm (1.7") tall. In 2011, its price was £45 ($74).

Lewis Chessmen Souvenirs Tip

If your Harry Potter holiday includes a visit to **Edinburgh**, we strongly suggest that you wait to buy Lewis Chessmen souvenirs until you're at the **National Museum of Scotland (Site #52)**. Although it houses far fewer of the actual chessmen than the British Museum, the **NMS** offers a far greater variety of Lewis Chessmen souvenirs.

Several Lewis Chessmen chess sets are available at the NMS, ranging from £52.50 ($86) to £130 ($213). Additionally, only the NMS sells a wide selection of *individual*, poly-resin Lewis Chessmen replicas. In 2011, full-sized replicas cost £11.99 ($20), and slightly smaller replicas cost only £9.95 ($16) each.

British Museum's Lewis Chessmen Souvenir Collection
http://www.britishmuseumshoponline.org/icat/shoponline

National Museum of Scotland's Lewis Chessmen Souvenirs
http://shop.nms.ac.uk/categories/Gifts/Lewis-Chessmen

Nearby Non-Potter Places

In front of the British Museum, along the south side of Great Russell Street, are several London tourist souvenir shops. Yes, much of what they sell is cheap and tacky. But, cheap and tacky stuff can be fun! Also, bargains can occasionally be found at these places. For instance, keep your eyes open for **Dunoon Stoneware** mugs and cups (the Dunoon name and symbol will be printed on the bottom). At £10 or less, they're a great buy.

Nearby Potter Places

 The Diagon Alley Wizard Entrance (Site #3): A 10 minute walk.

Going to the British Museum

Tip: If your route takes you along **Tottenham Court Road**, snap a street sign pic. The Muggle all-night Café was located on this street in the *Deathly Hallows* book.

Please Note: Saint Giles Circus is the junction of Charing Cross Road, Tottenham Court Road, Oxford Street, and New Oxford Street.

The Original Tour Bus Blue Museum Link Stops in Front of the Museum

Walk to the British Museum's main entrance.

From Tottenham Court Road Tube Station

A 6 minute walk.

Tottenham Court Road tube station has exits at each corner of **Saint Giles Circus**. Follow the station signs to the **New Oxford St/Tottenham Court Rd** exit. ♦ Walk northwest along the east side of **Tottenham Court Road** to **Great Russell Street**. ♦ Turn right and walk northeast for approximately 3 blocks to the British Museum's main entrance.

From Big Bus Stops 74 & 75

An 8 minute walk.

Walk southeast on the west side of **Woburn Place** until you've crossed to the northeast corner of **Russell Square Gardens**. ♦ Turn right and walk southwest along the garden-side of the street until you've just begun to round the next corner of the park. ♦ Turn right and cross over to the west side of **Russell Square Street**. ♦ Turn left and walk southeast to **Montague Place**. ♦ Turn right and walk southwest. The British Museum's modest north entrance will be on your left.

From the Diagon Alley Wizard Entrance (Site #3)

A 10 minute walk.

Walk north on the east side of **Charing Cross Road** to **Saint Giles Circus**. ♦ Cross north to the east side of **Tottenham Court Road** and walk northwest to **Great Russell Street**. ♦ Turn right and walk northeast for approximately 3 blocks to the British Museum's main entrance.

19

GODRIC'S HOLLOW

The Village of Lavenham, Suffolk, England
http://www.lavenham.co.uk/
http://www.historic-uk.com/DestinationsUK/Lavenham.htm
http://en.wikipedia.org/wiki/Lavenham
http://www.suffolktouristguide.com/Lavenham.asp

Google Maps UK: Market Place, Lavenham, Sudbury, Suffolk CO10 9QZ
🚄 London's Liverpool Street Railway Station [**LST**]
🚄 Sudbury Railway Station [**SUY**], in Suffolk.
🚌 Bus 753 between Sudbury and Lavenham
TAXI Taxi between Sudbury and Lavenham

London Station to Side-Along *One-Way* Travel Time:
Via Train and Bus, 2 hours.
Via Train and Taxi, 1.5 hours.

Operation Hours: See the Lavenham Guildhall and Tapestry Gallery info below.

Visit Time: If you're going to pay the pounds to Potter here, allow at least 2 hours for visiting the village–staying for 3 or more hours if you can.

Please Note: Lavenham is designated a **London Side-Along Apparation** only because it is located *northeast* of London, and cannot be conveniently included in any outside-London *Harry Potter Places* travel guidebook.

Parseltongue Pointers:
- Lavenham = "LAV-in-um"
- Suffolk = "SUFF-uck"
- Sudbury = "SUD-bree"

All **Godric's Hollow** scenes for *Deathly Hallows* Parts 1 and 2 were shot on a **set** constructed at **Pinewood Studios**. The Godric's Hollow set consisted of a few building-lined streets, a church front, and the graveyard where Harry's parents were buried.

No graveyard exactly resembling the one seen on screen exists in *any* real-life UK location–that we know of. But, like so many other Harry Potter movie sets, much of the set's **building architecture** *was* designed based on buildings found in a real-life place, the **village of Lavenham**.

Lavenham is widely recognized as being the best surviving example of a **Medieval Wool Town** in all of England. Despite its small size, Lavenham was considered the fourteenth-wealthiest town in England during **Tudor times** (1485 to 1603). And, although the majority of Lavenham's distinctive timber-framed buildings were built in the 15th century, a few village structures date back to **Saxon times** (early 5th century AD) and the **Norman Conquest** of 1066.

Warner Bros. location scouts were thrilled with Lavenham's appearance, primarily because so many of the village's oldest structures were built with **green wood**. As the unseasoned wood aged over the centuries, these buildings became twisted and tweaked out of alignment, creating scores of crooked houses–just the kind of distorted architecture *perfect* for a Potterverse village!

In January of 2010, several Godric's Hollow **architectural reference shots** and **background plates** were filmed in Lavenham. According to Jane Gosling, manager of the National Trust's Lavenham Guildhall, filmmakers had planned to fly "a squadron of helicopters over the village to dump fake snow across the Market Place" prior to filming background plates. But, just before the shoot date, Lavenham was lavished with an unusually deep *natural* snowfall. Thus, not a single fake snowflake was required for filming Godric's Hollow background plates for *Deathly Hallows*.

Site Rating

Godric's Hollow/Lavenham is Assigned a Might-be-Fun Rating Because:

- Being a **1.5 to 2-hour** *one-way* journey from Central London, Lavenham is the most distant London Side-Along Apparation. Visiting Godric's Hollow for only 2 hours will require at least 6 hours of one day's itinerary.

- Lavenham is an expensive Side-Along, costing as much as £50 ($80) round-trip from London.

- Only one real-life Lavenham building can be recognized on screen.

In spite of the points described above, Lavenham is such a lovely village that we couldn't bear to give Godric's Hollow a **Skip It** rating. If you can afford the travel time and expense, you're sure to enjoy a visit to Lavenham.

The Godric's Hollow Potter Home Saga

For the first Harry Potter movie, *Sorcerer's Stone*, scenes of Voldemort approaching James and Lily Potter's Godric's Hollow home were filmed outside a real-life cottage located in the village of **Lacock**. [*Harry Potter Places* Book 3–Snitch-Seeking in Southern England and Wales, Site #40.]

[*SS* screenshot (enhanced)]

However, as sometimes happens when shooting a series of several movies, the Godric's Hollow Potter home looked decidedly *different* in the 7th and 8th movies.

[*DHp1* screenshot (enhanced)]

233

Decayed and dilapidated during 16 years of abandonment, only a skeleton of the house remained when Harry and Hermione found his parents' Godric's Hollow home in *Deathly Hallows Part One*.

[*DHp2* screenshot (enhanced)]

In a *Deathly Hallows Part Two* Pensieve flashback, however, Professor Snape is seen approaching the Godric's Hollow Potter home on the night that Voldemort killed Harry's parents. In these scenes, Lavenham's architectural influence on the Potter home's set design can clearly be recognized.

Prior to the release of *DHp1*, it was widely reported that the *Deathly Hallows* Potter home would look exactly like the **Lavenham Guildhall**. Although its design is architecturally *similar*, the *DH* Potter home set is not a Guildhall building recreation. However, Lavenham's Guildhall ended up having a **cameo appearance** in *DHp1*.

Directions for Pottering around Lavenham

Our Lavenham Potter Trek is a circular route designed to accommodate Potterites who reach Lavenham from Sudbury by bus *or* taxi. Thus, the trek begins and ends at the Bus 753 stop on **High Street**, across from **The Swan At Lavenham** hotel and restaurant. From there, our route takes you north along High Street.

Both sides of Lavenham's High Street are lined with interesting antique shops, knitwear stores, curio sellers and art galleries, as well as a pub or two. But, because the Lavenham Potter Trek ends where it begins–in front of the Swan–it's best to save your Non-Potter High Street shopping for later.

Godric's Hollow Potter Architecture Pix

[©2011 Tara Bellers]

The moment you reach Lavenham, you can start snapping pix of buildings reminiscent of **Potterverse architecture**, beginning with the Swan Hotel–parts of which are structurally similar to the Godric's Hollow Potter home.

> "The Swan was built in about 1400 and comprises three houses dating from the same era. The oldest part dates back to the late 14th Century. It is not known when conversion to an Inn took place, but it was well established by 1667, when the then Landlord, John Girling, issued a 'Trader's Token'. The Girling family still live in Lavenham to this day."

After snapping exterior Swan Hotel building pix, turn left and walk a few steps north on High Street.

Hogwarts-Castle-Related Potter Pix in Godric's Hollow

[*Sorcerer's Stone* screenshot segment (enhanced)]

Adjacent to the north end of the Swan Hotel on High Street is **The Tapestry Gallery**, which is open every day from 10am to 5:30 pm.
http://www.tapestrygallery.co.uk/

This shop sells high-quality reproductions of *all* the gorgeous tapestries that adorned the **Gryffindor Common Room** walls, as well as reproductions of a particularly iconic tapestry often spied within **The Place Where Everything is Hidden**.

See the **Hogwarts Tapestries Supplementum** to learn all about the tapestries seen in Harry Potter movies, and in Lavenham's Tapestry Gallery.
http://HarryPotterPlaces.com/b1/TapestrySupplementum.pdf

Be forewarned, this is not a cheap souvenir shop! You'll not find mass-produced knockoffs or inexpensive imitations here. The Tapestry Gallery sells **woven** *artwork*. Each of their authentic reproductions is a top quality, loom-woven tapestry. Thus, the least expensive items–tapestry pillows–cost anywhere from £35 ($56) to £46 ($73). Fully-lined tapestry wall hangings start at £99 ($158), with the largest costing up to £895 ($1,425).

Keep in mind that, if you pay the pounds to purchase something from the Tapestry Gallery, you'll not only be buying a valuable work of art, you'll be buying a **Hogwarts Castle** work of art, from a shop in **Godric's Hollow**.

Please Note: If you make a purchase here, ask the Tapestry Gallery proprietor to hold it for you so that you can resume your Lavenham Potter Trek unencumbered.

Happily, Potterites on a tight budget can *browse* **the Tapestry Gallery without buying anything.** Please remember to be Potterly Polite and very discreet when snapping pix of the Hogwarts Castle tapestries displayed herein: *!!!Flash OFF!!!*

Additional Godric's Hollow Potter Architecture Pix

When you exit the Tapestry Gallery, turn right and walk about half a block farther north. Then, look across to High Street's westside, and you'll see **The Crooked House Gallery**.

Originally built in 1395 by a wealthy cloth merchant as part of his Grand Hall's service wing, this peach-colored building is a perfect example of Potterverse architecture.

The Crooked House Gallery sells original artwork created by local Lavenham artists, such as paintings, pottery, sculptures, ceramics, jewelry, and stained glass.
http://www.crookedhousegallery.co.uk/

Opening Hours: 10am to 5pm daily, except Wednesdays.

[©2011 Tara Bellers]

After snapping Potterverse architecture pix of the Crooked House *from* the east side of High Street, cross to the Crooked House Gallery's front entrance and spin about to snap pix of the buildings that are directly across from it, *on* the east side of High Street. These buildings also are gorgeous examples of Godric's Hollow Potterverse architecture.

When finished at the Crooked House, cross back to the east side of High Street. ♦ Turn left and walk north to **Market Lane**. ♦ Turn right and walk northeast. ♦ At the end of that short block, you'll reach **Lavenham's Market Place**. Look to your right. On the southwest corner of the Market Place you'll see **The Lavenham Guildhall**.

[©2011 Tara Bellers]

237

The Lavenham Guildhall is an impressive timber-framed building constructed sometime around 1530. The National Trust assumed its management in 1951, and created a marvelous museum of local history, complete with a Tea Room and Gift Shop.
http://www.nationaltrust.org.uk/main/w-lavenham

Guildhall Entry Fee: Adult £4.50 ($7), Child £1.90 ($3), Family £10.90 ($18)

Guildhall Operation Hours: Opening days and times vary throughout the year. From the end of March to the end of October, the Guildhall Museum, Tea Room and Gift Shop, are open 7-days-a-week, from 11am to 5pm. During all other months, opening hours are 11am to 4pm every Saturday and Sunday. In November, December and early March, the Guildhall is also open on a few weekdays.

Visit the Lavenham Guildhall's website for opening times during your holiday.

The Lavenham Guildhall's *DHp1* Cameo

Deathly Hallows Part One scenes of Harry and Hermione arriving in Godric's Hollow were shot on the Pinewood Studios set with a green screen in the background.

[*DHp1* Special Features screenshot (enhanced)]

For the finished film, the green screen at the end of this street was replaced with a background plate actually shot in Lavenham–featuring the west end of the Guildhall!

[*DHp1* screenshot (enhanced)]

Because this is the only *recognizable* Lavenham background plate used for Godric's Hollow footage seen in Parts 1 and 2 of *Deathly Hallows*, be sure to have your photo taken in front of the Lavenham Guildhall.

When Finished at the Guildhall, Check the Time

Consider visiting the shops surrounding Lavenham's Market Place, such as *Grannie's Attic antique store, or Sparling & Faiers Bakers & Confectioners, or the Vintage Pink gift shop.*

There's also a marvelous museum situated in a lovely 14th Century Hall House, found just off of the southeast corner of the Market Place, **The Little Hall Museum**. One hour is suggested for a visit. Accompanied children are admitted free. The entry fee for adults is only £3 ($5). Check The Little Hall Museum website to learn more about the museum, including opening hours in effect during your holiday.
http://www.littlehall.org.uk/littlehall/index.htm

When ready to leave the Lavenham Market Place, head for the **southwest corner** (just beyond the Guildhall). ♦ Turn left and walk south on **Lady Street**. ♦ Watch on your right for the sign that hangs above the rear parking entry for **The Swan At Lavenham** hotel and restaurant.

Another Other *Deathly Hallows* Godric's Hollow Potter Pic

[*Dhp1* Special Features screenshot (enhanced)] [©2011 Tara Bellers]

If you **Google** "The Swan, England"–or "The Swan, Scotland"–you'll learn that scores of UK villages and towns have a Swan Hotel or Pub. But, it is *this* sign in Lavenham that inspired the Pinewood Studios Godric's Hollow set design of the **Seven Swans Free House** sign.

After snapping your Swan sign pix, continue south on Lady Street to **Water Street.** ♦ Turn right and walk west to High Street, returning to the starting point of your Lavenham Potter Trek.

Your Lavenham Potter Trek is Done–Check the Time

If time allows, wander north on High Street again, this time visiting the many interesting Non-Potter shops that line both sides. Do you have purchases to pick up at the Tapestry Gallery? Do you have time to pop into the Swan and enjoy a sip or sup in this historic Inn before catching the next bus or meeting your prebooked taxi?

Lavenham Lodgings

Potterites who plan to enjoy an entire day touring Godric's Hollow may wish to lodge in Lavenham. Visit **Discover Lavenham**'s Where-to-Stay webpage to explore several options for Lavenham lodgings:
http://www.discoverlavenham.co.uk/where-to-stay-c44.html

It's difficult to go wrong when lodging in Lavenham. So, hunt for a place that suits your budget.

The Byes Barn B&B in Lavenham
http://www.byesbarn.co.uk/

In July of 2011, Tara Bellers–Potterite Researcher Extraordinaire–spent a night here.

"It was wonderful! While the exterior wasn't the breath-taking traditional Lavenham architecture, the interior was absolutely gorgeous. Plus, it was the most affordable place I could find, and an easy walk to the Guildhall and town center. The Landlady was very nice, and the Full English Breakfast was marvelous. I'd stay here again!"

The accommodation at Byes Barn is limited to *one* ensuite double-bed room, which includes tea and coffee amenities, as well as a Full English Breakfast. The 2011 tariff for this room: £80 ($127) per night, double occupancy; £70 ($111) per night, single occupancy.

The Swan At Lavenham Hotel

The Swan At Lavenham (aka, the Godric's Hollow **Seven Swans Free House**) would be a fabulous accommodation for Potterites planning an overnight in Lavenham.
http://www.theswanatlavenham.co.uk/

However, staying here ain't cheap. Below are 2011 tariff examples for a Bed & Breakfast one-night stay at the Swan Hotel.
Suite: £300 ($486)
Four Poster: £280 ($453)
Junior Suite: £260 ($421)
Classic Double/Twin: £200 ($324)
Single occupancy: £105 ($170)

The Angel Hotel and Pub

The Angel Hotel and Pub is another potentially wonderful Potterite accommodation, because it is located *in* the Lavenham Market Place.
http://www.maypolehotels.com/angelhotel/

First licensed in 1420, the Angel Hotel and Pub is believed to be the **oldest inn** in Lavenham. In spite of being periodically renovated over the centuries, the Angel is famous for having retained much of its original Tudor character.
    Less expensive than the Swan Hotel, the Angel Hotel still ain't cheap. Below are some 2011 tariff examples for a one-night Bed & Breakfast stay.

Bed & Breakfast tariff per night; Sunday through Friday:
Double or Twin, £110 ($178)
Single, £85 ($138)
Family of three, £135 ($219)

Saturday stays are slightly more expensive, and **Saturday-Night-Only bookings** aren't available unless a short-notice cancellation frees a room.

Going to Godric's Hollow / Lavenham

🚞 Leave from London's **Liverpool Street Railway Station** [LST], and go to **Sudbury Railway Station** [SUY], in Suffolk. Use the National Rail website to check the train schedules, and consider pre-purchasing your tickets.
http://www.nationalrail.co.uk/

The 2011 LST to SUY round trip train fare: £25.60 ($41).

Please Note: SUY is outside the **London Travelcard** (and London Pass w/ Travel) zones, and the **Oyster Card** may not be accepted for this journey.

Trains between LST and SUY run only once each hour, and the one-way rail journey is commonly 1 hour and 20 minutes long.

Taking the Bus

🚌 **Bus 753** runs between Sudbury and Lavenham on Mondays through Saturdays. It leaves once each hour, about 15 minutes after each SUY train arrival. The bus stop is a 5 minute walk from the train shelter. Bus fare between Sudbury and Lavenham is only £3.30 ($5.50) each way, but the bus trip is about 38 minutes long.

Please Note: Bus 753 does *not* run on Sundays.

To reach the Sudbury Bus Stops, walk west on **Station Road** from the SUY train shelter. ♦ Turn right at **Great Eastern Road** and walk north, keeping right to reach the **Hamilton Road** stop light and cross walk. ♦ Turn left to cross the street and walk west on Hamilton Road to the Sudbury Bus Stops. **Bus 753 leaves from bus stand F.**

Bus 753 arrives in Lavenham on **High Street**, just across from The Swan Hotel. The stop where the bus arrives is *opposite* to the stop where the return Bus 753 departs.

When finished in Lavenham, if you prefer taking a taxi back to the SUY train shelter, pop into the Swan and ask for help to call a taxi. Enjoy a sip or sup there while you wait.

Taking a Taxi

TAXI SUY is only a 10 to 15 minute drive from Lavenham.

Sudbury Railway Station isn't actually a *station*. It's a small, open train shelter. And, there is **no Taxi stand there**. Thus, you'll need to **prebook a taxi** to take you from SUY to the Swan Hotel in Lavenham (and back).
http://www.taxiregister.com/Sudbury

We recommend either the **Sudbury Cab Company** (01787 373222); a £12 ($19) one-way trip to Lavenham for up to 4 passengers:
http://www.sudburycabcompany.co.uk/

Or, the **Elite Taxi** company (01787 881212); an £11.70 ($19) one-way trip to Lavenham for up to 4 passengers:
http://www.elite-taxis.co.uk

If you discover that you'd like to spend more time than previously-planned while Pottering in Lavenham, pop into any Pub or Hotel/B&B and ask for help to call and change your prebooked taxi pickup appointment.

Bus vs Taxi Summary

LST to SUY 2011 round trip Train fare: £25.60 ($41).
One-way travel time from LST to Lavenham via SUY and Bus 753 is 2 hours.
One-way travel time from LST to Lavenham via SUY and Taxi is 1.5 hours.
Round-trip Godric's Hollow travel expense via Train and Bus 753 is £32.20 ($52).
Round-trip Godric's Hollow travel expense via Train and Taxi is £50 ($80).

Happily, the SUY to Lavenham taxi tariff can be split between up to 4 travelers, decreasing the total round-trip travel expense for each.

🚗 Driving to Godric's Hollow / Lavenham

Some Potterites may elect to design a personal travel plan that includes renting a car and driving to Lavenham. After all, you can head north from Lavenham to reach most of the **NEWTs** (*Harry Potter Places* Book 4–NEWTs: Northeastern England Wizarding Treks). In that event, use the coordinates below to reach Lavenham's largest parking area, Market Place.

SatNav/GPS: Market Place, Lavenham, Sudbury, Suffolk CO10 9QZ

If you'll be lodging in Lavenham, reserved parking may be included. Use your lodging's coordinates to reach the village.

HₚP Train
Station Café

Surbiton Railway Station
http://en.wikipedia.org/wiki/Surbiton_railway_station
http://www.nationalrail.co.uk/stations/sur/details.html

Google Maps UK: Surbiton Rail Station @51.392460,-0.303960
Address: Victoria Road, Surbiton, KT6 4PE
≋ London's Waterloo Railway Station
≋ Surbiton Railway Station
Travelcard Zone 6

Central London to Side-Along One-Way Travel Time: 25 to 45 minutes, depending on departure point and time of travel.

Operation Hours (Ticket Office): Mon-Fri 6:20am to 9:45pm; Saturday 6:20am to 9:30pm; Sunday 7:20am to 9:30pm

Entry Fee: None.

Visit Time: Schedule at least 30 to 45 minutes here.

!!!Flash OFF!!! For security reasons, photography is forbidden in underground and surface train stations.

Potter Props: Creative Potterites should bring a **newspaper** along.

Parseltongue Pointer:
- Café Chaud = "kaff-ay SHOW"

Surbiton Railway Station is located southwest of London, in the **Royal Borough of Kingston upon Thames**. The station's building was designed by J Robb Scott in an art deco style, and is considered to be one of the finest modernist stations in Great Britain. Surbiton station has two islands, both flanked by two train platforms. In the center of each island is a diner-like coffee house and snack shop called, **Café Chaud**. (Café Chaud is French for *"hot coffee."*)

Filming of exterior scenes for *Half-Blood Prince* took place on both Surbiton Railway Station islands in November of 2007. Much that was seen in the movie can be recognized in real-life.

Unfortunately for Potterites, a Leavesden Studios **set** was constructed to film the interior train station café *HbP* scenes (Harry reading his *Daily Prophet* newspaper, then making a date with the flirtatious Muggle waitress). Happily, the café set design was inspired by the real-life interior of the Café Chaud found between Surbiton Railway Station's **Platforms 1 and 2**.

When visiting this site on a weekday, it is best to avoid rush hours. Apart from keeping travel time to a minimum, avoiding rush hours will ensure that there won't be crowds of commuting Muggles interfering with your Potter Pix. Weekday rush hours are commonly from 7am to 9:30am, and 4pm to 6:30pm.

Because trains from London arrive at Surbiton Railway Station on **Platforms 3 or 4**, the **Surbiton Station Potter Pix** shot on or from that island are presented first.

Please remember to turn your camera flash off before snapping. Even with your flash off, station personnel who observe you taking pictures may ask you to stop taking them. Be Potterly polite, and they won't confiscate your camera.

Surbiton Station Potter Pic #1

[*Half-Blood Prince* screenshot, enhanced]

The scene above was filmed on Platform 4. When taking your screenshot recreation pix, be far enough away from the Exit to include a section of the dividing wall between Platforms 3 and 4 behind your Dumbledore and Harry stand-ins.

[©2009 Tara Bellers]

Surbiton Station Potter Pic #2

[© 2007 Marc Lechtenfeld of www.harrypotter-xperts.de]

Potter Pic #2 was taken by a **Fan** during *HbP* filming of the Surbiton Station Potter Pic #8 screenshot (below). This view of Dumbledore standing on **Platform 3** doesn't appear in the movie, but we think it's fun. If you agree, snap this pic after positioning your Dumbledore stand-in so that her/his body hides the hanging rubbish bin.

[©2008 C.D. Miller]

To obtain Marc's fan photo, go to:
http://www.harrypotter-xperts.de/movie6/setreport

If you don't speak German, paste his site's address into **Google Translate**.
http://translate.google.com/

Surbiton Station Potter Pic #3

[*Half-Blood Prince* screenshot, enhanced]

The Café Chaud seen in this screenshot is the one between Platforms 1 and 2.
Snap this pic while standing on Platform 3. If you're not in a rush, take turns
with others in your party being the Muggle Waitress stand-in. It's a very
short jaunt back and forth between the two Surbiton islands.

[©2008 C.D. Miller]

After taking your Platforms 3 and 4 Potter Pix, go up the steps and turn left. Make your way to the steps leading down to **Platforms 1 and 2**. The following screenshots are snapped on or from that island. Conveniently, your return train to London will leave from Platform 1 or 2.

Platform 2 and Café Chaud Pic Tips

Café Chaud employees have sometimes denied permission to Potterites wishing to take photos within the café, so don't ask. When you arrive on Platforms 1 and 2, **Sneakoscope your two interior-café screenshot pix first.** Taking exterior pix on the platform before you enter may alert staff to your intentions. Plus, after having snapped so many pix on Platforms 3 and 4, it's probably best to be out of sight for awhile.

Ensure that your **flash is off** before you go inside the café. If you're noticed and asked to stop taking pictures, be Potterly polite. Apologize for causing concern and discontinue interior photography.

Surbiton Station Potter Pic #4

[*Half-Blood Prince* screenshot, enhanced]

[©2009 Tara Bellers]

There are no tables and chairs within the real-life Café Chaud, and the service counter is very different from the one built for the set. But, this is the café that inspired *Half-Blood Prince* set design! You'll want these pix.

Surbiton Station Potter Pic #5

[*Half-Blood Prince* screenshot, enhanced]

Creative Potterites can angle their pix of a *kneeling* Harry Potter stand-in holding a **newspaper** so as to snap photos similar to this screenshot. Unfortunately, this is guaranteed to attract attention. Happily, it's the last interior pic.

Buy Something Before Leaving Café Chaud

Even if it's just a cuppa tea or coffee, you should contribute to their business before romping away. After all, you've had a great time here.

Surbiton Station Potter Pic #6

[*Half-Blood Prince* screenshot, enhanced]

When this exterior Surbiton station screenshot was filmed **on site**, Harry was standing behind the Platform-2-side Café Chaud window closest to the exit.

By saving this café shot for last, members of your party can take turns being the Harry Potter stand-in. Even if you were noticed Sneakoscoping interior pix and asked to stop, café employees likely won't complain about you taking these *exterior* pix.

Surbiton Station Potter Pic #7

[*Half-Blood Prince* screenshot, enhanced]

251

Stand on Platform 2 with your back up against Café Chaud (the more distance, the better) to shoot this wide view of Platform 3. If you have time, wait until a train is stopped at Platform 4 to snap. Shoot Potter Pic #8 from the same position, zooming in on the area where Dumbledore stands.

[©2009 Tara Bellers]

Surbiton Station Potter Pic #8

[*Half-Blood Prince* screenshot, enhanced]

This is the scene that was being filmed when Marc Lechtenfeld took his fan pic (Surbiton Station Potter Pic #2, above).

[©2009 Tara Bellers]

Prior to filming, the silver mesh Telephone box, hanging rubbish bin, and flower boxes were removed from the site. Additionally, filmmakers installed the **bill board** seen behind Dumbledore in the screenshot. Even so, your screenshot recreation pix will be quite recognizable. Again, if you're not in a rush, take turns with others in your party being the Dumbledore stand-in for this shot.

Going to the *HbP* Train Station Café Site

≋ Make Your Way from London's Waterloo Railway Station [WAT] to Surbiton Railway Station [SUR]
http://www.nationalrail.co.uk/

WAT to SUR is commonly a 15 to 23 minute direct trip (no train changes). The average 2011 Return (round trip) train fare is £8 ($13).

From the Leaky Cauldron, *Prisoner of Azkaban* in Borough Market (Site #7): Quick-Quill Trip/Kwikspell Crusade *POA* Day
A 10 minute walk, a 40 minute train/walk/train journey.

⫟ If leaving from the southern Borough Market entrance, walk southeast on **Stoney Street** to the intersection of **Southwark Street** and **Borough High Street**.

If leaving from the northern Borough Market entrance, walk southeast on **Bedale Street** to **Borough High Street**.

A stairway leading down to the **London Bridge Underground Station** lies on Borough High Street, between Stoney Street and Bedale Street. Follow station signs to **London Bridge Railway Station [LBG]**.

⇌ Take a **Southeastern** train towards Charing Cross Rail Station to reach **Waterloo East Railway Station**.

🏃 Follow signs to **Waterloo Railway Station**.

⇌ Take **South West Trains** towards Basingstoke Rail Station to reach Surbiton Railway Station.

From the Wizard Chessmen, British Museum (Site #18): the *SS* Day of the Huffandpuff Expedition, Padfoot Prowl, or Potter Promenade
A walk/tube/walk/train journey lasting approximately 40 minutes.

🏃 Exit from the British Museum's main entrance to **Great Russell Street** and cross to the south side. ♦ Turn right and walk southwest for approximately 3 blocks to **Tottenham Court Road**. ♦ Turn left and walk southeast to **Saint Giles Circus**. Enter the **Tottenham Court Road Tube Station**.

⊖ Take the **Northern Line** towards Kennington or Morden to reach **Waterloo Railway Station**.

⇌ Take **South West Trains** towards Basingstoke, Guildford, or Hampton Court to reach Surbiton Railway Station.

21

HERMIONE'S HOME

Hampstead Garden, London Borough of Barnet

Google Maps UK: 9 Heathgate, Barnet, Greater London NW11 7AR
🚇 **Golders Green Tube Station**
🚌 **H2 Golders Green** Bus
Travelcard Zone 3

Central London to Side-Along One-Way Travel Time: 68 minutes

Operation Hours and Entry Fee: None. This is a private Muggle Neighborhood.

Visit Time: Schedule 30 minutes on site to take a few Potter Pix. (If you have a taxi waiting, 15 minutes should be plenty.)

ೲ

In Chapter Six of *Deathly Hallows*, the trio were gathered at the Weasley's home when Hermione described how she'd used an **Obliviate Charm** to replace her parents' memories, giving them false names and causing them to move to Australia so that they would be out of danger while she searched for Horcruxes with Harry and Ron. Hermione's only regret was that she'd also had to erase *herself* from their memories.

> "Wendell and Monica Williams don't know that they've got a daughter, you see."

Filmmakers elected to actually show Hermione's act. At the beginning of *Deathly Hallows Part One*, Hermione is seen obliviating her parents' memories, and tearfully watching as her image magically faded from every photo in their home. Afterwards, Hermione leaves her home, turns left at the end of the neighbor's driveway, and walks down the street toward a spire-topped building in the distance.

Plenty of paparazzi were present on July 18th, 2009, when exterior *DHp1* Hermione's Home scenes were shot on location. Oddly enough, they all kept mum about the address where filming took place. In fact, they offered *misleading* location information, some reporting that these scenes were shot as Emma Watson "made her way out of Golders Hill Park in North London."

Thanks to **Tara Bellers'** tenacity, we kept searching until finally finding the true film site. *DHp1* scenes of Hermione leaving her home were shot outside **#9 Heathgate**, a modest home in the **Hampstead Gardens** suburb of the northern London **Borough of Barnet**—a location quite a bit north of Golders Hill Park. Footage of Hermione walking away from her home (toward the spire of **Saint Jude's church**) was also shot on Heathgate (street).

Because **no set pieces** were constructed for filming these exterior scenes, everything seen in the screenshots below is exactly the way this location looks in real-life.

Site Rating

Hermione's Home is Assigned a Might-be-Fun Rating Because:
- It may take **2 to 2.5 hours** to visit this site, snap your pix, and return to London.

- Only *two* screenshot reproduction pix are available here. However, in real-life they will look almost exactly as they did on screen.

Many Potterites consider this time expenditure excessive in relationship to what little can be photographed.

Number 9 Heathgate is a Private Muggle Neighborhood

Please remember the Potterite Prime Directive:

To *POLITELY* Go Where Potterites Need to Go
— without **PERTURBING** anybody —
So That Other Potterites Can *Continue* to
ENJOY GOING THERE!

Your behavior while visiting Hermione's Home will significantly affect how Potterites are greeted here long after you're gone. Please be as quiet and unobtrusive as Potterly possible.

Prime Directive Pointers:

- Visit on a **weekday**, during hours when indigenous Muggles are likely to be at work.
- Invoke the **Quietus Spell**, or activate a **Silencio Charm**, while visiting.
- **Stay *OFF* Muggle property.** Keep to the street while taking your Potter Pix.
- Do not approach, nor take any *photos* of, indigenous Muggles who might be out and about.
- **Get IN … Get your Potter Pix … Get OUT!**

Hermione's Home Potter Pic #1

[*Deathly Hallows Part 1* screenshot (enhanced)]

The screenshot above is only offered to ensure that you correctly identify the house that is **Hermione's Home**. Because you're being **Potterly Polite** and *not* walking up to the door of this Muggle residence, snap reproduction pix similar to the screenshot below.

[*Deathly Hallows Part 1* screenshot (enhanced)]

In order to reproduce a *combination* of these two screenshots, be sure to capture all of Hermione's Home and the neighbor's driveway when taking pix of your Hermione stand-in walking into the street **from the *end* of the driveway next door to her home.**

Hermione's Home Potter Pic #2

[*Deathly Hallows Part 1* screenshot (enhanced)]

Happily, Heathgate has very little traffic. You'll have no problem safely reproducing this screenshot while standing in the middle of the road. Unfortunately, in July of 2011, Tara discovered that there are commonly several cars parked here, even on weekdays when indigenous Muggles are away at work. Filmmakers obviously cleared the street prior to filming.

[©2011 Tara Bellers]

Hermione's Home—Site 21

Nearby Non-Potter Place
Saint Jude's Church
http://www.stjudeonthehill.com/

Saint Jude-On-The-Hill (Saint Jude's) is the Parish Church of Hampstead Garden Suburb. It is the *back* of Saint Jude's church and spire that is seen in *DHp1*. In addition to holding Sunday services, Saint Jude's is regularly used on weekdays for recordings, concerts, and miscellaneous cultural events. Potterites who enjoy visiting historically interesting churches (and can afford to spend an hour or more at the Hermione's Home site) should contact Saint Jude's ahead of time to determine whether or not you can obtain access to the church on the date you plan to visit.

Going to Hermione's Home
Part One: A Tube Journey from Central London to Golders Green

⊖ Consult **Transport For London** to make your way from any Central London lodgings to **Golders Green Tube Station**.
http://www.tfl.gov.uk/

⊖ Golders Green is on the **Edgware** branch of the **Northern Line**, between Brent Cross and Hampstead stations. From King's Cross/Saint Pancras Tube Station, Golders Green is a 22 minute trip with one train change. From other points in Central London, the trip may take up to 50 minutes.

Both an **Oyster** card and the **London Travelcard** (or London Pass w/Travel) should cover your fare from anywhere in Central London to Golders Green Tube Station.

Part Two: Journey from Golders Green Tube Station to Hermione's Home

There are three options, with travel time ranging from 7 minutes to 17 minutes, one-way.

Take a Taxi to Hermione's Home

TAXI If you're pressed for time or have plenty of pounds, there is a taxi rank just outside Golders Green Tube Station on **North End Road**. Your destination is **Number 9 Heathgate, NW11 7AR**. Consider asking the Taxi to wait for you while you snap your two Hermione's Home Potter Pix. Otherwise, you'll have to walk back to Golders Green Tube Station.

259

Take a Bus to Hermione's Home
A 5 to 7 minute one-way journey.

Exit Golders Green Tube Station and head right to reach **North End Road**. ◆ Turn right and you'll see the "former trolleybus turning circle" off of **Finchley Road**. Find the **H2 Golders Green** bus stop.

🚌 The H2 Golders Green bus runs every 12 minutes during the day from the former trolleybus turning circle to a stop on Meadway, between Linnell Close and Heathgate.

The **H3 Golders Green** bus and the **H1 Henrietta Barnett School** bus do *not* go to the Meadway's Linnell Close / Heathgate stop. Do not board them.

When boarding the H2 Golders Green bus, ask to get off at the Heathgate stop near Saint Jude's. When disembarking, ask the driver where you should go to get a bus *back* to Golders Green Tube Station.

According to Saint Jude's website:

> "The [H2 busses] run on the **'hail and ride'** system, so if you set off walking you will not find any stops—just wave at the driver."

Walk to Hermione's Home
A 17 minute walk.

🚶 Exit Golders Green Tube Station and head right to walk to **North End Road**. ◆ Turn right and walk north on **Finchley Road**, continuing until you've passed Corringham Road and reach **Hoop Lane** (approximately 4 blocks). ◆ Turn right and walk northeast for approximately 3 blocks, until you've passed Hoop Lane Cemetery (on your left) and reach the **Meadway Gate** roundabout. ◆ Cross to the roundabout's center island and make your way to the opposite side, where you'll reach **Meadway**. ◆ Resume walking northeast for another 200 yards, passing Linnell Close, until you reach **Heathgate**. ◆ Turn right and walk southeast, watching on your right for #9 Heathgate.

Leaving from Hermione's Home
Padfoot Prowl or Potter Promenade Zoo Day Itineraries
Return to **Golders Green Tube Station**.

⊖ Take the **Northern Line** towards Kennington or Morden to reach **Camden Town Tube Station**.

The tube journey between Golders Green and Camden Town is 11 minutes.

🚶 🚌 **TAXI** Follow directions to **Little Whinging Zoo** in Site #9.

22

Knight Bus
Pickup Playground

Abbots Langley, Hertfordshire

Google Maps UK: Gadeside Roundabout, Leavesden, Hertfordshire

[The address above identifies a point just south of the **roundabout** nearest this site, and the entrance to the **Warner Bros. Studio Tour (Site #27).**]

Please Note: Although officially titled, *Warner Brothers Studio Tour—the Making of Harry Potter*, we prefer to call this attraction the **Harry Potter WB Studio Tour**, abbreviated **HPST.**

🚊 London's Euston Railway Station [**EUS**]
🚊 Watford Junction Railway Station [**WFJ**]

Travelcard Zone: Site #22 is located *outside* the London Travelcard Zones, but Oyster cards are accepted at EUS and WFJ.

Central London to Side-Along One-Way Travel Time: 37 to 45 minutes

🚌 A special Shuttle Bus runs between WFJ and the HPST every 20 minutes.

TAXI Taxis are available at WFJ.

Operation Hours or **Entry Fee:** None. This is a private Muggle Neighborhood.

Visit Time: See the **Warner Bros. Studio Tour (Site #27)**, and the site rating information below.

Potter Props: Potterites who drive to the HPST should consider bringing an **empty roll-along suitcase** to the Knight Bus Pickup Playground—trunk-sized, if possible.

Site Rating Explanation

👓 The Knight Bus Pickup Playground Earns a Great Site Rating:
- When combined with a visit to the Harry Potter WB Studio Tour via public transportation or rental car.

In **Specialis Revelio London Part Two,** you'll find a link to the **Harry Potter Warner Bros. Studio Tour Itinerary Planning Supplementum.** Directions for including a Knight Bus Pickup Playground visit on your HPST day are provided there.

👓 If Not Visited During Your HPST Day Itinerary, the Knight Bus Pickup Playground Earns a SKIP-IT Rating Because:
- Including round-trip travel time, at least **2 hours and 10 minutes** must be scheduled for this trip.

- Although there are several screenshot reproduction opportunities in this area, only one of them will look exactly like what was seen on screen.

Many Potterites consider this time expenditure excessive in relationship to what little can be photographed.

Please Note: The Knight Bus Pickup Playground is **not** included on any of the *Harry Potter Places* Suggested London Itineraries.

The Knight Bus Pickup Playground Film Sites

After inflating **Aunt Marge** in *Prisoner of Azkaban*, Harry ran away from the Dursley's home, dragging his trunk behind him. After only a few blocks, Harry realized he had no place to go, and collapsed on the curb next to a playground. Much to his surprise, **The Knight Bus** magically arrived to pick him up.

These *POA* scenes were filmed on two streets in a Muggle Neighborhood located just east of the **southern Aerodrome Way roundabout** in Abbots Langley, Hertfordshire. At the time of filming (2003), this neighborhood was across from the **Leavesden Studios back lot fence.** Today, the southern Aerodrome Way roundabout is where the **Harry Potter WB Studio Tour entrance** is located.

[©2011 Tara Bellers—the HPST under construction in July of 2011.]

Please Note: For some unknown reason, **Google Maps UK** images identify the road north of this roundabout as **Airfield Way**. According to real-life road signs, it is **Aerodrome Way**.

[©2011 Tara Bellers]

The *POA* **Playground Set** was built in an open space just east of the roundabout, on the north side of **Dowding Way**.

[©2009 Tara Bellers]

A few trunk-dragging scenes were also filmed on Dowding Way. Earlier trunk-dragging scenes were filmed on another street, found about 3 blocks further east in this neighborhood.

As with many other Harry Potter film sites, screenshots associated with this location are all **night** scenes. It's rarely convenient (or *safe*) for Potterites to travel to Harry Potter locations at night. Happily, pix taken here during the daytime are perfectly wonderful.

The Playground Is in a Private Muggle Neighborhood

Please remember the Potterite Prime Directive:

To **POLITELY** Go Where Potterites Need to Go
— without **PERTURBING** anybody —
So That Other Potterites Can *Continue* to
ENJOY GOING THERE!

Your behavior will significantly affect how visiting Potterites are greeted here long after you're gone. Please be as quiet and unobtrusive as Potterly possible—especially since, beginning in 2012, these Muggles will daily have to deal with increased area traffic associated with the Harry Potter WB Studio Tour.

Prime Directive Pointers:

• Visit on a **weekday**, during hours when indigenous Muggles are likely to be at work.

• Invoke the **Quietus Spell**, or activate a **Silencio Charm**, while visiting.

• Stay *OFF* **Muggle property.** Keep to the street while taking your Potter Pix.

• Do not approach, nor take any *photos* of, indigenous Muggles who might be out and about.

• Get IN ... Get your Potter Pix ... Get OUT!

Follow Harry's Footsteps to Get the Best Playground Pix

When you arrive at the southern Aerodrome Way roundabout, walk east on Dowding Way *past* the playground set clearing to the next street, **Royce Grove**. ♦ Turn left and walk north on Royce Grove past **Whittle Close** (on your right), until you reach **Griffon Way** (also on you right). ♦ Perform an *about-face* while still on Royce Grove, and look back the way you came. Here is where you should start snapping your KBPP Potter Pix.

Knight Bus Pickup Playground Pic #1

[*Prisoner of Azkaban* screenshot (enhanced)]

The screenshot above shows Harry dragging his trunk south on Royce Grove from Griffon Way. The little DOT seen in the sky above him is **inflated Aunt Marge**, wafting in the wind. Consider Photoshopping a similar dot into your screenshot recreation pic.

[©2009 Tara Bellers]

Knight Bus Pickup Playground Pic #2

[*Prisoner of Azkaban* screenshot (enhanced)]

265

Walk back down Royce Grove to Dowding Way and cross to the south side. ♦ Turn right and walk west, passing by a wooden fence that extends east from a brick building. ♦ When you reach the wrought iron fence on the west end of that building, stop and look across the street. The brick garage and fence behind Harry in KBPP Pic #2 is on the north side of Dowding Way.

[©2009 Tara Bellers]

Although the illuminated signs mounted on this garage for filming do not exist in real-life, you can take great screenshot recreation pix here—especially if your Harry-stand-in is dragging **an empty roll-along suitcase** behind her/him.

For the remaining KBPP pix, snap your photos while **standing in the street**. Thus, each person in your party should take a turn acting as a **Traffic Scout**. If you're a duo or alone, *please* be careful!

Please Note: We are *not* advising you to risk getting run over while snapping pix on Dowding Way. We hereby disclaim responsibility for any liability, loss or risk, resulting directly or indirectly from any person or persons who independently elect(s) to remain in the street long enough to get run over by oncoming motorists.

Knight Bus Pickup Playground Pic #3

[*Prisoner of Azkaban* screenshot (enhanced)]

After snapping your #2 KBPP Pix, step *into* Dowding Way and turn left to face west and shoot #3 KBPP Pix. Be sure to include the clearing that once contained the playground set in the right side of your camera frame (something Tara unfortunately forgot to do).

[©2009 Tara Bellers]

Knight Bus Pickup Playground Pic #4

[*Prisoner of Azkaban* screenshot (enhanced)]

Next, cross to the gutter on the north side of Dowding Way, turn left and walk just a few steps toward the roundabout. To best recreate KBPP screenshot #4, get as low to the ground as possible.

[©2009 Tara Bellers]

Knight Bus Pickup Playground Pic #5

[*Prisoner of Azkaban* screenshot (enhanced)]

There is no lamp post in the middle of the clearing that once contained the KBPP set. Happily, there is a **speed zone sign post** here. Go to that sign post. Carefully back into the street a few feet and get as low to the ground as possible to snap your KBPP #5 screenshot recreation pix.

[©2009 Tara Bellers]

Knight Bus Pickup Playground Pic #6

[*Prisoner of Azkaban* screenshot (enhanced)]

While out in the middle of Dowding Way, turn right to face east and shoot your #6 KBPP Pix. Do your best to have most of *both* doors of the blonde-brick garage inside your camera frame on the **left**, and *both* of the sphere-topped brick gate supports inside your camera frame on the **right**.

[©2009 Tara Bellers]

Since the Knight Bus won't be in your picture, consider taking turns snapping pix of everyone else in your party standing at the point where the Knight Bus is seen in the screenshot, facing the camera and waving. If a seemingly-friendly Muggle happens to be passing by, politely ask if she/he would take a few **group pix** for you.

Knight Bus Pickup Playground Pic #7

[*Prisoner of Azkaban* screenshot (enhanced)]

For your final KBPP pix, move back to the northern Dowding Way sidewalk and slide slightly to the right (east) of the speed zone sign post. From there you can back up into the street and snap bus-less recreation shots of KBPP Pic #7. Line up the barn-shaped building behind and slightly to the left, of your Harry Potter and Stan Shunpike stand-ins—or the sign post.

[©2009 Tara Bellers]

Nearby Potter Places

😎 **Warner Bros. Studios Tour, Leavesden (Site #27):** If you haven't already, read that entry!

Going to the Knight Bus Pickup Playground Site

See Site #27 Including the Knight Bus Pickup Playground When Visiting the HPST

The directions below are provided for Potterites divinely inspired to visit the Knight Bus Pickup Playground *separately* from visiting the HPST.

☮ Consult **Transport For London** to make your way from any point in Central London to **Euston Railway Station** [EUS], and then to **Watford Junction Railway Station** [WFJ].
http://www.tfl.gov.uk/

🚆 The National Rail website can also be used.
http://www.nationalrail.co.uk/

WFJ is located *outside* the London Travelcard Zones. However, Oyster cards are accepted at EUS and WFJ.
  EUS to WFJ is a 20 minute direct trip (no train changes).
  The 2011 Return (round trip) train fare between EUS and WFJ ranges from £14 ($22) if departing before 9 am, to £9.50 ($15) if departing after 9 am.

📺 The WB Studio Tour Shuttle Bus

Warner Bros. has partnered with a company that will operate a special Shuttle Bus between the WFJ and the HPST, leaving at 20 minute intervals throughout the day, and requiring approximately 15 minutes of one-way travel time.

At this writing (December, 2011), it is unknown whether or not the WB Studio Shuttle Bus will be available to travelers *without* a ticket to the HPST. The shuttle's fee and daily operational hours are also unknown.

When performing your **Pre-Trip Transport Times Check** two weeks before your holiday, visit the Warner Bros. Studio Tour website to obtain more information about the WB Shuttle Bus and its schedule.
http://www.wbstudiotour.co.uk/en/your-visit/getting-here

If use of the WB Studio Shuttle Bus is available to travelers *without* a ticket to the HPST: Board the Shuttle Bus at WFJ and ride to the HPST compound. ♦ Exit the HPST compound and walk across the **Gadeside Roundabout** to **Dowding Way**. From there, follow our **Knight Bus Pickup Playground** pix directions. ♦ When finished, return to the HPST compound to catch the next return shuttle bus.

🚕 Taxis are available at WFJ

Potterites with limited time or plenty of pounds can take a Taxi to the Gadeside Roundabout.

🚶📺🚶 From WFJ to the Knight Bus Pickup Playground
A 17 minute Walk/Bus/Walk journey.

🚶 When you arrive at Watford Junction Rail Station, ask for directions to Bus 10's **Woodside-Holywell Estate Stop #3**: a 1 minute walk.

📺 Ride Bus 10 to the **Woodside, Ashfields Stop**: a 9 minute trip.

When disembarking, ask where to catch the Bus 10 that will *return you* to the railway station. It may be across the street.

🚶 Walk west to Aerodrome Way. ♦ Turn right and walk north to the next roundabout—the **southern Aerodrome Way roundabout** at the HPST entrance: a 3 minute walk. From there, follow our **Knight Bus Pickup Playground** pix directions.

23

KNIGHT BUS
STREETS

Palmers Green, London Borough of Enfield
http://en.wikipedia.org/wiki/Palmers_Green

Google Maps UK: 370 Green Lanes, London, N13 5PE

[See our explanation of these coordinates below.]

🚇 Palmers Green Railway Station [PAL]

Travelcard Zone 4

Central London to Side-Along One-Way Travel Time: 55 minutes

Operation Hours or **Entry Fee:** None. This site includes a street lined with commercial venues and a private Muggle neighborhood.

Visit Time: Schedule at least 30 minutes here to snap your Potter Pix. Interesting non-Potter evening entertainment offerings are described below.

☙

In *Prisoner of Azkaban*, the Knight Bus delivered Harry to the Leaky Cauldron's **Charing Cross Road** Muggle entrance. Many scenes showing the Knight Bus careening down streets while enroute to the Leaky Cauldron *were* filmed on Charing Cross Road. Unfortunately, not a single Charing Cross Road building can be recognized during those rapid and blurry *POA* scenes. In fact, throughout all of the *POA* Knight Bus street-careening footage, only one building can be recognized with certainty—the **Chester Stevens Estate Agents** office building.

The Chester Stevens building and street exist exactly as they appear on screen, but they're nowhere near Charing Cross Road. The Chester Stevens building is on the northeast corner of **Green Lanes** and **Park Avenue** in **Palmers Green**, an intersection found within the northern **London Borough**

of Enfield. Additionally, film footage of the Knight Bus almost running into an elderly woman slowly crossing the street with her walker was shot on Park Avenue, just around the corner from the Chester Stevens building.

Our **Going to the Knight Bus Streets in Palmers Green** directions (below) will guide you to the first photo vantage point: across the street from the Chester Stevens building.

Knight Bus Streets Potter Pic #1

[Prisoner of Azkaban screenshot (enhanced)]

KBS Potter Pic #1 is of the Knight Bus traveling south on Green Lanes, just before reaching the Chester Stevens building at Park Avenue.

[©2009 Tara Bellers]

Knight Bus Streets Potter Pic #2

[*Prisoner of Azkaban* screenshot (enhanced)]

Potter Pic #2 is of the Knight Bus turning left from Green Lanes, to travel *east* on Park Avenue.

[©2009 Tara Bellers]

After the Knight Bus made this turn, **movie magic** caused the **direction of the travel to *flip***. In the scenes that followed, the Knight Bus was traveling *west* on Park Avenue, *toward* the Chester Stevens building.

When you walk down Park Avenue from Green Lanes you'll be entering a relatively private Muggle neighborhood.

Please remember the Potterite Prime Directive:

To **POLITELY** Go Where Potterites Need to Go
— without **PERTURBING** anybody —
So That Other Potterites Can *Continue* to
ENJOY GOING THERE!

Be as quiet and unobtrusive as Potterly possible while taking pix along Park Avenue.

To reach a good point for taking KBS Potter Pic #3, cross Green Lanes and walk east on Park Avenue until you see the **Maple Durham Court** apartment building on your right. Perform an about-face, and you'll be in position.

Knight Bus Streets Potter Pic #3

[*Prisoner of Azkaban* screenshot (enhanced)]

In the screenshot above (and Tara's pic below), the Chester Stevens building is seen at the end of Park Avenue, on the right.

[©2009 Tara Bellers]

Discerning eyes might notice that neither the buildings seen on the *left* side of screenshot #3, nor the building at the street's *end* (across the street from the Chester Stevens building), look the same as those seen in the real-life location pic: **movie magic** again.

Although the lady-with-walker scenes were filmed on Park Avenue, only the **north** side of Park Avenue (the buildings seen at the *right* of screenshot #3 and Tara's pic above) appeared in the film.

To snap KBS screenshot #4, walk *almost* all the way back to the Chester Stevens building, watching on your *left* for the first **alley** before reaching Green Lanes—an alley that extends **south** from Park Avenue (opposite of the Chester Stevens building side). At the mouth of this alley, turn about so that you're facing east (away from Green Lanes), **check for traffic** and step into Park Avenue.

Knight Bus Streets Potter Pic #4

[*Prisoner of Azkaban* screenshot (enhanced)]

Yes. This shot could have been taken when you first walked east on Park Avenue from Green Lanes. But, it's almost always best to shoot screenshot reproduction pix in the order they appeared on film.

[©2009 Tara Bellers]

In screenshot #4, the buildings on the right side were CGI altered. The buildings on the left side look exactly as they do in real-life.

For the last KBS screenshot pix (screenshot #5), walk *into* the alley you stopped at—the alley that extends **south** from Park Avenue, opposite of the Chester Stevens building side—turn around and face Park Avenue. KBS screenshot #5 was filmed from within this alley.

Knight Bus Streets Potter Pic #5

[*Prisoner of Azkaban* screenshot (enhanced)]

The sign post and brick fence seen above at left are set pieces. The real-life dumpsters found on the right were removed for filming. The real-life brick fence behind the dumpsters looks almost exactly like the set piece brick fence built for the opposite side. CGI alteration of the building seen on the left, behind the bus, was performed.

[©2009 Tara Bellers]

Google Maps UK Coordinates Conundrum

Located on the *northeast* corner of Green Lanes and Park Avenue, the Chester Stevens building address is **372 Green Lanes, Palmers Green, London, N13 5XQ**. For some unknown reason, no version of this address identifies the correct building when using **Google** or **bing** maps.

However, the **Flowerzone** store is located on the *southeast* corner of Green Lanes and Park Avenue. Its address **does** identify the correct corner when using **Google** or **bing** maps. That's why we suggest using the Flowerzone's address for your Chester Stevens **Google, bing**, or **SatNav/GPS** coordinates: **370 Green Lanes, London, N13 5PE**.

Nearby Non-Potter Places

The Waiting Rooms Café
http://waitingroomscafe.co.uk/

Located within **Palmers Green Rail Station**, this café has a liquor license and offers live music on Friday and Saturday nights—sometimes Wednesday nights.

"Open every day from 9am to 4pm, with evening events as scheduled."

[©2009 Tara Bellers]

The Fox
http://www.thefoxpalmersgreen.com/

The Fox is a friendly pub housed in a gorgeous old hotel that sprawls across the southwest curve of the Fox Lane and Green Lanes roundabout (within sight of the Chester Stevens building). In addition to the standard English Pub Fare and Vegetarian food offered everyday, weekday lunches include a Thai menu. And, on Sunday afternoons you can enjoy a **Traditional English Carvery** here: a buffet where freshly-cooked meat is sliced to order.

The Fox has live music on Thursday, Saturday, and Sunday nights.

On at least two Friday nights each month, the Fox hosts **The Electric Mouse Comedy Club**.

Please Note: Visiting the Knight Bus Streets in Palmers Green is best scheduled in the early evening, at the end of any Potter itinerary day. Thus, we highly recommend that you consult the websites of these two non-Potter places to determine whether or not you can enjoy dinner and live music or comedy before returning to your London lodgings.

Going to the Knight Bus Streets in Palmers Green

Consult the Transport for London Website
http://www.tfl.gov.uk/

Palmers Green Railway Station [PAL] can be reached from any Central London Underground Station. Once there, follow the directions below for walking to the first Knight Bus Streets Screenshot Vantage Point.

From the Fly-By Bridges & Buildings (Site #4) Tour End: Padfoot Prowl or Potter Promenade Zoo Day

🚶☉☉🚆 A 15 minute walk, two tube trips (15 minutes), a 15 minute train trip.

🚶 After crossing over Lambeth Bridge, follow our end-of-tour option (2): Get off at the next bus stop and follow Site #4 directions for walking to **Westminster Underground Station.**

☉ Take the **Jubilee Line** towards Stanmore, Wembley Park, or Willesden Green, to reach **Green Park Tube Station.**

☉ Take the **Victoria Line** towards Seven Sisters or Walthamstow Central to reach **Highbury & Islington Rail Station** [HHY].

🚆 Take **First Capital Connect** towards Gordon Hill, Hertford North, or Stevenage, to reach **Palmers Green Railway Station.**

Walk to the First Knight Bus Streets Screenshot Vantage Point from PAL

A 10 minute walk.

🚶 Exit the PAL station and turn left to walk southeast on the east side of **Alderman's Hill.** ◆ After passing Devonshire Road, keep left as the street curves to meet **Green Lanes.** ◆ Turn left and walk northeast on Green Lanes. When you reach the **Fox Lane roundabout**, the **Chester Stevens building** and **Park Avenue** will be ahead of you, on the right. ◆ Cross Fox Lane, staying on the west side of Green Lanes, to reach the point where you can take **Knight Bus Streets Potter Pix #1 and 2.** ◆ Follow **Knight Bus Streets Potter Pix** directions (above) for reaching the places where you can snap **Park Avenue** pix.

Number 4 Privet Drive

Number 12 Picket Post Close, Martin's Heron
http://harrypotter.wikia.com/wiki/4_Privet_Drive

Google Maps UK: 12 Picket Post Close, Bracknell, Berkshire, RG12 9FG

🚕 **SatNav/GPS:** Whitton Road, Bracknell RG12 9TZ (These coordinates are explained below.)

🚄 Martins Heron Railway Station [MAO]

Martins Heron is outside the London Travelcard Zones

London Station to Side-Along One-Way Travel Time: 1 to 1.5 hours

Operation Hours or **Entry Fee:** None. This is a private Muggle Neighborhood.

Visit Time: If you arrive by train, spend only 25 minutes snapping your Potter Pix before hustling back to catch a return train. If you drive there (while **Snitch-Seeking in Southern England and Wales**), spend as much time as you'd like.

When location Scouts for *Harry Potter and the Sorcerer's Stone* stumbled upon the **Picket Post Close** neighborhood, they immediately recognized that this location was perfect for filming the **Dursleys' #4 Privet Drive neighborhood**.

[*COS* Ultimate Edition extras screenshot segment (enhanced)]

In 2000, the owners of **#12 Picket Post Close**, along with all their neighbors, granted permission for exterior *Sorcerer's Stone* Dursley home scenes to be filmed here. According to the *Harry Potter Film Wizardry* book, however, production ran longer than originally scheduled. After that, "the neighborhood requested too much money to make the location available again for *Chamber of Secrets*."

Thus, in 2001, Warner Brothers built an almost exact replica of the Picket Post Close neighborhood on the **Leavesden Studios' backlot**. All Privet Drive exterior scenes have been shot on this set since *Sorcerer's Stone*.

[*SS* Ultimate Edition extras screenshot (enhanced)]

Beginning in 2012, Potterites who visit the Harry Potter **Warner Bros. Studio Tour (Site #27)** will be able to walk around on this set! Although this opportunity may diminish traffic to the real-life location, many Potterites will still want to visit Picket Post Close.

The Muggles who owned #12 Picket Post Close during *Sorcerer's Stone* filming sold the home within a few years. It is unclear whether the next owners were advised of the location's popularity prior to the purchase. What is clear, is that they do not want to be troubled by Potterites. In fact, they asked us not to mention their home's location in *Harry Potter Places*.

> "Only the outside of the house was used in the film and the inside looks nothing like the house in the movie. As we did not own the property at the time of filming we do not have any film related memorabilia, etc. and have no plans to allow the general public into our house. … I'm sure that you understand that we wish to maintain our privacy and the security of our property as much as possible."

Although we would like to accommodate their request, we cannot disregard the fact that #12 Picket Post Close is forever identified on the Internet as the address where #4 Privet Drive scenes were filmed. What we can do, is remind all Potterites to please remember the **Potterite Prime Directive:**

To *POLITELY* Go Where Potterites Need to Go — without **PERTURBING** anybody — So That Other Potterites Can *Continue* to ENJOY GOING THERE!

Number 12 Picket Post Close is a Private Muggle Neighborhood. Your behavior while visiting will significantly affect how Potterites are greeted here long after you're gone. Please be as unobtrusive as Potterly possible.

Prime Directive Pointers:

• **Do not drive to Picket Post Close.** (Nearby parking information is provided below.)

• Visit on a **weekday**, during hours when indigenous Muggles are likely to be at work.

• Invoke the **Quietus Spell**, or activate a **Silencio Charm**, while visiting.

• Stay *OFF* **Muggle property.** Keep to the street while taking your Potter Pix.

• Do not approach, nor take any *photos* of, indigenous Muggles who might be out and about.

• **Get IN … Get your Potter Pix … Get OUT!**

Potter pic opportunities begin when reaching the **Setley Way** corner of Picket Post Close.

Privet Drive Potter Pic #1

[©2009 Tara Bellers] [*Sorcerer's Stone* screenshot segment (enhanced)]

Use Photoshop to replace "Picket Post Close" with "Privet Drive."

Privet Drive Potter Pic #2

[*Sorcerer's Stone* screenshot (enhanced)]

The only **set pieces** added to #12 Picket Post Close when filming *SS* Privet Drive scenes were a couple of bird baths, black property boundary posts with chains between them, and the automobile **license plates**.

[©2008 C.D. Miller]

Please Note: If you're going to post your Picket Post Close Potter Pix anywhere on the Internet (such as in Photobuckets or Flickr accounts, or on any Blog), be sure that you **obscure** all real-life Muggle license plates seen in your photos before posting them.

[©2009 Tara Bellers]

Privet Drive Potter Pix #3 and #4

[*Order of the Phoenix* screenshots (enhanced) above and below]

287

If an indigenous Muggle is out and about—and doesn't appear bothered by your pic taking—politely ask if she/he would take a group photo for you.

Privet Drive Potter Pic #5

[*DHp1* promotional screenshot (enhanced)]

Invading Muggle private property by standing on #12's doorstep with your arm outstretched is right out. However, if you stand on the street between the door and your photographer, you can snap a shot that will look similar.

Privet Drive Potter Pic #6

In Special Features footage of the Dursleys preparing to evacuate Privet Drive, the buildings *across the street* from the house are seen in the background.

The biggest difference between the location and the set is that both sides of the Privet Drive set are lined with homes exactly like the Dursley's. In real-life, the houses across the street look quite different.

[*Deathly Hallows Part One* Special Features screenshot (enhanced)]

However, because the set's opposite side is a repeat of the real-life #12 Picket Post Close side of the street, you can snap a similar shot with the Dursley's home in the background. You simply can't stand on a neighbor's doorstep to shoot it.

[©2009 Tara Bellers]

Going to #12 Picket Post Close (#4 Privet Drive)

⊖⇌ Travel via Public Transportation from London

Martins Heron Rail Station [MAO] can be reached from any London Railway station. However, it is cheaper to use the Underground system to reach **Waterloo Rail Station [WAT]** from your London departure point, and purchase a return railway ticket to MAO from there.

For instance, the 2011 MAO return fare from Paddington Railway Station is £18.50 ($29), while the MAO return fare from WAT is £12.60 ($20). It won't cost you $9 to reach WAT via the tube from a London location.

Consult the **Transport for London** website to obtain directions from your departure point to WAT.
http://www.tfl.gov.uk/

You can pre-purchase your ticket on the **National Rail** website.
http://www.nationalrail.co.uk/

Potterites who wish to depart from the Railway station nearest to your London departure point should consult the National Rail website.

If following *Harry Potter Places* Suggested London Itineraries, adjust your departure time so that you arrive MAO no later than 9:20am (Kwikspell Crusade or Huffandpuff Expedition *SS* day), or 10:20am (Padfoot Prowl or Potter Promenade *SS* day).

From any Central London location, the one-way journey to Martins Heron ranges between 1 and 1.5 hours, depending on the time of day.

🚶 Walk to Picket Post Close from Martins Heron Railway Station
A 5 minute walk.

🚶 Walk north to **Whitton Road** and cross to the north side. ♦ Turn right and walk east. ♦ Keep left at the roundabout and walk northeast on **Setley Way**. ♦ The first right is **Picket Post Close**, and the site of your first Privet Drive Potter Pic.

🚗 Drive to Martins Heron

Please Note: Do NOT drive to the Dursley's Home! There are no public parking spaces on *any* of the streets in or around Picket Post Close, and residents become upset when strangers park in front of their property. Instead, drive to the **Tesco Store** parking lot adjacent to the Martins Heron Railway Station.

SatNav/GPS: Whitton Road, Bracknell RG12 9TZ
Park in the northeastern area of the Tesco parking lot. Parking here is free. However, if you stay over 3 hours, you will be ticketed (cameras clock your entry time). Happily, there is no reason for any Potterite to park here longer than an hour or so—max.

After parking, go inside the Tesco Store and buy a candy bar or something. (Besides wanting the cameras to catch you actually using the store, it's polite to actually use the store.) When you exit the store, head north (right) to Whitton Road, and follow the walking directions above.

25

PROFESSOR
FLITWICK'S CLASSROOM

Harrow School's Fourth Form Room

http://www.harrowschool.org.uk/
http://en.wikipedia.org/wiki/Harrow_School

Google Maps UK: 34 High Street, Harrow on the Hill, Middlesex, HA1 3HL (This is the Harrow School Hill Shop address.)

Harrow-on-the-Hill Underground or Railway Station [HOH]

Bus 258

Travelcard Zone 5

London Station to Side-Along One-Way Travel Time: Approximately 30 minutes

Operation Hours, Entry Fee, and Visit Time: Conundrum explained below.

[©2011 Google, Street View image segment (enhanced)]

Harrow School is a private school for boys, ages 13 to 18, which has been operating in this area since 1243. The first building specifically erected for Harrow was completed in 1615 and was called the **School House**. Between 1818 and 1820, a *duplicate* of the School House was constructed beside it, with a structure built to connect the two houses into one building: the **Old Schools Building**.

[©2008 C.D. Miller]

Located within the original School House (the Old Schools Building's west wing), the **Fourth Form Room** is considered the best preserved 17th century classroom in Britain. Professor Flitwick's Charms Class **Wingardium Leviosa** lesson was filmed here for *Harry Potter and the Sorcerer's Stone*.

Site Rating

Professor Flitwick's Classroom is Assigned a Might-be-Fun Rating Because:

• The Fourth Form Room door is padlocked. Access is only granted during a guided Harrow School Tour.

• The most frequently offered Harrow School tours are extremely expensive, unless you're traveling with a **group of 5 to 9 people**.

• The less expensive Harrow School Open Tours (tours that can be enjoyed by individuals) are offered only **three times a year**. You'd have to schedule your holiday around one of those dates to inexpensively visit Professor Flitwick classroom.

Harrow School Tours

A **Standard Harrow School Guided Tour** is offered once in the morning and once in the afternoon on almost every weekday during each term, but costs a whopping £70 ($108) for a tour group of 1 to 9 people. For 10 or more tourists, an additional £7 ($11) is charged per extra person. Lasting about 90 minutes, the tour begins between 10 and 11:30am, or between 2 and 4:00pm. These tours have become more popular over the past few years, and must be **pre-booked** *months* **in advance.**
http://www.harrowschoolenterprises.com/html/tours/information/

If your Harry Potter UK holiday dates are flexible, email tours@harrowschool. org.uk and ask to be notified of the upcoming Harrow School **Open Tour** dates. Open Tours are available only once each term:
- Spring Term, January to March.
- Summer Term, April to July.
- Autumn Term, September to December.

Open Tours are far less expensive and pre-booking is not required (though it sure wouldn't hurt to do so). Usually offered on a Saturday afternoon, the fee to join a 90 minute Open Tour is £5 ($8) for an adult, £4 ($6) for Students or Pensioners (Seniors). Children accompanied by an adult are allowed to tour for free.

All tours of Harrow School are coordinated by the folks who run the **Harrow School Hill Shop**. Mr. John Lee, Christine Zuchelkowski, and Jill Thomas are **Friends of Potterites**, and will be happy to assist you.
http://www.harrowschoolenterprises.com/html/shop/

Tips for Those Who Tour Harrow School

- All Harrow tours begin in the **School Yard**, directly in front of the Old Schools Building.

- **When you arrive, notify the Tour Guide that you're a Potterite.** Guides often cater the pace of the tour to a group's special interest, and may arrange for Potterites to spend extra time in the Fourth Form Room.

- If you'll be *leaving* the tour after visiting the Fourth Form Room, politely notify your guide when you leave. We are assured that guides will not be offended by your disinterest in the non-Potter parts of Harrow School. Please do not cause the launch of an unwarranted **Search and Rescue mission** by neglecting to notify your Tour Guide when you leave early!

- **Consider enjoying the entire 90 minute tour.** This school has been in existence for nearly 800 years—it has a lot to offer.

Potter Pix Available in the Fourth Form Room
Professor Flitwick's Classroom Pic #1

[*Sorcerer's Stone* screenshot (enhanced)]

Professor Flitwick's piles of books and the desks seen in front of the students were **set pieces**. Apart from those items, everything seen on film can be seen in the real-life Fourth Form Room.

[©2008 C.D. Miller]

Climbing on the Instructor's Chair, or on student benches, is potentially damaging and shouldn't even be considered. But, any walking surface within the Fourth Form Room is fair game. Since your Professor Flitwick stand-in will likely not be a **little person** (dwarf), have her/him stand between the Instructor's Chair and its desk to snap your pix.

Professor Flitwick's Classroom Pic #2

[*Sorcerer's Stone* screenshot (enhanced)]

In Miller's pic below, the buckled spot in the front row bench seen at the right of Professor Flitwick's chair is the precise place that Daniel Radcliffe sat while *SS* Charms Class scenes were filmed.

[©2008 C.D. Miller]

Consider asking a fellow tourist—or your Tour Guide—to snap a straight-on group shot while all in your party are seated on this bench.

Professor Flitwick's Classroom Pic #3

[*Sorcerer's Stone* screenshot (enhanced)]

Have the tallest person in your party snap Classroom Pic #3 while extending the camera above her/his head. Perhaps a very tall fellow tourist would help you by snapping a group shot from this angle.

Professor Flitwick's Classroom Pic #4

[*Sorcerer's Stone* screenshot (enhanced)]

Being the very surprised recipient of a **private** Fourth Form Room tour in 2008, Miller was in a rush and didn't line-up her Classroom Pic #4 recreation shot as well as **you** can during a scheduled tour.

[©2008 C.D. Miller]

Back up *past* the entryway door and the fireplace directly across from it. Then, gently climb up to stand in front of the **top bench** on the entry-door-side, so that you can snap this pic from the correct viewpoint.

Professor Flitwick's Classroom Pic #5

[©2007 Brian Wilson]

The end of the Fourth Form Room *opposite* from Flitwick's chair was never seen on film. But, since you're there, snap a pic of **Professor Flitwick's view** while standing in front of the Instructor's Chair.

Warwick Davis and Professor Flitwick

Throughout all eight Harry Potter films, the primary role of actor **Warwick Davis** has been that of **Professor Filius Flitwick**, the kindly and loveable Hogwarts' Charms Instructor. However, Warwick's very first Harry Potter appearance was as a **Gringotts Goblin Bank Teller** in *Sorcerer's Stone*.

Because we discovered so many interesting facts about the **five** characters Warwick has portrayed in the Harry Potter films, we created a **Warwick Davis Revelio Supplementum**.
http://HarryPotterPlaces.com/b1/WarwickDavisRevelio.pdf

This Supplementum includes a discussion of Professor Flitwick's magical transformation—how he *grew younger* in *Goblet of Fire!*

[*Order of the Phoenix* screenshot (enhanced)]

During Your Harrow School Visit, Pop into the Hill Shop

There are no Harry Potter souvenirs in the Hill Shop. But, the Hill Shop is staffed by incredibly Potter-Friendly people, and you really ought to buy *some* kind of souvenir to commemorate your Harrow School visit.

A booklet sporting the Old Schools building on its cover contains photos and historical info about Harrow, and is available for only £2.50 ($4). Inexpensive postcards (50 pence apiece) featuring the Fourth Form Room are also available.

- **During term times**, the Hill Shop is open Monday, Tuesday, Thursday, and Friday from 8:20am to 5pm. It is also open on Wednesday from 8:20am until 2pm, but is closed on Saturday and Sunday.

- **During holidays**, the Hill Shop is open Tuesday through Friday from 11am until 3pm.

- **During the month of August**, the Hill Shop is closed.

Going to Professor Flitwick's Classroom

⊖ Consult the **Transport for London** website to explore Underground transportation options from your London departure point to **Harrow-on-the-Hill Tube Station**. These options may or may not require slightly more travel time than using Railway Stations. But, traveling via the Underground will be less expensive.
http://www.tfl.gov.uk/

≋ Consult the **National Rail** website to explore options for traveling via train from Central London to the **Harrow-on-the-Hill Railway Station [HOH]**.
http://www.nationalrail.co.uk/

🏃 We Do Not Recommend Walking to Harrow School From the HOH Underground or Railway Station

It's only a 15 minute walk from the HOH station to the Old Schools Building. However, the bulk of that walk is *UP* a **very steep hill**. The walk is lovely, and we highly recommend it for your journey **back** (*downhill*) to the station. But, when going *TO* Harrow School from HOH, follow directions for the 10 minute Walk/Bus journey below.

🏃🚌 Walk/Bus From HOH to Harrow School

A 10 minute journey.

🏃 After arriving at Harrow-on-the-Hill Railway or Tube Station, follow station signs to the **Station Approach/Lowlands Road Exit**. ♦ Turn left to walk east on **Station Approach** to its end, then cross to the east side of **Peterborough Road**. ♦ Turn right and walk south, keeping left, to reach the first of *two* **Bus 258** stops: one on the east side of Peterborough Road, one slightly farther away and on the west side of Peterborough Road.

Please Note: We are unsure from which stop you catch the Bus 258 that goes *to* Harrow School. (In 2008, Miller huffed-and-puffed up the very steep hill!) If the bus stop signs are unclear, as soon as a bus arrives at either stop, ask the driver for instructions.

🚌 **Board the Bus 258 going to Harrow School.** When the bus arrives at Harrow and curves left to pass in front of the gorgeous, grey stone **Harrow Chapel** (on the left), ring the bell to request the bus stop closest to the **Old Schools Building.** If you miss this stop, never fear. The bus will automatically stop only a block farther away, near the **Hill Shop.**

🏃 Walk Back to the HOH Station

A lovely *down-hill* 15 minute walk.

[©2011 Google, Street View image segment (enhanced)]

🚶 Head north toward the gorgeous, grey stone **Harrow Chapel**, crossing to the west side of **Peterborough Road** before reaching the **Do-Not-Enter** signs that bar automobiles from entering **Grove Hill** (seen above). ♦ Turn left and walk north on Grove Hill. Enjoy the lovely woodland that lines the steep descent to **Lowlands Road**. ♦ Turn left and walk west to **Lansdowne Road**. ♦ Turn right and walk straight ahead to the HOH Station.

🚌🚶 Bus/Walk Back to the HOH Station

A 10 minute journey.

🚌 The Bus 258 stop *nearest* the Old Schools building is where you catch the bus that returns to the area of Peterborough Road found just south of the **Station Approach** intersection (near **Harrow Central Police Station**).

🚶 Walk west on Station Approach to reach the HOH station.

QUIDDITCH WORLD CUP
PORTKEY LANDING

Eastbourne, Beachy Head
http://www.beachyhead.org.uk
http://en.wikipedia.org/wiki/Eastbourne
http://en.wikipedia.org/wiki/Seven_Sisters,_Sussex

Google Maps UK: Birling Gap Hotel, Seven Sisters Cliffs, East Dean,
Eastbourne BN20 0AB
≥ London's Victoria Railway Station [VIC]
≥ Eastbourne Railway Station [EBN]
Eastbourne is outside the London Travelcard Zones

Victoria Station to Side-Along One-Way Travel Time: up to 2 hours

🚶 🚌 **TAXI** Options for reaching the screenshot search site from EBN are
provided below

Operation Hours or **Entry Fee:** None

Visit Time: We guestimate at least an hour of searching to find screenshot
views

Parseltongue Pointer:
 • Eastbourne = "EAST-born"

Scores of films, television commercials, and documentaries have been shot
on the gently undulating downs above Beachy Head's iconic white cliffs.
Known as the **Seven Sisters**, these cliffs are relatively free of modern
development and are often filmed as a stand-in for the more famous **White
Cliffs of Dover.**
http://en.wikipedia.org/wiki/White_Cliffs_of_Dover

Unfortunately for Potterites, the actual location where *Goblet of Fire* **Portkey Landing** scenes were filmed is entirely unknown. In fact, the scenes with Beachy Head's cliffs in the background may have been filmed on a green-screen set, with **background plates** of the Seven Sisters digitally inserted.

Site Rating

The Quidditch World Cup Portkey Landing Earns a Skip-It Rating Because:

- It is possible that principle characters never came here for filming.

- The location for snapping screenshot recreation pix is unknown.

- Up to **5 or 6 hours** is required to reach the screenshot-search place, perform your search, and return to London.

That said, the views from this area are so magnificent, we've spent several hours researching instructions for finding the best screenshot search point (see below). If you can afford the time and expense of traveling to Eastbourne, the following screenshots demonstrate the views to watch for while hiking o'er the downs above the beach.

Portkey Landing Potter Pic #1

[*Goblet of Fire* screenshot (enhanced)]

In this scene, Harry, Ron, Hermione, and the Weasley Twins crash-landed at the end of their Portkey journey to an area near the Quidditch World Cup Tent City.

Portkey Landing Potter Pix #2 and 3

[Goblet of Fire screenshot (enhanced) above and below]

Being experienced Portkey travelers, Mr. Weasley, Amos Diggory and his son, Cedric, alighted in a far more controlled manner.

Portkey Landing Potter Pic #4

[Goblet of Fire screenshot (enhanced)]

Once all were on their feet, the group set off on a short hike from the Portkey Landing site to the Tent City.

Nearby Non-Potter Places

Visit the following **Beachy Head** website link to learn about the many activity options available in this area, options as diverse as a **Sheep Centre** visit or **horseback riding**. Potterites interested in longer and more scenic hikes than those we describe in the **Going To** section will find several route options here.
http://www.beachyhead.org.uk/activities_for_all/

The Tiger Inn, East Dean
http://www.beachyhead.org.uk/eating_drinking/food_at_the_tiger_inn/
http://www.facebook.com/group.php?gid=159915929185&v=wall

Google Maps UK, SatNav/GPS: The Tiger Inn, The Green, East Dean, Eastbourne, East Sussex BN20 0DA

Located west of Eastbourne in **East Dean**, this friendly country pub dates back to the 14th century and is a wonderful place to enjoy a meal before or after your search for the screenshot views site.

The Tiger Inn also is the start point of a lovely hike that will take you to Birling Gap, searching for the screenshot site along the way: the **Seven Sisters Walk** (link below). This hike is 4 miles long if you walk to Birling Gap and back to the pub. Alternatively, after a 2 mile hike, on Sundays and public holidays you can catch a bus from Birling Gap back to Eastbourne Railway Station.

For Potterites traveling via rental car, a free car park is available near the pub (see below). Additionally, the Tiger Inn is a 5-room, four star B&B.
http://www.beachyhead.org.uk/staying_here/staying_at_the_tiger_inn/

*Birling Gap
http://en.wikipedia.org/wiki/Birling_Gap#Birling_Gap

Google Maps UK, SatNav/GPS: Birling Gap Hotel, Seven Sisters Cliffs, East Dean, Eastbourne BN20 0AB

Birling Gap is the ultimate destination for accomplishing your Quidditch World Cup Portkey Landing screenshot site search. Visit the wikipedia link above to learn why this historic location soon may cease to exist!

Going to the Quidditch World Cup Portkey Landing Area

Below we provide directions for reaching **Birling Gap** via **public transportation** from **London**, or via **rental car**.

No matter how you arrive, show your screenshots to a **Birling Gap Café** employee and ask directions for hiking to a place with similar views. They may know precisely where you should go. Better yet, they may have Potter-related information that you can blog about on the *Harry Potter Places* website.

Please Note: Although the area of your screenshot views search is described as "gently undulating downland," some of the low hills are slightly steep and the area can become quite muddy at times. **Sturdy walking shoes or boots are strongly recommended.**

The Seven Sisters Walk
http://www.beachyhead.org.uk/fileadmin/uploads/Walk_PDFs/Seven_Sisters_Walk.pdf

This file is important to **all directions** for reaching Burling Gap and the screenshot views search area, *except* when taking a **Taxi** from Eastbourne Railway Station.

Reach Birling Gap via Public Transportation from London
Step One: Go to Eastbourne

≋ Travel from London's Victoria Railway Station [VIC] to Eastbourne Railway Station [EBN]
http://www.nationalrail.co.uk/

Google Maps UK: Eastbourne Rail Station @50.769370,0.281260

The journey from VIC to EBN is commonly a 90 minute direct trip (no train changes), but sometimes can take up to 1 hour and 40 minutes. The 2011 Return train fare between VIC and EBN ranges from £15 ($23)—if you can leave and return during a Cheapest Fare time slot—to £26.30 ($41).

Step Two: Decide How Much Hiking You Want to Do
Only the Hike o'er the Downs: Take a Taxi

TAXI The drive from EBN to Birling Gap is approximately 20 minutes. If the driver will make a return trip appointment, allow at least 2 hours to hike o'er the Downs, shoot your screenshot pix, and enjoy a sip or sup in the café.

If you're visiting on a Sunday or public holiday, consider following the directions below for taking a **Bus** back to EBN from Birling Gap.

A Two Mile Hike Plus the Hike o'er the Downs

Please Note: This option is only available on Sundays or public holidays. Those are the only days that Bus 13 runs from Birling Gap to Eastbourne.

🚶 Upon arriving at EBN, ask a Station employee for directions to the **Eastbourne Town Centre, Terminus Road Bus Stop J.**
A 2 minute walk from the station.

🚌 **Board the #12 bus towards Brighton.** Ensure that you're on the right bus (and that you'll get off at the correct stop) by letting the driver know your destination: the **Tiger Inn** on **Village Green Lane** in **East Dean.**
A 15 to 20 minute bus ride.

🚶 From the bus stop on **East Dean Road,** walk south on **Gilberts Drive,** watching on your right for **Village Green Lane** and the sign for the **Tiger Inn Free House.**
A 1 minute walk.

Go to the Tiger Inn, enjoy a sip or sup. When finished, ask a Tiger Inn employee to point you in the right direction to find **Went Way.**

🚶 Follow the **Seven Sisters Walk** instructions (link above) for hiking from Went Way to **Birling Gap.**
A 2 mile hike.

Please Note: It's possible that you'll find the screenshot view site before reaching Birling Gap and won't have to hike o'er the Downs.

🚌 **Board the #13 bus towards Eastbourne.** Advise the Driver that your destination is the **Eastbourne Railway Station.**
A 23 minute bus ride.

A Four Mile Hike Plus the Hike o'er the Downs

Follow the Two Mile Hike directions above for reaching the Tiger Inn and hiking from Went Way to Birling Gap. After shooting your screenshots, hike back to the Tiger Inn.

🚶 Walk back to the bus stops on **East Dean Road.**

🚌 **Board the #12A bus towards Eastbourne.** Ensure that you're on the right bus by letting the driver know that your destination is the **Eastbourne Railway Station.**
A 15 to 20 minute bus ride.

Reach Birling Gap via Rental Car
🚗 Drive Directly to Birling Gap

SatNav/GPS: Birling Gap Hotel, Seven Sisters Cliffs, East Dean, Eastbourne BN20 0AB

The Birling Gap Pay & Display car park fee is £2 ($3) per half day, £4 ($6) per day.

🚗 Drive to the Tiger Inn and Hike to Birling Gap

SatNav/GPS: The Tiger Inn, The Green, East Dean, Eastbourne, East Sussex BN20 0DA

The East Dean Free Car Park entrance is found where **Village Green Lane** meets **Gilberts Drive**.

Go to the **Tiger Inn Free House** and enjoy a sip or sup. When finished, ask a Tiger Inn employee to point you in the right direction to find **Went Way**.

🚶 Follow the **Seven Sisters Walk** instructions (link above) for hiking from Went Way to **Birling Gap** and back. If you find the screenshot view site before reaching Birling Gap, your hike will total only 4 miles.

27

WARNER BROTHERS STUDIO TOUR LONDON*

*The Making of Harry Potter

Warner Brothers Studios, Leavesden

http://www.wbstudiotour.co.uk/
http://www.facebook.com/wbstudiotourlondon

Please Note: Although officially titled, *Warner Brothers Studio Tour—the Making of Harry Potter*, we prefer to call this attraction the **Harry Potter WB Studio Tour**, abbreviated **HPST**.

Google Maps UK: Gadeside Roundabout, Leavesden, Hertfordshire WD25 7

(See Driving Directions for SatNav/GPS information.)

🚄 London's Euston Railway Station [**EUS**]

🚄 Watford Junction Railway Station [**WFJ**]

The HPST is located outside the London Travelcard Zones, but Oyster cards are accepted at EUS and WFJ.

🚌 When the HPST opens (March 31, 2012), a special Shuttle Bus will run between WFJ and the HPST every 20 minutes.

TAXI Taxis are available at WFJ

🚌 A Golden Tours WB Studio Tour Coach Package leaves from London three times each day

Operation Hours, Ticket Prices, and Visit Time are discussed below.

Lumos Warner Brothers Studios, Leavesden

Originally built in 1940, **Leavesden Aerodrome** was an aircraft production complex owned and operated by England's Ministry of Defense. After the end of World War II, it was sold to the Rolls-Royce Company, and became a helicopter engine factory that continued production until closing in June of 1993. In November of 1994, the site was purchased by **Leavesden Studios**, and the aircraft hangers were transformed into gigantic movie stages. The first major motion picture filmed at Leavesden Studios was the James Bond film, *GoldenEye*, released in 1995.

Leavesden Studios were rented by Warner Bros. [WB] to film *Harry Potter and the Sorcerer's Stone*, which began production in October of 2000. Ten years and seven additional Harry Potter movies later, WB purchased Leavesden Studios, becoming the only US studio to have a permanent base in Britain.

WB has renovated Leavesden Studio buildings A, B, C, D, and F, the studio's backlot, and all ancillary workshops and production facilities. WB also constructed two *new* buildings; **J** and **K**—buildings solely dedicated to the **Warner Brothers Studio Tour—the Making of Harry Potter** attraction. Is the alphabetical identification of these buildings a coincidence? We don't think so!

[TM ©2011 Warner Bros. Entertainment Inc.; promotional art (enhanced)]

The Harry Potter Warner Brothers Studio Tour

In September of 2011, Nicholas Myers of *Mugglenet.com* enjoyed a behind-the-scenes sneak peek tour of the HPST. His excellent article is well worth reading. It included a few set photos and revealed some surprising news (at the time) about which sets have been preserved for the attraction.
http://www.mugglenet.com/studiotour/report.shtml

Highlights From Nick's Report:
• You'll be able to walk within the Great Hall set, and even have your photo taken while sitting at one of the Hogwarts House tables.

- The Gryffindor Common Room and Boys Dormitory sets are here, though you'll only be able to walk partway into them—"a decision that was rightly made to allow them to furnish the rooms full of props for you to admire."

- Other Hogwarts sets displayed include Dumbledore's Office, parts of Hogwarts' Library, the Potions Classroom, and Hagrid's Hut.

- Non-Hogwarts HPST sets include the Weasley Kitchen, the Black Family Tapestry, the Cupboard Under The Stairs (which you can go inside), and several Ministry of Magic features; such as Floo Network fireplaces, the evil Magic is Might statue, and Dolores Umbridge's Office.

- Outdoor sets available for visiting include Number 4 Privet Drive, the Riddle Tomb, Hogwarts' Bridge, and the giant Chess Pieces seen in *Sorcerer's Stone*.

- Three of the 15 Ford Anglia sedans used for filming are also present— one of which can be entered and posed in, for your pic-snapping pleasure.

- Given the vast store of props and set pieces that have accumulated over 11 years of filming, HPST exhibit items may be periodically rotated and replaced. Obviously, the WB wants to encourage repeat visits!

- Photography is allowed throughout the entire tour.

An Equally-Excellent Sneak Preview by "Emma Riddle" of *SnitchSeeker.com*:

http://www.snitchseeker.com/harry-potter-news/snitchseeker-previews-warner-bros-studio-tour-london-the-making-of-harry-potter-85804/

"Fans will have a chance to get hands-on with some of the props, for example items (frying pan, knitting needles, iron) in the Weasley kitchen which they can bring to life with a flick of a wand or a little bit of wandless magic.

... you'll be able to see not just the sets but what's behind them (e.g. scaffolding, plastering, polystyrene, etc.) You will truly get to experience these sets as the cast and crew did while shooting on them. On top of that, there will be video screens interspersed throughout, with contributions from cast and crew, talking about filming from both a technical and personal perspective, guiding you through the journey they've had working on these stories."

The only sad news reported by both Nick and Emma: No Butterbeer is available at the Harry Potter WB Studio Tour's Café!

Visiting the Harry Potter WB Studio Tour

Warner Bros. learned a lesson from the *Wizarding World of Harry Potter*. http://www.universalorlando.com/harrypotter/

[©2010 Tara Bellers]

On June 18th, 2010, the *Wizarding World of Harry Potter* [**WWoHP**] opened within a 20-acre corner of the enormous **Universal Orlando Resort's** *Islands of Adventure* theme park in Florida, USA. During the first few months after its opening, hundreds of thousands of Potterites from all over the planet flocked to the WWoHP. Waiting in line simply to get *into* the park (which was only open for 10 hours each weekday, 11 hours some weekends) took **up to 8 hours** in June and July of 2010.

If they didn't quit the ridiculously-long entrance queue and move to the slightly-less-long **ticket refund** queue, Potterites who finally gained entrance to the WWoHP had to wait in even more lines to **get into the individual shops**, where they found *standing-room-only* crowds and lengthy cash register queues.

Lines to board the rides (especially the fantabulous **Forbidden Journey** ride inside **Hogwarts' Castle**) were rarely less than 90 minutes long during the first six months of WWoHP operation.

The Harry Potter WB Studio Tour Ticket System

To ensure that no visitor ever has to wait more than 30 minutes to enter the HPST, Warner Bros. developed an advanced-purchase, timed-ticketing system.

Tickets are *NOT* Available for Sale at the Studio Tour Attraction

All HPST tickets must be purchased in advance, for a **specific day** *and* **a specific timeslot**. The 13 entry timeslots available each day begin at 10am, then every 30 minutes thereafter, until the last entry timeslot at 4pm.

Warner Bros. anticipates accommodating 5000 visitors each day. Thus, with up to 385 tickets available for each day's 13 entry timeslots, the earliest timeslots are the least crowded. **Weekend** timeslots sellout quickly, making **weekdays** better (hopefully) for avoiding huge crowds.

If You're Late for Your Timeslot, You May be Turned Away!

Plan to arrive *no less than* 20 minutes before your entry timeslot, especially if you have an Email booking confirmation and need to pickup tickets from the kiosks outside the attraction.

If you pay extra to have actual tickets mailed to you, you can go straight to the Studio Tour entrance queue. However, it still would be best to arrive 20 to 30 minutes before your timeslot, in case the HPST ticket-holders entrance queue is rather long.

No Time Limit for Enjoying the Harry Potter WB Studio Tour

The freedom to stay as long as you like is a wonderful thing. Unfortunately, unlimited visit time means that with each entry timeslot following the first one (10am), the HPST becomes more and more crowded. Afternoon timeslots may be *very* crowded. Thus, the best daily timeslot tickets are the earliest ones.

Visiting time for those with late afternoon timeslots is limited to the hours that the Studio Tour remains open. Happily, according to WB Visitor Services:

> "At present the closing time is 7 pm ... this fluctuates depending on the time of year ... [But] we can assure you that you will not be forcibly removed if you are still here at closing time."

The One-Way-Route *IMPERIO CURSE*

Although there is no time limit for traveling through the HPST, Warner Bros. designed the Studio Tour route so that there is only **one direction of travel**. After leaving any exhibit or set, you *cannot* double-back to revisit it. And, once the HPST **end point** is reached, you *cannot reenter*.

Spend plenty of time at each display, exhibit, and set as you encounter it! A full Harry Potter Studio Tour is estimated to last approximately three hours, but you'll not be hustled along the route. **Go SLOW.** Stay long enough at each place to exhaust every single ounce of enjoyment before Pottering to the next stop.

Only One Portion of the Harry Potter WB Studio Tour is Guided

The HPST tour starts in a small **Cinema Room** with a short introductory video. After that, Potterites are free to wander through the many props and costumes exhibits—the indoor and outdoor sets—as they encounter them.

The Great Hall set is the only area where **Guides** will escort you, describing the history associated with the longest-standing and most frequently-filmed Harry Potter set.

Please Note: It is possible that Potterites wishing to repeat the Great Hall set Guided Tour may do so immediately after returning to the Start Point after enjoying their first tour. **If this proves true,** please blog about it on the *Harry Potter Places* website.

The Studio Café & Gift Shop are *Outside* the Studio Tour Area

The Studio Café and Gift Shop are in an area apart from the Studio Tour, and are open daily from 9:30am to 7pm. Potterites with early ticket timeslots will have plenty of time to visit the café and shop after exiting the tour. Early afternoon ticket-holders can shop before and after the tour. Potterites who purchase 3, 3:30, or 4pm tickets should plan to **arrive two or three hours early** so that your shopping can be fully accomplished *before* queuing-up to enter the HPST.

Miscellaneous Harry Potter WB Studio Tour Info

- Personal, handheld cameras are welcomed in all areas of the HPST, and exciting photo opportunities have been designed throughout the attraction.

- Video recording equipment and tripods are *not* permitted within the HPST.

- Because space is limited, a free **Buggy Park** is available outside the attraction, where strollers and prams (or the like) should be checked.

- A cloakroom is available for checking coats, bags, or pre-tour shop purchases—for a small fee.

Harry Potter WB Studio Tour Tickets

The HPST opens at 10am every day of the year, except for Christmas Day and Boxing Day—December 25th and 26th.

Tickets can be purchased online from the HPST website:
http://www.wbstudiotour.co.uk/en/tickets/individuals

If something unforeseen alters your holiday dates, you can contact the WB Studio Tour Call Centre at 08450 840 900, and *change* your HPST ticket for a £10 ($16) administration fee. Unfortunately, if all timeslots on your new visit date(s) are sold out, **HPST tickets are non-refundable.**
   Adult Ticket (16 years old & older); £28 ($44)
   Child Ticket (5 to 15 years old); £21 ($33)
   Family Ticket (2 adults & 2 children, or 1 adult & 3 children); £83 ($130)
   Children under 5 years old get in free, but a ticket must be obtained.
   The UK's VAT (Value Added Tax) is *included* in each ticket price.
   No Concession (senior or student) discounted tickets are available.
   Group Discount Tickets are available for parties of 10 or more:
http://www.wbstudiotour.co.uk/en/tickets/groups

Harry Potter WB Studio Tour Extras
   • **Rent a Digital Guide:** This is a handheld audio-visual device that provides fascinating facts about all the sets, costumes and props you'll see during your visit, as well as video interviews with cast and crew and behind-the-scenes footage. Digital Guides are available in eight languages and can be reserved when you buy your ticket. £4.95 ($8)

   • **Buy a Souvenir Guidebook:** The ultimate Harry Potter WB Studio Tour souvenir can be pre-purchased when you buy your ticket and picked up upon arrival, or purchased when you visit the Studio Tour Gift Shop. £9.95 ($16)

   • **Save £4.95 ($8) by Buying the Complete Studio Tour Package:** This discounted package includes your HPST entrance ticket, a Souvenir Guidebook, and a Digital Guide reservation.

   Adult Complete Studio Tour Package; £37.95 ($60)
   Child Complete Studio Tour Package; £30.95 ($49)

If your party is small, and includes at least one child aged 5 to 15 years old, buy the Complete Studio Tour Package (including a free Digital Guide reservation and a Souvenir Guidebook) for a child. All others in your party can purchase individual HPST tickets, *share* the Child's Digital Guide, and buy their own Souvenir Guidebook at the Studio Tour Gift Shop.

Plan Your HPST Day Itinerary

Including travel time, a *minimum* of 6 hours are required to visit the Harry Potter WB Studio Tour—far more time than any other London Potter Place or Side-Along Apparation requires. Thus, the HPST must have its very own itinerary day, which may include no more than two other Potter Places.

In **Specialis Revelio London Part Two**, you'll find a link to the **Harry Potter WB Studio Tour Day Itinerary Planning Supplementum**. Directions for designing your HPST day itinerary, based on the mode of transportation you choose and the Studio Tour ticket you purchase, are provided there.

Nearby Potter Places
Knight Bus Pickup Playground (Site #22)

If you travel to the HPST via public transportation or rental car (rather than booking a Golden Tours London Coach package), add another hour to your itinerary so that you can walk across Gadeside Roundabout from the Studio Tour's entrance and snap pix within the private Muggle neighborhood where *Prisoner of Azkaban* filming occurred. Scenes of Harry dragging his trunk through the streets to a playground, and being picked up by the Knight Bus, were shot here.

Please Note: The Knight Bus Pickup Playground is a **Skip-It** rated site if not visited during an HPST itinerary day.

Going to the Harry Potter WB Studio Tour
The London Coach WB Studio Packages

Offered by **Golden Tours** (a Gray Line bus company), in partnership with the Warner Brothers Studio Tour, this is the most convenient way to visit the HPST during your London holiday. A Golden Tours WB Studio Coach package includes roundtrip transportation between Central London and the Studio Tour location, as well as your HPST entry ticket.
http://www.wbstudiotour.co.uk/en/your-visit/coaches
http://www.goldentours.com/partner/wbsstudiotour/\

Three Golden Tours WB Studio Coach Packages Each Day
• **The 10am HPST entry timeslot Golden Tours WB Coach Package:** Coach check-in *closes* at 7:45am (arrive no later than 7:30). London departure at 8am, arriving HPST between 9 and 9:30am. HPST departure, 12noon. Return arrival in London, between 1 and 1:30pm.

• **The 1pm HPST entry timeslot Golden Tours WB Coach Package:** Coach check-in *closes* at 10:45am (arrive no later than at 10:30). London departure at 11am, arriving HPST between 12 and 12:30pm. HPST departure, 3pm. Return arrival in London, between 4 and 4:30pm.

• **The 4pm HPST entry timeslot Golden Tours WB Coach Package:**
Coach check-in *closes* at 1:45pm (arrive no later than at 1:30). London departure at 2pm, arriving HPST between 3 and 3:30pm. HPST departure, 6pm. Return arrival in London, between 7 and 7:30pm.

Total Golden Tours HPST Package Itinerary Time:
Approximately 6 hours, including check-in and travel time.

Departure Point for all Golden Tours HPST Coaches:

#4 Fountain Square, 123-151 Buckingham Palace Road, London, SW1W 9SH—a block southwest of London's Victoria Railway & Underground Station.

Golden Tours HPST Package Fees:
  Adults, £55 ($86).
  Children aged 5-15, £50 ($78).

Drawbacks to the Golden Tours HPST Coach Packages

(**#1**) WB Studio Family Package tickets are not available from Golden Tours.

(**#2**) Golden Tours Packages do not include HPST Souvenir Guidebooks or free HPST Digital Guides.

(**#3**) **Only 2 hours are allowed** *within* **the Harry Potter WB Studio Tour!**

When traffic is moving well, coach travel time between London and the Studio is only 1 hour. To ensure that you'll arrive well before your HPST entry timeslot—even when traffic is heavy—each Golden Tours WB Studio Coach departs 2 hours early. Arriving up to 1 hour before your entry timeslot would be a good thing, except for the fact that **each Golden Tours Return Coach leaves the Studio 3 hours after its** *scheduled* **arrival, allowing only 2 hours within the attraction.**
  The Studio Café and Gift Shop open at 9:30am. No matter how light the traffic is, Potterites who purchase the 10am HPST ticket Golden Tours package will have **barely 10 minutes** to visit the Café or Gift Shop before queuing up for the Studio Tour.
  When traffic is moving well, Potterites who purchase the 1pm or 4pm HPST ticket Golden Tours packages will have only 40 minutes to visit the Studio Café and Gift Shop before queuing up for the Studio Tour—an exceptionally *insufficient* time. And, being afternoon timeslots, these may be the most crowded times to tour the HPST.

(**#4**) **Visiting the Knight Bus Pickup Playground (Site #22) is** *right out.*

Granted, this isn't one of the best London Side-Along Apparations. In fact, if you cannot visit Site #22 during your HPST day itinerary, the Knight Bus Pickup Playground area is a **Skip-It**-rated site. Still, we mention this additional drawback to booking a Golden Tours Coach HPST package.

Avid Potterites Will *NOT* Want to Book a Golden Tours WB Coach Package!

Although less convenient, it is far cheaper to purchase your HPST ticket independently and travel from London to the Studio via the **National Rail system** and **WB Shuttle Bus**. But, most importantly, by using public transportation (or a rental car), you'll be able to enjoy *unlimited time* within the Harry Potter WB Studio Tour, *and* have the option of visiting Site #22!

Use the National Rail System to Reach the HPST from London
http://www.nationalrail.co.uk/

Make your way from London's **Euston Railway Station** [EUS] to **Watford Junction Railway Station** [WFJ]. WFJ is located *outside* the London Travelcard Zones. However, Oyster cards are accepted at EUS and WFJ.

EUS to WFJ is a 20 minute direct trip (no train changes).

The 2011 Return (round trip) train fare between EUS and WFJ ranges from £14 ($22) if departing before 9 am, to £9.50 ($15) if departing after 9 am.

Be sure to arrive at the Watford Junction Railway Station no less than 45 minutes before your HPST entry timeslot.

The WB Studio Tour Shuttle Bus

Warner Bros. has partnered with a company that will operate a special Shuttle Bus between the WFJ and the HPST, leaving at 20 minute intervals throughout the day, and requiring approximately 15 minutes of one-way travel time. Have your HPST ticket or Email booking confirmation handy when boarding the bus.

At this writing (December, 2011), it is unknown whether the WB Studio Shuttle Bus is free to ticket holders, or if a fee is charged. The shuttle's daily operational hours are also unknown.

When performing your **Pre-Trip Transport Times Check** two weeks before your holiday, visit the Warner Bros. Studio Tour website to obtain the WB Shuttle Bus schedule and plan your WFJ arrival time.
http://www.wbstudiotour.co.uk/en/your-visit/getting-here

![TAXI] Taxis are available at WFJ

The drive time between WFJ and the HPST is only 10 minutes. Especially if a fee is charged for using the WB Studio Shuttle Bus, this may be a relatively inexpensive option.

🚗 Drive to the Harry Potter Warner Brothers Studio Tour

Potterites who will be renting a car to travel outside of London have a marvelous opportunity to make the HPST their first driving destination, and will also be able to visit the Knight Bus Pickup Playground.

SatNav/GPS: Gadeside Roundabout, Leavesden, Hertfordshire

The address above identifies a point just south of the roundabout where the HPST entrance is located—the roundabout that also leads to the Knight Bus Pickup Playground.

Please Note: the Gadeside Roundabout is at the junction of Gadeside and **Aerodrome Way**, not Airfield Way (as identified by Google Maps UK).

Brief written directions for driving to the HPST are provided on the Warner Bros. Studio Tour website. However, a SatNav/GPS device is invaluable for getting here, especially if you take a wrong turn along the way.

The HPST Visitor Car Park is *free* and has 598 parking spaces available. Have your ticket or Email booking confirmation handy when you arrive at the gate.

28

WHOMPING WILLOWS
KEW GARDENS

Kew Gardens

http://www.kew.org/
http://en.wikipedia.org/wiki/Royal_Botanic_Gardens,_Kew

Google Maps UK: Kew, Kew Gardens, Victoria Gate *or* 51.474667, -0.295467

🚄 London's Waterloo Railway Station [WAT]

🚄 Kew Gardens Railway Station [KWG]

🚇 Underground and Overground travel alternatives are discussed below KWG is in Travelcard Zones 3 and 4

London Station to Side-Along One-Way Travel Time: 35 to 45 minutes

Operation Hours: Kew Gardens is open at 9:30am every day of the year except for Christmas Eve and Christmas day. Consult the Kew Gardens website for seasonal closing times. The restaurants and gift shops are commonly open at 10am daily.

Entry Fee: In 2011, entry cost £13.90 ($22) for Adults, £11.90 ($19) for Concessions (Students with valid IDs and Seniors 60+), and adult-accompanied children under 17 enter for free. The London Pass allows free entry.

Visit Time: If you visit this site, allow **2 or 3 hours** to get merely a small taste of what Kew Gardens has to offer.

Parseltongue Pointer:
- Kew Gardens = "CUE" Gardens (as in "Pool **Cue** Stick")

The **Royal Botanic Gardens at Kew** occupy the site of what once was a royal estate in the London borough of **Richmond upon Thames**, belonging to the mother of **King George III**. In 1759, Augusta designated a portion of her private estate to become a place where plants from all over the world could be collected for botanical research and educational purposes. Between 1778 and 1820, the Kew facilities became known as an eminent scientific institution and in 1840 the gardens were donated to the United Kingdom.

Today, the Royal Botanic Gardens at Kew span more than 300 acres of land and contain over 40 heritage-listed buildings, including an impressive collection of **Victorian glasshouses**. Kew is home to 50,000 different types of plants, a herbarium that houses more than 5 *million* dried specimens, and a library of more than 130,000 botanical texts. Kew's three museums are largely devoted to economic plant products and a laboratory specializing in plant genetics and classification.

Site Rating

The Whomping Willow / Kew Gardens Earns a Skip-It Rating Because:
- Nothing here looks anything like a Potter screenshot.
- Kew Gardens is not a quick or inexpensive place to visit.

That said, it is important for us to acknowledge that there are **Three Points of Association** between **Kew Gardens** and **Harry Potter**—points some Potterites may consider important.

Point One: In several interviews, J.K. Rowling has reported that—although she's not entirely sure—she thinks that she came up with the name for Harry's school based on a visit to Kew Gardens seven years before writing *Harry Potter and the Sorcerer's Stone*. She recalls being charmed by the **Hogwarts lilies** (*Croton capitatus*) she'd seen there.

Point Two: When *Chamber of Secrets* scouts searched for a real-life location to film **Professor Sprout's Greenhouse Classroom** scenes, the very first place they thought of was Kew Gardens.

> "We do not want things to be purely fantastical. ... The greenhouse had to feel like it's existed hundreds of years. And it had to feel like a very earthy, natural place. ... The best greenhouses ... are in Kew Gardens."

Unfortunately, within minutes of their arrival, the frequency of roaring airline traffic above Kew Gardens entirely quashed the thought of filming there. Instead, a **greenhouse set** was built.

Point Three:

> "The beautiful twisted bark of one of Kew's elderly sweet chestnuts (*Castanea sativa*) was used as a model for a very different and more mischievous tree—the Whomping Willow in the Harry Potter films. A mould was taken of the bark by enveloping the tree in a plaster cast."

One last consideration: Potterites who particularly enjoy gardens will not want to miss Kew Gardens when visiting London.

Kew Gardens and Loosely-Associated Screenshots

The **Temperate House** at Kew Gardens is the largest surviving Victorian glass building in the world, as well as home to the world's tallest indoor plant (over 58 feet high), the **Chilean Wine Palm**. Construction of the Temperate House began in 1860. The octagons and center block were completed in 1862, but bureaucratic issues arose in 1863 that caused work to be discontinued. It wasn't until 32 years later, in1895, that construction was resumed. The south and north wings of the Temperate House were finally completed in 1898.

[©2008 David Iliff, license CC-BY-SA 3.0]

Of all the structures at Kew Gardens, only the Temperate House has design elements *somewhat* similar to the **CGI-generated** exterior images of Professor Sprout's greenhouses.

[*Chamber of Secrets* screenshots (enhanced)]

The interior of the Temperate House also boasts ground level glass panels and overhead steel arches (far above ground level) *similar* to those designed for Professor Sprout's greenhouse set.

[*Chamber of Secrets* screenshots (enhanced)]

[©2003 Averil Duncan]

Unfortunately for screenshot-seeking Potterites, only the *atmosphere*—the sense that these structures have existed for hundreds of years—is actually shared by the Temperate House and Prof. Sprout's Greenhouse classroom.

he Kew Gardens Whomping Willow

[©2009 Tara Bellers]

Yes, filmmakers made a mold of the uniquely twisted trunk of Kew Gardens' oldest **Sweet Chestnut Tree** prior to designing the original Whomping Willow. However, only a *hint* of that real-life twisted trunk has ever been seen on screen. Furthermore, the Whomping Willow's design has been significantly altered over the years, as has its Hogwarts' location.

[*Chamber of Secrets* screenshot (enhanced)]

The Whomping Willow first appeared on screen in *Chamber of Secrets*, when Ron crashed his father's flying Ford Anglia into its branches. At that time, the tree was located within Hogwarts' Training Grounds, near to the castle. Scenes surrounding that crash were filmed at **Alnwick Castle**, in northeastern England.

In *Prisoner of Azkaban* the Whomping Willow looked very different, and had been magically relocated far outside of the Hogwarts grounds, on a hill overlooking Hagrid's Hut.

[*Prisoner of Azkaban* screenshot (enhanced)]

We don't know why the Whomping Willow was relocated between *COS* and *POA*. Perhaps the tree was magically moved to give it sufficient space to recover from the flying car damage. Perhaps the tree decides for *itself* where it will stand, and simply wanted a change of scenery. Whatever the reason for its relocation, the Whomping Willow has looked less and less like the Kew Gardens Sweet Chestnut Tree with each cinematic reappearance.

Going to the Whomping Willow / Kew Gardens Site

⊖ ▣ For Potterites with Lots of Time

⊖ Consult the **Transport for London** website to explore Underground and Overground transportation options from your London departure point to the Kew Gardens Tube Station or Main Gate. These options generally require more travel time, but are less expensive than traveling by rail.
http://www.tfl.gov.uk/

≩ Make Your Way from London's Waterloo Railway Station [WAT] to Kew Gardens Railway Station [KWG]
http://www.nationalrail.co.uk/

KWG can be reached from any London Railway station. However, KWG is most swiftly and economically reached from WAT. Journey to WAT from your London departure point via the Underground system, and purchase a Return (round trip) railway ticket to KWG from there.

WAT to KWG is commonly a 30 to 40 minute trip including one train
hange. The 2011 Return train fare between WAT and KWG is £7.30 ($6)
uring off-peak travel, £10 ($8) during peak hours.

Walk from Kew Gardens Underground or Railway Station to e Kew Gardens Victoria Gate Entrance
5 minute walk.

Follow station signs to the **Station Approach (Eastbound)** exit. Once
utside, watch for street signs pointing the way to Kew Gardens as you
ollow our directions.

[©2009 Tara Bellers]

Exit the station and keep left to follow **Station Parade** to **High Park Road**.
♦ Turn right and walk to **Sandycombe Road**. ♦ Turn right and walk to
Lichfield Road. ♦ Turn left and walk to **Kew Road**, where you'll see the Kew
Gardens **Victoria Gate** entrance.

When you arrive at the Kew Gardens Victoria Gate entrance, obtain a free
Visitor Information map. Ask one of the Kew Gardens employees to mark
the location of the Whomping Willow/Sweet Chestnut Tree on your map.
(It's just north of the Temperate House, and west of Holly Walk.) Then, head
to the **Temperate House**.

THE END

Thus ends the adventures of
Harry Potter Places Book One ...

Please join us in Harry Potter Places
Book Two—OWLs: Oxford
Wizarding Locations

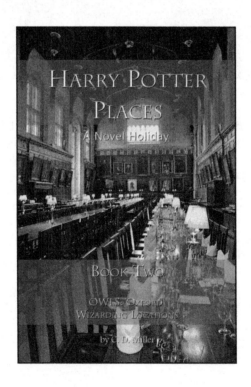

INDEX

Smith
Duncan vii
Sommerville
Tony viii
Southwark Bridge 83
Southwark Cathedral 118
Specialis Revelio 4
Spencer
Stephen viii
Spirit of London 187
Steves
Rick 7, 8
Stoehr
Karen viii
Surbiton Railway Station 245
Swan At Lavenham Hotel 241
Swiss Re Building 80

T

Tate Modern Art Museum 45, 118
Temple Church 97
Terminology Used 2
Thames River City Cruise 22
The Fox 280
The Globe Exhibition and Theater
Tour 46
Tiger Inn 304
Tower Bridge 76, 86
Tower of London 90
Trafalgar Square 153
Trafalgar Studios 155
Travelodge 30
Trip Advisor 26
Trocadero 51, 57
Twinings Tea 97

U

UK Car Rental 11
UK Internet Access 11
UK Photography 11
UK Telephones 11
UK Terminology 11
UK Youth Hostel Association 26
US Department of State 8

V

VAT Tax 9
Vauxhall Bridge 77
Village of Lavenham 231
Visit Britain 9

W

Waiting Rooms Café 279
Warner Brothers Entertainment iii
Warner Brothers Studio Tour 309
Westminster Abbey 179
Westminster Bridge 76
Westminster Millennium Pier 78
Westminster Palace 178
Westminster Tube Station 171
Whomping Willow 321
Wikimedia viii
Wikipedia viii
Wizard Chessmen 225
Wizarding World of Harry Potter
312

CPSIA information can be obtained at www.ICGtesting.com
Printed in the USA
BVOW07s2057040116

431695BV00009B/48/P

9 781938 285165